24,95

# Creating Spaniards

D0555933

# Creating Spaniards

## Culture and National Identity in Republican Spain

SANDIE HOLGUÍN

THE UNIVERSITY OF WISCONSIN PRESS

Colo. Christian Univ. Library
8787 W. Alameda Ave.
Lakewood, CO 80226

The University of Wisconsin Press
1930 Monroe Street, 3$^{rd}$ floor
Madison, Wisconsin 53711-2059
uwpress.wisc.edu

3 Henrietta Street
London WC2E 8LU, England
eurospanbookstore.com

Copyright © 2002
The Board of Regents of the University of Wisconsin System
All rights reserved. No part of this publication may be
reproduced, stored in a retrieval system, or transmitted, in any
format or by any means, digital, electronic, mechanical,
photocopying, recording, or otherwise, or conveyed via the
Internet or a Web site without written permission of the
University of Wisconsin Press, except in the case of brief
quotations embedded in critical articles and reviews.

This book is published with the assistance of the Program for
Cultural Cooperation between Spain's Ministry of Education,
Culture, and Sports and United States Universities.

Printed in the United States of America

Library of Congress Cataloging-in-Publication Data
Holguín, Sandie Eleanor.
Creating Spaniards : culture and national identity in
Republican Spain / Sandie Holguín.
p. cm.
Includes bibliographical references.
ISBN 0-299-17630-4 (cloth: alk. paper)—
ISBN 0-299-17634-7 (paper: alk. paper)
1. Spain—Intellectual life—20th century. 2. Spain—Politics and
government—1931–1939. 3. Spain—Cultural policy—History—20th century.
4. National characteristics, Spanish. 5. Nationalism—Spain—History—
20th century. 6. Nationalism and art—Spain—History—20th century.
7. Popular culture—Spain—History—20th century. I. Title.
DP223.5 .H64 2002
306'.0946—dc21
2001005414

ISBN-13: 978-0-299-17634-1 (pbk.: alk. paper)

# CONTENTS

# ILLUSTRATIONS

## Figures

## Maps

## Table

# ACKNOWLEDGMENTS

I have traveled a long, circuitous road from my dissertation to this book, and I have taken many captives and companions with me on the journey. I am grateful for their stamina and patience, for I certainly would not have made it to the end of this trip without them.

My interest in cultural and intellectual history was nurtured in graduate school at the University of California, Los Angeles (UCLA), by my advisor, Robert Wohl, and by Debora Silverman. Their classes stimulated me to think comparatively about cultural trends in nineteenth- and twentieth-century Europe, and they inspired me to try and write a book of the caliber of those they had me read. Thanks to C. Brian Morris, who taught me much about modern Spanish literature, and to Kathryn Norberg, whose classes on gender and European history were always interesting, even if what I learned is not expressly in this book. Her sense of humor sustained me through much of the dissertation writing.

I could not have written this work without receiving funding to do my research. For the dissertation, the Fulbright Commission, in conjunction with the Spanish government, funded a year of research in Spain, as did a fellowship from UCLA's Del Amo Foundation. A UCLA Chancellor's Dissertation Fellowship in 1992 enabled me to write the dissertation. When I came to the University of Oklahoma in 1995, the university was generous enough to provide me Junior Faculty Grants through the College of Arts and Sciences and the Research Council so that I could do more research in Europe.

I would also like to thank the staffs at the following archives and libraries for helping ease the research process: in Madrid, the Biblioteca Nacional, Archivo Histórico Nacional, Hemeroteca Municipal, Fundación García Lorca, Fundación Pablo Iglesias, Consejo Superior de Investigaciones Científicas, and Academia de la Historia; in Salamanca, the Archivo Histórico Nacional, Sección Guerra Civil; in Barcelona, the Arxiu Nacional de Catalunya, Instituto Municipal de Historia, and Centre de Documentació Històrico-Social-Ateneu Enciclopèdic Popular, Biblioteca Arus; in Amsterdam, the International Institut voor Sociale Geschiedenis; in Los Angeles, the UCLA library; in Oklahoma, the University of Oklahoma library and its interlibrary loan staff.

Once I wrote the dissertation, I needed readers to suggest how I might revise it for a book. Thanks to Pamela Radcliff at the University of California, San Diego, and Adrian Shubert at York University for their good suggestions. Thanks also to my colleague at the University of Oklahoma, David Levy, who, although he is an American historian, actually took the time to read my dissertation in a field he knew little about and wrote detailed, helpful comments.

My acquisitions editor, Raphael Kadushin, and his assistant, Sheila Moermond, took a chance on my book, for which I am eternally grateful. They also took care in finding good readers who provided me with excellent comments for revision. My book is much better for the readers' advice.

In my five-plus years at the University of Oklahoma, I have had many friends and supporters. The chair of the history department, Robert Griswold, has gone to great lengths to juggle my teaching load in different ways so that I could write this book. Gary Cohen took me under his wing early on and helped me adjust to academic life. I cannot thank Melissa Stockdale enough for being my advocate and for mentoring and guiding me safely through the minefield of the publishing process. She has been a great friend since I've been here. Roberta Magnusson and A. Kipp have amused and supported me since we arrived at OU together, and I vow that one day I will beat them at cards. Toward the final months of doing these revisions, my beautiful son, Miguel, was born. Although I wanted to play with him all the time, I had a book deadline. Corinne Pernet and my newest friend and colleague, Cathy Kelly, went beyond collegial duty and cheerfully volunteered to baby-sit during these last months so that I could meet this deadline. Miguel and I thank you. Finally, thanks to Luci Gouin for helping me unsnarl computer foul-ups whenever they arose and to Josie Adams for creating great maps on such short notice.

The friends I met in graduate school provided both intellectual and moral support. Their mark is in this book, whether or not they want it to be. Ellen Healy, Sharon Gillerman, Louise Townsend, Tamara Zwick, Carolyn Eichner, Muriel McClendon, Karen Nissen, Tom Mertes, Greg Kendrick, Holly Brewer, Brad Reed, Philip Minehan—thank you so much.

And now, my family. My parents, Eva and Saulo Holguín, have seen me throughout the various stages of this project and have provided the support I needed to persevere through the rough spots. I thank them for not pushing me to get an MBA after college. My son, Miguel, entered this world right before this manuscript left town. He has opened up a new world to me and brought me such joy. Finally, I come to my husband, Bob Rundstrom. Bob has never known me without this book project hanging over my head like Damocles' sword. In fact, in getting to know each other over the years, we have had to ask, where do I begin and the book end? Despite the many frustrations that writing this book has brought us, he has stayed by my side, delicately balancing his roles as both cheerleader and commandant. He made the base maps for this book and, with careful attention to detail, located the over five hundred villages where the *misioneros* went. He took up slack around the house, and he petted the cats for me when I shoved them off my computer keyboard. He reined in my propensity to be a social animal so that I would work on my book when I was sick of doing so. But, most important, he has taken the partnership part of our marriage seriously, and this has made all the difference. His love has sustained me, and I only hope that he will be pleased with the new me, shed of this book.

*Creating Spaniards*

# Introduction

Beginning on the night of October 5, 1934, and continuing throughout the month of October, the Spanish Republic faced the gravest crisis of its five-year tenure. Horrified by what they saw as the prospect of encroaching fascism embodied in the appointment of Alejandro Lerroux as prime minister and three cabinet members belonging to Gil Robles's conservative-Catholic Confederación Española de Derechas Autónomas (CEDA) Party, Socialists all over Spain called for an armed insurrection to overthrow the government. General strikes flared up in Spain's major cities; Luis Companys, the president of Catalonia's autonomous regional government, established an independent Catalan Republic; and miners in Asturias went on strike, set up a revolutionary commune, and, declaring a "proletarian revolution," battled police forces in Oviedo. Meanwhile, in the villages of Sanabria, unaware that the October Revolution had broken out, students, schoolteachers, intellectuals, and artists subsidized by the government were busy reading poetry, showing films, performing plays, and illustrating hygiene and farming techniques to illiterate villagers who were barely able to eke out an existence. While workers sought to foment the social revolution, members of the intelligentsia attempted to sow the seeds of a cultural revolution.

The reader might ask: What could have possessed these urban intellectuals to venture into Spain's hinterlands on a seemingly quixotic mission, when it was obvious to most politically informed people that Spain was a tinderbox waiting to explode? This question assumes that Spanish intellectuals were hopelessly naive about their country's problems. They were

3

not. They knew, for example, of successful cases like the Soviet Union, where state-approved artists and intellectuals engaged in cultural projects even *during* their civil war. Indeed, many European intellectuals of the interwar period believed in the transforming power of culture. How else do we explain the enormous resources poured into Soviet cultural programs, as well as those in Fascist Italy and Nazi Germany, at the very moment when these governments were attempting to consolidate their regimes? Obviously, the Soviets, Fascists, and Nazis ranked cultural transformations on a par with political and economic ones, just as Spaniards did. But they were more successful than Spain at imposing at least some measure of cultural hegemony over their respective citizens.[1] Even more striking, however, is that these other countries imposed their cultural programs during dictatorships, while Spain tried to implement them in the context of a fragile democracy. So, rather than taking Republican and Socialist politicians and intellectuals in Spain to task for expending too much energy on cultural projects instead of getting down to the dirty business of governing, perhaps we should ask different questions, ones that recognize that Spaniards were not alone in their desire to deploy culture in the service of the nation: How important is cultural unity in consolidating a regime? What purpose does a cultural revolution serve, and under what conditions can it be successful? In particular, why did Spanish culture and, by extension, the Spanish state not cohere? Did Spain's "culture wars" lead to the Spanish Civil War? My work seeks to answer these questions.

This study explores the relationship between politics, culture, and the formation of national identity during Spain's Second Republic, 1931–1936. It begins in the nineteenth century and ends with the Spanish Civil War, but it centers primarily on the Second Republic, the tumultuous years before the war, when radical changes to thus-far intractable problems actually seemed possible. In their efforts to grapple with the problems associated with modernization, the rise of mass politics, and the shift to new political structures, various intellectuals and politicians of the Republican–Socialist coalition used cultural projects like theater, literature, and film as avenues for constructing a unified history and culture out of Spain's seemingly aimless history and fragmented society, while others resisted their claims to cultural hegemony.

Following on the heels of a military dictatorship, the founding of Spain's Second Republic in April 1931 held out to its citizens the promise of political, social, economic, and cultural transformation. Whereas much of the rest of Europe had rejected parliamentary politics in favor of authoritarian regimes, Spain embraced leftist-liberal democracy as the cure-all for its ills. And its ills up until then were many: the political system reeked of corruption and inefficiency; peasants and landless rural laborers—especially in southern Spain—faced severe economic shortages, while absentee landlords living in Spain's major cities extracted high rents from them; the Roman Catholic Church interfered in the workings of the state and allied itself with the forces of reaction; the military remained bloated with a top-heavy command structure; Socialist and anarchist workers threatened middle-class interests; illiteracy was rampant; and regional nationalisms, especially in Catalonia, threatened to dismantle the already precarious state known as Spain.

The Provisional Government tackled these myriad problems from the beginning, but, curiously, amid all of these difficulties, the government set itself apart from previous ones by making the dissemination of culture one of its primary goals. During the Republic, government officials sponsored a host of cultural projects in the hopes that these programs would foster nationalism, wrest political and educational control from the Catholic Church, and create a nation of republican citizens from the shards of a shattered body politic. They believed that these projects would rescue Spain from its sickly status as a third-rate power, restore the glory it had enjoyed in the sixteenth century, and foster a national unity based on both "Castilianized" and "Europeanized" conceptions of Spain.

While Socialists and Republicans pushed for cultural programs that reflected their beliefs and that seemingly provided a means to solidify their power, other groups contested that power and challenged the Republican–Socialist coalition's versions of identity and the nation. The radical right and the traditionalist right pushed for a more virulent and less foreign-seeming nationalism based on a vision of Spain that was drawn from the sixteenth century, when politics, empire, and religion were fused in the rule of the Catholic monarchs, Ferdinand and Isabel. Although the right shared some goals with the new Republicans namely, the desire to forge a Castilian-based nationalism, they promoted programs that would strengthen the bonds of church and state. They sought to nurture in Spain and its former Spanish colonies an ideology based on a notion of shared values of religion, language, and culture known as *Hispanidad*. Others, however, wanted to remain untainted by Spanish nationalism altogether. On the one hand, Catalan nationalists hoped to disassociate themselves from Spain and eventually create a separate Catalan state based on a distinct Catalan culture. On the other hand, anarchists, because of their internationalist bent and their disdain for nationalism of any sort, sought to abolish the state completely and establish a revolutionary culture. In addition, quests for national unity were embedded within the wider context of contemporary worldwide developments. Spaniards and those who resisted this label took many of their cues from cultural revolutions that were occurring in places as widely disparate as Mexico, the Soviet Union, Fascist Italy, and Nazi Germany.

Using the Republican cultural projects as touchstones, I chart a path through this welter of competing ideas of identity to show the process by which various groups competed for cultural hegemony and to demonstrate how the failure of any one group to achieve hegemony led to a power vacuum that would eventually result in civil war. Thus, the process of negotiating the boundaries of Spanish culture, identity, and history is at the center of this study.

Historians of Spain have published many political and social histories of the Second Republic, but unlike the historiographical changes that have transpired in the last two decades in other fields of European history, the field of cultural history in Spain is only in its incipient phases.[2] Much work has been done on the educational system and the role of intellectuals during the Second Republic, and there is some degree of consensus indicating that the educational reforms embarked on during this period had their roots in liberal ideologies that were propounded during the late nineteenth century.[3] The few studies that look at the flourishing of culture during the Republic tend to cover the period only very briefly or fail to ground their cultural analysis in the realm of Spanish politics.[4] Although the new cultural histories are slowly trickling into contemporary Spanish historiography, no one has yet made the connection between the flourishing of state-sponsored cultural programs and the attempt to create a stable national identity, especially during the Second Republic.

When I first conceived of this project in the early 1990s, the study of Spanish nationalism and national identity was also in its infancy. Since then, a number of important books and articles about the strength—or lack thereof—of Spanish national identity in the nineteenth and twentieth centuries have appeared.[5] Most of this scholarship contends that Spanish nationalism, that is to say, peoples' identification with the Spanish state over all other forms of identification, failed to achieve a mass following before 1936. My study concurs with these conclusions. But I part company with those scholars who believe that politicians of the Second Republic "tended to assume that the republican nation already existed," or that "they failed to understand the need actively to take on the political and cultural task of 'making the nation,' as a dynamic project vis-à-vis the future," or that "there was little sense of the political need to invent new traditions or revivify old ones."[6] In fact, as I see it, the Republican–Socialist coalition clearly understood the need to invent traditions, as well as to "revivify old ones." And those opposed to the Republican–Socialist vision of Spanish identity understood all too well the powerful potential of these traditions—that is why they took every opportunity to dismantle the cultural programs that were implemented during the Second Republic.

## THEORIES ABOUT NATIONALISM

The most influential theorists of nationalism have differed over how and when groups of people privileged national identity over all other forms of identity. Some scholars credit a confluence of modern forces—including print capitalism, the French revolution, industrialization, and urbanization—as necessary to create the infrastructure and ideology of an "imagined community" that would eventually imagine itself as a modern nation.[7] Others, however, argue that nationalism was not a radical break from the pre-modern era.[8] As Miroslav Hroch has pointed out, the most fervent nationalist clashes actually occurred in nations that had not begun full-scale industrialization.[9]

Despite some of their disagreements, most of these scholars stress the "constructedness" of nationalism in the nineteenth century. According to them, identification with the nation was not something that poured forth naturally from the soul of the people, as Herder and other German Romantics would have us believe, but, in fact, was inculcated deliberately by various elites who tried to direct peoples' loyalties from a local community, religion, or class to the nation. This process included creating national myths; inventing traditions; binding people to a particular language, geographical territory, or religion; and solidifying this attachment through the schools (which spread both literacy and ideologies of the state), the press, public spectacles, and increasingly sophisticated networks of communications.

Some people have recently begun to challenge the idea of the nation as a constructed or imagined community and have instead offered more flexible analyses of national formation, national identity, and nationalism.[10] Prasenjit Duara demonstrates how other ideologies often compete with nationalism. He questions both the modernity of nationalism and the "constructivists'" tendency to essentialize the nation. The constructivists assume that the nation is a fixed entity, a collective historical subject and, therefore, nationalism becomes the master narrative for modern history. Duara counters these essentialist arguments by viewing nationalism and national identity as fluid relationships: "[National identity] thus resembles and is interchangeable with other political identities."[11] For him, "nationalism is rarely the nationalism of the nation, but rather represents the site where very different views of the nation contest and negotiate with each other." The meaning or meanings of the nation are constantly in flux; individuals and groups in both agrarian and industrial societies can imagine themselves in several types of communities simultaneously. And, he points out, "these identifications are historically changeable, and often conflicted with each other."[12]

The complexities of modern Spanish history, with its competing and splintering nationalisms, class warfare, and pockets of unwavering traditionalism, provide us with the basis for analyzing the multivalent aspects of national identity. While I certainly do not discount the modernizers' and constructivists' analyses of national identity, I prefer Duara's concept of national identity as a fluid relationship. He provides a theoretical framework for uncovering the oft-hidden political, social, economic, and cultural strategies of anarchists, Republicans, Socialists, Catalan nationalists, and traditionalists of the late nineteenth and early twentieth centuries.

## HEGEMONY

But this study is not only about the shifting sands of identity. It also attempts to demonstrate how various groups used cultural projects to build consensus—or, to use a more cynical turn of phrase—to orchestrate consent. And here, Antonio Gramsci's concepts of hegemony and counter-hegemony, defined broadly, help explain how and why the Republican–Socialist coalition used cultural projects as a means to construct a particular kind of national identity and how other groups sought ways to erode those efforts.[13]

Instead of securing and maintaining power through violence, a group vying for power can attain domination by consent—that is, by exercising hegemony—via politics and ideology. To establish hegemony, a group must build alliances among other groups who may share a common vision of the world, at least superficially,[14] and to sustain it, a group needs to transform popular consciousness and moral conduct in civil society.[15] This task is not easy because hegemony is never stable. Subordinate groups in the same civil society often try to counteract the influence of the hegemonic power by carving out an alternative hegemony, or counterhegemony.

Because the terms *hegemony* and *counterhegemony* imply both a constant negotiation of power and consent within the broad framework of domination and the quest to change popular consciousness around particular ideological issues, they help demonstrate the mechanisms by which Spanish Republicans sought to fight their war of position against the fraying elites represented by traditional groups such as the church, the military, and the large landholders, as well as how those elites tried to fight back. When the Republican–Socialist coalition triumphed on April 14, 1931, they had by no means a firm hold on the reins of power. They won the national elections by building a broad coalition that included Republicans, Socialists, and Catalan nationalists, whose common—if only temporary—conception of the world centered around eliminating the dictatorship and monarchy and replacing these tired forms of leadership with some breed of liberal democracy. Attaining power was relatively easy. Maintaining it would not be.

With the help of intellectuals, the coalition would try to use education and cultural programs to bring the inhabitants of rural areas and workers in the cities into the Republican fold and to instill in them the values of civic duty, voluntary association, and secularism. But others sought to dismantle the hegemonic edifice that the coalition tried so fiercely to erect. Anarchists and the radical right—to name but two groups—sought to construct counterhegemonies to the Republican's hegemony-in-process. It is perhaps this failure of any one group to achieve cultural hegemony that resulted in the Spanish Civil War.[16]

## CULTURE

Culture meant different things to Spanish and Catalan intellectuals and artists, and they applied their ideas about culture to such abstract notions as national or class identity. At its most basic level, *cultura* could mean either education or culture—or both—and Spanish speakers used these meanings interchangeably. But Republicans, Socialists, and anarchists used the term expansively, with meanings that ranged from education and literacy to arts and crafts to philosophy and sociology. As the Republican pedagogue Lorenzo Luzuriaga put it, culture encompasses "all of the products of the activity of mankind, from the most humble and utilitarian, such as domestic utensils and instruments of work, to the most elevated and spiritual [activities] of art and science."[17] When it came to disseminating their idea of culture, however, Republicans and their allies emphasized what historians call the products of elite culture, works that had reached canonical status in Spain and western Europe, while, paradoxically, they presented elements of the peasantry's own popular culture refracted through the prism of nationalism.[18]

By using the term *elite culture*, I do not want to imply that I mean *official culture*, although the terms are often seen as synonymous and, in the Spanish case, their meanings sometimes elide. Official culture—that is, urban culture sanctioned by the state and taught in the universities— did not always coincide with the culture practiced by intellectuals who felt disaffected by the corrupt Restoration System and the Primo de Rivera regime. From 1875 until the Second Republic, official culture represented religious and political elitism and corruption, a stagnant pool that drowned all new ideas. As José Ortega y Gasset stated in "Old and New Politics," there were two Spains, an official Spain and a vital Spain. The corrupt bureaucracy, politicians, and press inhabited the dying, official Spain, while young intellectuals alienated from the political process represented the vital Spain.[19] Those "vital Spaniards" who took part in the Republican cultural projects generally came from social elites, but their study of culture was incubated in schools like the Institución Libre de Enseñanza that had deliberately set itself apart from the state apparatus. Many had been schooled abroad for some portion of their lives and felt an affinity for the cultural trends that were emanating from the rest of western Europe. All believed that Spain was hopelessly backward. Therefore, they thought that the Spanish people needed an infusion of both western European official culture and canonical Spanish culture, which generally, but not exclusively, meant art, theater, and belles lettres from the sixteenth and seventeenth centuries. Now that these proponents of elite culture had assumed the mantle of power, vital Spain might finally transform official Spain and elite culture would replace official culture.

My work is also a study, then, of how a regime tried to reconfigure an official culture and make it accessible to a popular audience, in the process turning one of the oldest European states into a modern nation. Using memoirs, journals, newspapers, parliamentary debates, and archival sources, I look at the formation, dissemination, and impact of the cultural reforms during the Second Republic and the Spanish Civil War. I focus specifically on internal debates and external arguments over such contested cultural spheres as theater, literature, and film because cultural reformers tried to apply their theoretical ideas about culture and its dissemination to these three areas.

Theater represented the highest art form for most Spanish intellectuals whether they were anarchists, Republicans, Socialists, or conservatives, for Spain had a rich theatrical tradition that reached its pinnacle in the sixteenth and seventeenth centuries. More important, they all saw theater as a didactic art form, and many intellectuals believed that restaging old theatrical performances could unite communities that industrialization had rent asunder. For Republicans, Socialists, and anarchists, literature, and by this I generally mean belles lettres, also functioned didactically, imparting lessons about social justice and the nation. The Republican–Socialist coalition and the anarchists believed that they first had to expose the peasantry and working classes to literature through public readings, but, ultimately, they wanted to increase urban and rural literacy as a way of promoting social change. I also chose to look at their discussions about film, for this was a new, comparatively untested artistic medium for disseminating ideas to the masses. Intellectuals were less unified in their conception of what film could do than they were in their attitudes toward theater and literature, but, given the overwhelming popularity of this new mass cultural form, intellectuals could hardly avoid grappling with it.

Within these cultural areas, I demonstrate how Spanish intellectuals of various stripes struggled to define and construct a unified vision of culture to inform Spaniards' understanding of their past and their future, how they tried to fend off attacks from those who sought to provide alternative visions of identity, and how this cultural hegemony was used in an attempt to build a coherent state.

## INTELLECTUALS

Intellectuals were the major conduits for disseminating these alternative visions, and this makes sense, given that the Second Republic is often referred to as a "government of intellectuals." In many respects, its intellectual character set it apart from the rest of Europe. Though certainly no one would deny that Lenin and Trotsky were intellectuals, or that Mussolini had close connections with the Italian avant-garde, Spain was unusual in having democratically elected a large number of intellectuals to its parliament, the Cortes, in 1931. Prime Minister Manuel Azaña, for example, in addition to writing numerous essays, journal articles, plays, and novels, became the president of Madrid's Ateneo—the literary club of the Spanish intelligentsia—in 1930. The renowned philosopher-writers José Ortega y Gasset and Miguel de Unamuno participated as Cortes members, helping to shape both political and cultural policies. In fact, almost one-quarter of the Cortes was composed of university professors, teachers, journalists, and writers.[20] This preponderance of intellectuals clearly affected the tenor of Spanish politics.

José Alvarez Junco's schema is particularly useful in defining the Spanish intelligentsia.[21] He argues for a three-tiered definition of intellectuals: (1) the intellectual elite, (2) liberal professionals, and (3) bureaucrats and public functionaries. He defines the intellectual elite as "those who create new artistic products or mental schema"; the liberal professionals as those who disseminate information, namely, lawyers, journalists, teachers, doctors, and engineers; and the bureaucrats as those who do not depend on the "cultural market" for a living, but who serve a cultural function by connecting outside communities with the centralized government, thus socializing new generations in the "national culture." The first group creates products of culture, whereas the latter groups disseminate or administer the products of the first group. Alvarez Junco adds that "the intellectual is, above all, a *publicist* or *educator,* in the broadest sense of the term."[22]

This three-tiered definition works well in analyzing the functions of the various groupings of the intelligentsia during the Second Republic. In many ways, it sheds light on why officials of the Second Republic chose the types of cultural policies they did, and why, as I will argue, their cultural reforms tended to espouse nineteenth-century notions of culture such as theater, novels, and poetry but were slow to accept twentieth-century ones, such as film. The intellectuals responsible for creating cultural policy during the Second Republic tended to reflect the liberal professional and the bureaucratic and functionary groups more than the elite intellectual groups. In other words, the intellectuals most closely tied to the political programs of this period were those who functioned as disseminators of already existing ideas. This is not to say that members of the intellectual elite did not participate in the cultural projects of the Republic—they did. In fact, writers such as Federico García Lorca, Antonio Machado, Luis Cernuda, and Pedro Salinas volunteered their artistic and intellectual services to the Republic. But these artists, and a whole cadre of others besides them, also inhabited and experimented in an artistic world very much separate from the Spanish government, and one that drew sustenance from and contributed to avant-garde trends in the rest of Europe. My study focuses more specifically on those intellectuals who were intimately tied to the functioning of the state, those who would later be at the center of national conflict during the Second Republic and the Spanish Civil War.

Chapter 1 traces the nineteenth- and early-twentieth-century intellectual and social roots of that conflict. It outlines the clashes between liberal intellectuals and reformers, who tried to build a liberal state, and traditionalists, who sought to shore up a shaky monarchy and a church that was seriously weakened by the revolutionary forces that had affected the entire European continent. As we move to the latter part of the nineteenth century, we see the beginnings of resistance to the liberal agenda and reactions to Spain's loss of empire in 1898 via the development of anarchism and socialism on the one hand and of Catalanism on the other. Despite the ideological divide among these various groups, they shared the belief that education and culture held the key to either regeneration or revolution, or both.

Chapter 2 introduces the advent of the Second Republic and the new government's search for a way to handle the myriad social, political, and economic problems that had been laid at its doorstep. To avoid the mistakes that rulers had committed in the previous century, the Republican–Socialist coalition sought means to consolidate their power and unify their country. Looking at the Mexican and Russian revolutions as models, they chose to use education and cultural projects as a means to inculcate in people of rural Spain the values of the educated classes from Madrid. This chapter illuminates the debate among intellectuals across the political spectrum over the nature and function of "Spanish culture." Left- and right-wing ideologues conceived of culture differently and attempted to impose their particular visions of it in the political arena. Leftist Republicans pushed through a cultural program known as the Misiones Pedagógicas, which contained the basic tenets of the Republican agenda: the secularization of culture, the centralization of government, and the tensions between the "Europeanization" and "Castilianization" of Spain.

Chapter 3 shows how Republicans and Socialists saw within Spain's seventeenth-century Golden Age theater the means to create a "long-lost" community and to resolve the tension between those who wanted to see Spain more Europeanized and those who wanted to see it more

Hispanified. Sensing that modernity had fractured all elements of commonality and community among the peasantry and the urban dwellers, Republicans, in an attempt to reestablish that community, subsidized itinerant theatrical troupes that performed Golden Age theater. The most famous of those troupes was García Lorca's La Barraca. In contrast, anarchists eschewed what they viewed as bourgeois theater and worked to create a new type of theater for the working classes. They hoped that this new theater would educate the working classes in the tenets of anarchism. And, finally, some members of the right wanted to invent new dramas and to reclaim Golden Age theater to propagate their own ideas about the nation, religion, hierarchy, and empire.

Chapter 4 investigates the ways the Republican–Socialist coalition grappled with film to bolster cultural unification. Because they trusted the pedagogical possibilities of theater more than the unfamiliar territory of film, reform-minded Republicans failed to harness film's potentially propagandistic power and employed it in a very limited way, concentrating mostly on documentary and educational films as opposed to revolutionary ones. The debate over film's ability to move the masses and define the Spanish character really occurred outside the sphere of the liberal state. It took place instead in partisan film journals and was dominated by members of the extreme left and right.

Chapter 5 demonstrates how those in charge of cultural policy at the beginning of the Republic relied heavily on the reformative and restorative powers of literature. Seeing words as the building blocks of culture and civilization, they sought to increase literacy—especially in the rural sectors—to instill a love of reading and eventually to foster an appreciation of Castilian literature and language as embodiments of the Spanish national character. Eventually, reformers believed, this newly literate citizenry would be ready to take on the mantle of the modern state. But others, such as the anarchists, who also believed in the liberating possibilities of literacy, took many of the same canonical texts and interpreted them as paeans to revolution. Finally, the Catalans, who prided themselves on their own language and literature, resisted this Castilian hegemony.

Chapter 6 discusses how all of the previous cultural reforms played out during the Spanish Civil War, demonstrating how they evolved (or disappeared) with the exigencies of war and how the destabilizing effects of the war changed the tenor of cultural reform within both the Republican and Nationalist sides. The war's outbreak and the subsequent revolution pushed the leaders of the antagonistic camps to take more radical stances than they had during the Republic. The calls for cultural reform became more shrill, and partisans of both sides were willing to fight to the death to preserve their respective cultural visions for Spain.

This study, then, looks at the years preceding the bloodbath to show how, for a few brief years, a cohort of intellectuals and artists sought to transform the cultural and intellectual landscape of Spain and incorporate disparate groups into the fold of the nation. Their journey, as we shall see, was perilous, as they attempted to steer a careful course between tradition and modernity, and between reform and revolution.

CHAPTER 1

# The Center Cannot Hold

## *Intellectual and Social Roots*
## *of Republican Spain*

IN SPAIN THE NINETEENTH CENTURY READS LIKE A FRENZIED CATALOGUE
of wars, coups d'état, and catastrophes. In the space of about one hundred
years (1808–1898) Spain experienced foreign occupation; the ban, restoration, and final elimination of the Spanish Inquisition; scores of *pronunciamientos* (military takeovers); revolutions; three civil wars; a monarchical
restoration supported by an intricate political system that institutionalized political corruption; and, finally, the loss of the last vestiges of its
overseas empire. The opening decades of the twentieth century seemed no
less chaotic. The working classes and rural laborers, long excluded from
participating in Spain's political and economic spheres, registered their
disaffection with the system through strikes and terrorist activity. Catalan
nationalists clamored for autonomy, and the Spanish military fought
tenaciously for control of Spanish Morocco. Even liberals lost faith in a
system that purported to be democratic but served the needs of a minus-
cule elite. By 1923, when General Miguel Primo de Rivera staged a pronunciamiento, many people welcomed his dictatorship as a balm for
Spain's seemingly perpetual social unrest. This period saw many groups
scramble to refashion a Spanish nation out of the wreckage of the dis-
solute Restoration System. To demonstrate the multitude of problems
that Spaniards encountered, this chapter will unravel the various social,
cultural, and intellectual threads that made up the fabric of Spain between
1875 and 1931.

In retrospect, much of the chaos of the nineteenth and early twentieth
centuries appears to be no different from that of the rest of the continent,

especially France and central Europe. Like its counterparts, Spain had to adjust to the residual ideological and political ramifications of the French Revolution and the subsequent Metternichean restoration. Although steeped in a militantly Catholic and absolutist past, Spaniards could not help but be altered by the ideologies that emerged from the revolution to the north. Spain experienced immense dislocations in its attempts to transform itself from an ostensibly feudal society to a liberal, industrial one.

Spain was not alone in its quest for stability—witness, for example, the European-wide revolutions of 1848 and the Paris Commune of 1871. Many disenfranchised Europeans demanded their individual rights from revanchist monarchs, while the growing working classes agitated for better working conditions, political rights, and, sometimes, revolution. European statesmen did their best to quash rebelliousness by force, but they also tried to lessen their populations' disaffection with industrialization and other by-products of modernization by encouraging an allegiance to the nation. The communal ties that had been destroyed by industrialization and urbanization could be re-created through nationalism. But some of the people who were most affected by the dislocations wrought by the transition to capitalist economies, namely, the working classes and displaced rural laborers, sought their communal ties not in the nation but in class solidarity.

For the first two-thirds of the nineteenth century, Spanish liberals attempted to transform Spain into their vision of a modern state, free from the encumbrances of absolutist monarchs and retrograde Catholics. The more radical liberals sought a constitutional representative government that gave sovereignty to the nation, the end of church authority in state affairs, the disentailment of land, the abolition of seigneurial privileges, and the development of a modern, capitalist economy. By 1840, much of the liberal program had been achieved, especially the creation of private property and, at least on paper, state centralization. But other qualities that scholars have used to judge the strength of the liberal state in Europe—universal primary education and an efficient transportation system to import and export goods and services—were sorely lacking in Spain at this time.[1] The liberal state benefited only a small minority at great cost. For example, the liberals' disentailment policies transferred one-quarter to one-third of the national land surface to different hands, but the structure of land ownership changed little.[2] The inability of Spanish liberals to spread the benefits of liberalism to the majority of the population also contributed to government instability and the numerous pronunciamientos that characterized nineteenth-century Spain.

The Restoration settlement of 1875, with its infamous *turno pacífico* (peaceful rotation), brought a measure of political stability for at least the next twenty years, but Spaniards paid a high economic and social price for this peace. Antonio Cánovas del Castillo developed the turno pacífico as a strategy to prevent the numerous pronunciamientos and civil wars that had threatened the Spanish state's stability. It allowed for the peaceful rotation of power between two groups, Liberals and Conservatives. When one party was deemed to be losing support, the king would dissolve the cabinet, appoint a new prime minister from the opposition party, and then that party would rule until the next crisis forced another change. This system achieved success through the machine politics known as *caciquismo*. Once the oligarchs in Madrid drew up their list of candidates, they would contact the local provincial and municipal notables who had ties with the local party bosses—the *caciques*. The caciques would then tell people in their districts how to vote, usually in exchange for things like exemption from military service or taxes, or employment. This system, most observable in rural areas, may have gotten the "right" people elected, but the government was rarely able to collect enough taxes to create the kinds of public works that might strengthen the state's infrastructure, and so the gap between rural and urban Spaniards increased.

The Restoration System began breaking down slightly with the Spanish defeat in Cuba and the Philippines in 1898. This colonial loss exacerbated tensions that had been brewing just beneath the surface of Cánovas's political politesse. Catalan nationalists, embarrassed and hurt economically by what they perceived to be the bungling of the centralized government in Madrid, put their nationalist throttle into high gear and began demanding Catalan autonomy and, sometimes, independence. The 1898 "disaster," so called because it ended Spanish colonialism, also spawned a giant wave of criticism from all parties and social classes against the Spanish state. Known collectively as the regenerationist movement, these reformers sought ways to regain the former glory of Spain in the sixteenth century and to bring about Spain's regeneration.[3]

Between 1898 and 1931, as fragmentation and social dislocation became even more pronounced, these quests for unity intensified. Believing that Spain's social disintegration had been caused by modernization, various groups harked back to a golden age when people felt connected to a greater community. They sought to re-create this communal sensibility by fostering an allegiance to the nation—however they defined it—or, in the case of the anarchists and sometimes the Socialists, an allegiance to one's class. Although one might claim that there was no serious national-ist movement on the scale of other European nations between 1808 and 1931, Spain was not devoid of nationalists. Different social and political groups tried to solidify and impose their particular vision for strengthen-ing the nation, or, in the case of the anarchists, their community, but their attempts to attain hegemony became but one of many in a din of competing ideologies. All of the groups concerned with changing the future of Spain believed that education was the key to social change, to forming community bonds, and to fostering Spain's regeneration.

## LIBERAL EDUCATION

By the late nineteenth century, Spain had the trappings of a liberal state— a constitution, universal manhood suffrage, an industrializing economy— but not the infrastructure or the popular support necessary to carry out the grand changes envisioned by the architects of liberalism. Liberals believed that Spain needed to open itself up to the progressive forces of Europeanization that is, to the ideas of the Enlightenment and the tech-nological innovations of industrialization. Because Spain had not kept up with western European trends, liberals believed, it had declined from its position as the world's greatest empire to become a third-bit player on the stage of international politics. Literacy statistics for this period bear out liberals' fears. As late as 1887, some 65 percent of the Spanish population was illiterate. Broken down regionally, the statistics become even more grim. For example, in the province of Granada, illiteracy was 80 percent, whereas in the province of Madrid, it was only 38 percent.[4] According to liberals, if Spain were going to compete on the international market, it would need a literate workforce. But the solidly entrenched Catholic Church rebuffed many attempts at modernization, seeing the devil's work in liberalism and blaming it for Spain's decline. During the early nine-teenth and early twentieth centuries, the liberals struggled incessantly with the Catholic Church to define Spanish identity. They thought Spain would not succeed as an international power until the last vestiges of retrograde Catholicism had been rooted out of politics and until Spaniards could compete in the industrial arena. Coming squarely out of the Enlighten-ment tradition, Spanish liberals saw education as the only hope for Span-ish regeneration.

## KRAUSISM

The most influential school of thought on nineteenth-century Spanish Liberals was Krausism. Named after Karl Krause (1781–1832), Krausism was a variant of German idealist philosophy. Brought from Germany to Spain in 1844 by the Spaniard Julián Sanz del Río, Krausism exerted a tremendous influence during the late nineteenth and early twentieth centuries in the spheres of education, politics, law, and culture. Sanz del Río's teachings were seminal in the founding of the Institución Libre de Enseñanza, which, in turn, produced many leaders responsible for the cultural reforms of the Second Republic. These two movements—and the backlash against them—mapped out the course that the cultural and intellectual fields would take in the hands of politicians, church activists, and intellectuals during the Second Republic.

In Spain, Krausism belonged to a cluster of reform movements that swept the universities in the first half of the nineteenth century. Given the wretched state of most Spanish universities (which lacked qualified professors, libraries, and laboratories), educational reformers sought to gut the entire university system and start anew. Based on the alarming state of Spanish education, some pedagogues and politicians began looking to France and Germany as models for reforming the Spanish educational system. Sanz del Río was the first person to bridge this "education gap." Hired in 1843 to fill the position of interim professor of philosophy at the University of Madrid, Sanz del Río was required by the Minister of the Interior, Pedro Gómez de la Serna, to spend two years in Germany to learn what he could about the major schools of German philosophy.[5] While in Germany, however, he gravitated toward Krause's work and dropped any pretensions of studying the most important nineteenth-century German philosophers. He returned to Madrid in 1844, but to the university only in 1854, where he influenced "the first generation of Spanish Krausists."[6]

As interpreted by Sanz del Río, Krausism melded the concepts of scientific reason, mysticism, positivism, and idealist philosophy into a totalizing theory for political, legal, educational, and economic reform.[7] Krause developed a philosophy of ethics that posited God as a moving force, without denying human action or culpability. Like many of his Enlightenment-minded contemporaries, he believed in human perfectibility, but this perfectibility came from attaining a knowledge of God through reason. He synthesized Enlightenment reason with idealist philosophy, and it is this seemingly harmonic synthesis that begins to explain the Spanish love affair with Krausism.

What attracted Spanish liberal intellectuals to follow Krause rather than Hegel, the philosophical giant? Some credit religion as the characteristic that most distinguished Krausism from other reformist ideologies that developed before or since.[8] People who wrote about the Krausists painted them as descendants of the reformist tradition that flourished in the sixteenth and seventeenth centuries.[9] Like those religious renegades of the Counter-Reformation, the nineteenth-century Krausists saw the need to overhaul church practices.

Reformers of the nineteenth century perceived the Catholic Church to be too closely allied to the forces of reaction, namely, the monarchy and the landed oligarchy. The church had turned its back on the downtrodden, had neglected their poverty, and chose instead to ingratiate itself with those who were prosperous enough to support its administrative and financial interests.[10] The church controlled the educational system, but the "policy of the religious orders in the early nineteenth century had been to prevent the poor from learning to read";[11] their fervent antiliberalism isolated middle-class Spaniards from the teachings available in the rest of western Europe. The Spanish church rejected any ideas associated with Enlightenment education and seriously discouraged importing any of the scientific and educational trends that were then emanating from northern and western Europe.

Krausism filled a need for those who had become disillusioned with the traditional Catholic Church. The Krausist God was a harmonious and loving one, whose world functioned best when all members of society cooperated with one another and when all people sought to lead their individual lives as morally as possible. Furthermore, He did not frown on the pursuit of scientific knowledge. People could attain knowledge of God and, consequently, could evolve toward human perfection through reason. This blending of reason and spirit offered an alternative to those who felt themselves intellectually stifled by the Catholic Church. But the Krausist melding of intellect and spirit did not connote any desire to break with the church.

Yet the religious aspects of Krausism do not completely or always convincingly explain its appeal to Spanish intellectuals. Krause's emphasis on finding harmony even within the most seemingly unresolvable conflicts may have been the balm that Spain longed for when such events as the War of Independence, the Carlist Wars, and waves of pronunciamientos

so painfully disrupted society and politics.[12] Therefore, Krausist philosophy suited the cultural, intellectual, and political needs of Spain during
the latter half of the nineteenth century more readily than someone like
Hegel could, and Krausism coincided most readily with liberal thought.[13]

In fact, while bathed in the language of harmonious rationalism, Sanz
del Ríos' political tracts read very much like textbook descriptions of
classical liberalism. He sought religious, political, economic, and intellectual liberty through "the gradual transformation of political institutions
for the peaceful and lawful development of all institutions." He also
called for limited state and clerical intervention to facilitate the "free
movement of social forces according to their nature and their relative
ends."[14] His desire for gradual reform within the political system bespoke
more of Krause's organic unity than of Hegel's dialectical clashes of
opposing ideas.

Education and "civilization" were seen as the tools for transforming
the state. Since every human had the potential to know God through
reason, all people could eventually use this reason—acquired through
education—to eliminate immoral behavior and attain God's goodness.
As each person reached a higher moral plane, the aggregation of all these
educated and "civilized" people would create a state that moved closer to
God's perfection. In the following decades, the theme of education as
a civilizing process would appear repeatedly in the calls for educational
and cultural reforms. But because it devalued homegrown Spanish
thought in favor of European intellectual trends, Krausist education
soon proved threatening to both church and state. More precisely, the
new intellectuals and educators looked toward the rational Europe of the
Enlightenment tradition as their model for cultural, spiritual, and material regeneration.

Sanz del Río's ideas put him into conflict almost immediately with the
neo-Catholics at the University of Granada. His teachings and popularity
incurred their wrath, and they accused him of practicing pantheism and
of espousing "anti-Catholic doctrines" and heterodox ideas "capable of
corrupting the heart of the youth." They charged Krausist philosophy
with propagating the "infection of contemporary society" and promised
to wage war against this new intellectual scourge. Hoping to rid higher
education of these toxic elements, the neo-Catholics called on the government to expel Krausist professors from the university.[15] In fact, between
1865 and 1875, the Krausist professors were regularly removed and then
reinstated, subject to the political tides of the volatile Spanish state.

The restoration of the Bourbon monarchy in 1875 signaled a return to the reactionary policies that preceded the 1868 September Revolution. The conservative Minister of Public Instruction, Manuel de Orovio, issued a decree to "remedy … the damage that has befallen education on account of free thinking" and warned rectors to watch over their professors so that they would not teach "anything contrary to dogma or healthy morality."[16] Once again, the professors protested, and they were tossed out of the university. In response, some of these disciples of Sanz del Río formed their own educational center, known as the Institución Libre de Enseñanza, a school that would train a significant number of people who would prove to be highly influential in developing cultural and political policies during the Second Republic. Many of the people who became government officials during the Republic had come of age during the regeneration debate of the late nineteenth century, and they had either taken part in molding the Institución Libre or, at least, flowered in the intellectual climate that it nurtured.[17]

This ongoing struggle for power between the Krausists and the forces allied with the Catholic Church had serious implications for the future of educational and cultural reform within Spain. As already noted, the early Krausists had no desire to topple the church. Instead, they hoped to infuse Catholicism with renewed spiritual vigor. But because of the church's intransigence, the Krausists severed their ties with it. This rupture resulted in the gradual evolution of Krausism from a deeply religious body of thought to an increasingly anticlerical one, and for the next half-century, the church vigorously opposed anything associated with Krausism or "freethinking," and this culminated in their extreme polarization during the Second Republic and the Civil War.

## INSTITUCIÓN LIBRE DE ENSEÑANZA

After the numerous clashes with the Spanish government and Catholic Church, Francisco Giner de los Ríos—a disciple of Sanz del Río—along with Nicolás Salmerón, Gumersindo de Azcárate, Montero Ríos, Segismundo Moret, and Joaquín Costa, formed the Institución Libre de Enseñanza (ILE) in 1876 as a private coeducational school designed to be free from any political or religious affiliation.[18] The ILE represented the first real practical application of Krausist philosophy. While many recognize Sanz del Río as bringing Krausist philosophy to Spain, they credit Giner de los Ríos for putting the practical spin on Krausist doctrines and inspiring generations of teachers and students to use education and culture to aid Spain's regeneration.

Giner, like many Krausists, thought that an uneducated populace posed the most fundamental problem for Spain. No social or political reforms could take place without reforming individual Spaniards themselves, and the only way to salvage individuals was through education,[19] thus demonstrating the Krausist emphasis on improvement of the organic whole through gradual reform of its individual parts. From 1876 until his death in 1915, Giner dedicated himself to revamping Spain's educational system under the auspices of the ILE.

When the ILE first began, its organizers self-consciously wrote a manifesto that aligned itself against the doctrines of people such as Minister Orovio. This new school proclaimed itself to be "completely free from any religious affiliation, philosophical school or political party; proclaiming only the inviolability and liberty of science, and the independence of its research and teaching, irrespective of any other authority than the conscience of the professor, the only one responsible to its doctrines."[20] Although one could question whether any form of education is politically neutral, the founders of the ILE were true nineteenth-century liberals who endeavored to further the education of a small class of students by teaching them scientific methods and other modern techniques lacking in a typical Spaniard's education. The ILE also revolutionized education by being the first school in Spain to have coeducational classes.

Although the *institucionistas* desired primarily to develop the students' scientific minds, they also saw the need to create an elite class of well-rounded individuals who were capable of serving the nation. Influenced by the educational theories of Locke, Rousseau, and Pestalozzi, the institucionistas believed that education should excite the students' interest, making learning joyous rather than a chore. They emphasized manual labor alongside intellectual pursuits, bringing together what Descartes had rent asunder: body and mind. The bulk of learning would occur outside the classroom. Instead of using textbooks (which were forbidden because they filled pages with dull prose, stagnant formulas, and tedious charts), teachers expected students to learn about art by visiting museums, about history by studying the architecture of a local building, and about science by conducting experiments in the natural world. Nevertheless, books became the students' most crucial avenues of enlightenment: "The Institution hopes that its students will avail themselves quickly and fully of *books* as the greatest fount of culture."[21] The educators were not talking about textbooks but, rather, what we might call "classics," works that had been included in the canon and that comprised what every learned person should know. According to the institucionistas, these canonized works gave students more insight into Spanish culture and fostered in their pupils a greater sense of loyalty to the Spanish nation.

For Krausists such as Giner de los Ríos, literature and art, but especially literature, contained the truest version of a nation's essence, its "internal history." Political history, what Krausists would characterize as "external history," was a mere chronicle devoid of spirit and morality, a "mute hulk made of events, a skeleton neither clothed in virile muscle nor quickened by the blood's life-giving heat."[22] History, according to Krause, "is the result of a clash between two aspects of man: the outer and the inner. The outer is considered temporary and superficial; the inner ideal and eternal."[23] Thus, events alone cannot offer us a glimpse of the inner essences of people because they are too random to offer any meaning. Instead, the combined inner essences of individuals add up to a collective essence that is the spirit—the *genio*—of the nation. In many ways, Krause's ideas as filtered through Giner represented a distillation of nineteenth-century German romanticism and nationalism best typified by Fichte and Hegel.[24]

History was not useful if it could not tell us something about the human spirit or provide a moral purpose. That is why, according to the Krausists and the institucionistas, literature, especially theater, provided the best forum for transmitting a nation's historical essence: "[Literature] offers with the greatest clarity and precision this happy harmony of the general with the individual.... Suppress the literature of the people, and in vain will they resort to reconstructing their past and their political history."[25] Thus, if one wanted to find out about the grandeur of the sixteenth century or the decline of the seventeenth, one needed only to look at the plays of Lope de Vega or Pedro Calderón de la Barca. For in these plays history "appears most truthfully in its fullest spirit, with all of the distinctive traces of its physiognomy, marvelously expressed by those immortal men."[26]

An aesthetic education, therefore, became a major tenet of the ILE's pedagogical philosophy and the basis of a culturally nationalist program. As we shall see, this belief in the moral attributes of aesthetic creations profoundly influenced those people who carried out the series of cultural programs during the Second Republic. At the same time, other groups generally opposed to liberal politics shared these same beliefs in education's power to effect radical ideological changes.

## ANARCHIST EDUCATION AND CULTURE

While liberals tried to build the foundations of a modern nation by extirpating the influence of the Catholic Church and cultivating a small, educated elite to lead Spain back to international prominence, other groups sought their support among urban and rural laborers to create identities to rival both the liberal and traditional Catholic conceptions of the nation. The most influential of these—the anarchists, Socialists, and Radical Republicans—targeted subaltern groups as the source of radical change and regeneration.[27] These three entities sought to significantly alter the Spanish state as conceived by liberals and traditionalists; like the liberals, however, supporters of these groups fastened onto education as the force for social transformation.[28] Of the three, the anarchists proved the most dogged educators, attempting to educate both rural and urban laborers and to create an alternative cultural framework within the constraints of a corrupt and often repressive political system.

Anarchism itself was a child of the Enlightenment. Proponents of anarchist thought took the Enlightenment ideals of individual freedom and faith in science and reason and used them to challenge the intellectual suppositions behind private property, state centralization, and religion. Individual freedom lay at the core of anarchist thought, and anything that impinged on that freedom, for example, the church and the state, had to be swept away like so many insistent cobwebs.

Although anarchism, like most "isms," never took the form of a monolithic, homogeneous movement,[29] various anarchist ideologies, no matter from whom they originated—Mikhail Bakunin, Peter Kropotkin, Errico Malatesta, or Elisée Réclus—possessed some common vision of an anarchist world. They longed in some ways for an antediluvian past when free individuals organized themselves into harmonious groups and worked for the benefit of the community. Like Rousseau, who wrote, "The first person who, having enclosed a piece of land, thought of saying 'This is mine' and found people simple enough to believe him, was the true founder of civil society,"[30] anarchists believed that all of the evils of society could be traced to private property. Property owners used the police, the military, the law courts, and religion to protect their possessions, dehumanizing others in the process. Therefore, the institutions at the service of private property had to be destroyed through revolution. Unlike the Marxists, whose revolution would result, at least for some time, in a centralized state run by a dictatorship of the proletariat, the anarchists eschewed any form of state centralization, preferring instead either some form of federalism or libertarian communism to encourage local control. In an anarchist world, an organization of free associations and collectivized agriculture and industry that united production and consumption would replace the dehumanizing and demoralizing pitting of landowner against laborer and of capitalist against proletariat. Humans would labor together in the spirit of cooperation, forming communities that were decidedly not nationalist. Through scientific education, humanity would finally reach its potential to do good in this world.

Anarchist ideology was first introduced into Spain by the Federal Republican Francisco Pi y Margall, who disseminated Pierre Joseph Proudhon's ideas, and later by Mikhail Bakunin's Italian disciple, Giuseppe Fanelli, who saw in the September Revolution of 1868 the opportunity to channel urban and rural laborers' discontent into a revolutionary social movement.[31] After the September Revolution and the subsequent tumultuous six-year period known as the Sexenial (1868–1874) failed to institute the economic and social reforms promised by the Federalists, many laborers turned to anarchism to ensure their newly developing class identity.[32] And from the outset, anarchists used education to recruit followers and to foment revolution.

In the early years of Spanish anarchism (and anarchism in general), acratic theorists debated the role of education in revolution. Should education be used as a method to eradicate peoples' religious and bourgeois prejudices *after* the revolution, or should it be a *tool* of revolution, providing individuals with the intellectual framework to carry out the necessary attacks on church and state?[33] During the 1870s and 1880s, Bakunin and his Spanish followers focused on bringing the revolution to fruition. For them, education could not succeed until the revolution decimated the corrupt vestiges of the old regime. Bakunin stressed the need for revolution before education. But after it became clear that the anarchist revolution would not come about immediately—which was attested to by the often violent and unsuccessful conflicts that ensued between anarchists and the state during these decades—the anarchist theorist Peter Kropotkin developed an evolutionary theory of change with education as the catalyst. Instead of arguing the social Darwinian idea of survival of the fittest, whereby creatures in the natural world had to pitch battles of strength and wit to survive in the cruel world, Kropotkin posited a natural world in which organisms evolved through an altruistic strategy of mutual aid. Having been inculcated with and perverted by the superstitions promulgated by the coercive forces of church and state, humans had lost this capacity for cooperation. Under Kropotkin's strategy, the school would free children from these superstitions and return them to their once natural state. Evolution, not revolution, would win out. Kropotkin's ideas about mutual aid and evolutionary education would begin to influence anarchist pedagogy at the turn of the century.[34]

Despite their differences about the role education would play in the revolution, many anarchist theorists espoused what they called "integrated education," a philosophy of education similar to that practiced by the ILE. Following the educational philosophies propounded by Locke, Rousseau, Pestalozzi, and Dewey, mixed in with a bit of Bakunin, Kropotkin, and Tolstoy, anarchists espoused an educational system that focused on the children's needs—not the instructor's—and, like the institucionistas, the anarchists insisted on maintaining their independence from church and state. While many Socialists and Republicans called for universal, state-supported education, anarchists balked at the proposal. To them, any education propounded by the state would mirror its bourgeois class prejudices. Children would not be free to develop a critical mind, nor would they receive the tools necessary to carry out radical social change. State education bred an anesthetized populace willing to do the bidding of the government. Anarchists also shared with the institucionistas the belief that manual and intellectual labor should be integrated into the curriculum (hence the name "integrated education") and that textbooks should be thrown into the nearest receptacle. Children had to be allowed to explore the world around them, to try experiments, to wander outside the confines of the classroom, to exercise body and mind.

For all of their discussion about integrated education, anarchists rarely attempted anything so grand. The early anarchist schools of the 1870s and 1880s were impromptu centers that worked clandestinely and unsystematically, forgoing the complexities of integrated education for the practicality of literacy training. Unlike the theorists who viewed education in revolutionary terms, most workers desired a practical education that emphasized basic literacy and mathematics, knowing that such skills might enhance their ability to climb the social and economic ladder.[35]

The first anarchist school to espouse the principles of integrated or rational education was the Modern School (Escuela Moderna) in Barcelona, although it did not always put these principles into practice. It was founded by the libertarian Francisco Ferrer y Guardia on September 8, 1901, with money he had inherited from his wealthy pupil, Ernestine

Meunié. The Modern School first opened its doors to thirty pupils, eighteen boys and twelve girls. Unlike most schools of its day, the Modern School accepted children from a variety of social classes, for Ferrer believed that no revolution could come about until members of different social classes became aware of entrenched social and economic inequality. Unfortunately for the working classes, whose wages rarely went beyond subsistence levels, the fees charged to students were prohibitive. Instead, because the school offered a more rigorous and progressive curriculum than many of the schools available in Barcelona at the time, many of the students came from the progressive segments of the middle class. Ferrer and the other teachers at the Modern School engaged in a radical anarchist pedagogy, treating every academic subject as an avenue for discussing the exploitation of laborers by capitalists, by the state, and by the church. Because he could not find textbooks that satisfied the needs of his libertarian pedagogy, he set up a publishing house to disseminate radical literature for his students and for those who were interested in anarchist ideas.

Ferrer's Modern School achieved a nominal amount of success, and every year the enrollment increased,[36] that is, until 1906 when Spanish authorities charged Ferrer with masterminding the plot—although not participating directly in it—to kill Alfonso XIII and his bride on their wedding day, May 31, 1906. Because the assassin Mateo Morral worked in Ferrer's publishing house, the authorities used this as evidence of Ferrer's complicity in the plot and immediately shut down the Modern School, blaming it for spreading the sorts of radical ideas that engendered political assassinations.[37] Although the authorities kept him in jail for a year, they eventually acquitted him at his trial for lack of evidence. But the events in Barcelona in August 1909, now known as Tragic Week, ended Ferrer's experiment in radical education. He was arrested on August 31 and charged with unleashing the anticlerical conflagration that leveled numerous monasteries and churches throughout the city. After a kangaroo-court trial, Ferrer was found guilty of inciting the working classes to violence and sentenced to death. Although his execution spurred worldwide protests, to Spanish authorities, his death and the subsequent repression against the working classes heralded the end of anarchist education and violence.

But they did not. In fact, despite the repression that followed, anarchist activists formed the Confederación Nacional del Trabajado (CNT) in 1911, a national anarchist organization dedicated to syndicalist tactics; that is, they employed trade unionist tactics to achieve revolutionary goals. More important, anarchist education continued, despite Ferrer's death. Other avenues of anarchist education had already developed alongside libertarian schools since the 1870s. *Ateneos* for the working classes and rural laborers—cultural centers where people could meet, hold conferences, sometimes take classes, or read—sprung up all around Spain. After 1911, many CNT headquarters served the same purpose as the ateneos: they became safe havens for anarchists to proselytize, to learn, and to educate. Volunteers in these community-based centers taught children and adults to read and write. As one participant described the classes: "The education in the school was a totally different kind of education.... Each person would talk about what he had read,... and then we would all talk about it, and think about what each had said.... As far as I am concerned, the school and the books were probably the greatest factors shaping my development."[38] Laborers who knew how to read could often browse among a vast range of texts and journals, from revolutionary anarchist and Socialist tracts, to works on the latest scientific discoveries, and on to canonical texts in literature. In the larger ateneos in urban areas, workers could go to conferences where speakers would discuss such things as anarchism, education, and the latest scientific achievements. Members of urban ateneos also organized trips out of the city to give people the opportunity to learn about the nature that had been denied them. One anarchist explained this practice as a way to "allow young people to experience freedom, so that they will want to live it and defend it."[39] Finally, these cultural centers prepared Spanish youths for a life of political activism. If successful, the ateneos and CNT headquarters could achieve the decentralization of education, provide the tools for self-education, and eventually encourage a radical change of thinking in individuals. These libertarian-educated individuals could then do the necessary legwork to prepare their communities for revolutionary change.

Anarchist journals were the third prong of the acratic educational agenda. Libertarian journals flourished between the 1880s and the 1930s, although they sometimes lived tenuous existences that depended on the vicissitudes of political repression. Such journals as *Acracia, Natura, Estudios, Tiempos Nuevos,* and the most famous, *La Revista Blanca,* as well as anarchist newspapers, *Tierra y Libertad* and *Solidaridad Obrera,* provided the intellectual framework for anarchist ideas, while *La Revista Blanca* disseminated scientific and revolutionary ideas from within and without Spain. The journals discussed a wide variety of subjects, including vegetarianism, free love, eugenics, abortion, revolutionary libertarian-ism, and the development of an anarchist culture, while the newspapers focused more on the daily struggles facing the working classes and rural laborers in Spain.[40] Those who published and wrote for the acratic presses tried to provide Spanish laborers with the intellectual tools necessary for articulating their grievances and for fomenting revolution. They also created an alternative space for workers, a counterhegemonic identity not found in the mainstream presses, that reflected the harsh circumstances of their lives.

## SOCIALIST EDUCATION

Anarchists may have attracted the most laborers to their cause, but they still had competition from groups such as the Socialists. After very slow beginnings in Spain, Socialists rivaled anarchists and Radical Republicans for working-class loyalty. Unlike anarchists, Socialists concentrated their efforts on radicalizing a smaller group, the traditionally defined working classes who were centered in urban areas.[41] Not as independent-minded as anarchists, Spanish Socialists relied both on Socialist educational pro-grams tried in other European countries and on educational methods as practiced by the institucionistas.

Unlike anarchism, which debuted rather spectacularly in Spain, social-ism took longer to take root there. Spain's Socialist Party (Partido Social-ista Obrero Español; PSOE) and its labor union, the General Union of Workers (Unión General de Trabajadores; UGT), were founded by Pablo Iglesias in 1879 and 1882, respectively, but until the Second Republic, they fought to increase working-class membership, maintaining strongholds only in Madrid, Bilbao, and Asturias. Spanish Socialists offered a more reformist path for the working classes than anarchism and adhered to an evolutionary socialism that was less radical than its European counter-parts.[42] Other historians have discussed the numerous reasons behind socialism's slow implantation and reformist course in Spain, but to help explain the path that Spanish Socialist cultural and educational reforms took, two reasons rank highest.

First, events such as Tragic Week in 1909 and the brutal government repression that followed led Socialists to ally with Republicans as a way to dismantle the long-discredited oligarchy cemented by Cánovas's turno pacífico. Pablo Iglesias had originally balked at any negotiations or alliances with "bourgeois" groups, but when it seemed that the inevitable revolution was not to be, he switched courses and decided that Spain needed a "bourgeois revolution" before it could reach the historically determined "proletariat revolution." This meant an electoral alliance with the Republicans and the tacit assumption that Spain would become a republic first. The 1909 alliance paved the way for more liberal intellectuals to join the PSOE, which also lent the party a reformist bent. The most prominent Spanish Socialist theoreticians, Luis Araquistáin and Julián Besteiro, both of whom joined the PSOE in 1909, and Fernando de los Ríos, who joined in 1919, were all schooled by the Institución Libre de Enseñanza. This background gave the Spanish Socialist Party its reform-oriented Krausist and institucionista stamp.[43] In other words, because many of the institucionistas formed the leadership of the Socialist Party, Socialist transformation was moderate, not extreme.

Second, the failure of the attempted 1917 general strike and the all too familiar government crackdown and jailing of Socialist leaders that followed, deterred the Socialists from engaging in revolutionary action until 1934. Membership in the UGT fell to 89,601 in 1918, a drop of 10,000 members in one year.[44] With its leadership jailed and its organization in tatters, the dominant *pablista* wing of the Socialists moved cautiously toward gradual reform instead of revolution. Therefore, when the Bolshevik revolution made gigantic waves in other parts of Europe, Spanish Socialists stayed away from the water. For the Socialists, a revolutionary course in Spain meant only bloodshed and defeat for workers.[45]

Change would have to come less sanguinarily. Spanish Socialists could still look to a Europe long fertilized by Marxist ideas to help transform the Spanish working classes along Socialist lines, while stopping short of revolution. What did they see as the answer to their dilemma? Culture and education. As one editorial in the Socialist newspaper, *El Socialista,* put it: "The emancipating ideal of socialism is economic and spiritual, and to reach it, the fundamental base is culture."[46]

When Pablo Iglesias first tackled the problem of workers' education and cultural development in the late nineteenth century, like the anarchists, he pushed for the creation of a separate workers' culture that would change the workers' morality and ethics to form a new prototype: the Socialist Man.[47] The Socialist Man, free from the taint of religious and bourgeois superstitions and educated along rational and scientific lines, would lead other workers out of their destitute condition and prepare them for the revolution that would end in a Socialist state. But, as we know, after 1917, the workers' eviscerated condition led them to forsake revolutionary tactics. Any of their attempts to create an alternative Socialist culture failed to cohere. Thus, after 1918, Spanish Socialists decided to concentrate their efforts on transforming the state educational system, although they did not completely abandon their hopes to create alternative educational centers for workers.

The Socialists differed from the anarchists in their willingness to use the state for social change.[48] They believed that as long as enough Socialist allies held positions of power within the state apparatus, the state could perform the function of disseminating Socialist ideology to the masses just as well as individual Socialist missionaries could. But, of course, until the Second Republic, the Catholic Church still exerted great influence over the educational curriculum, preventing the Socialists from making much headway in the process.[49] By the 1920s, Spanish Socialists were hell-bent on providing workers access to a solid education that would equip them with the tools for carrying on the task of socialism. They tried both informal and formal means to supply workers with a rational, integral education.

The Casa del Pueblo (The People's House) proved the most successful of these informal avenues. Similar to the anarchist and liberal ateneos, the Casa del Pueblo, which was usually located in each provincial capital, served multiple functions for workers: as a UGT meeting hall, a lending library, a conference and lecture hall, and a place for workers to socialize. It was the one place where workers felt free to be themselves and where they could shut out the conflicts of the working world. As one worker put it, it was "the workers' palace."[50] Madrid's Casa del Pueblo, inaugurated on November 28, 1908, became the model for all of Spain. At its height it had a food cooperative, a cafe and salon for meetings, a theater with 4,000 seats, a library with over 8,000 volumes, a sport team, a choral society, a performance group, and a mutual aid society. A world unto its own, the Casa del Pueblo provided a separate space for working-class cultural activities. It both nurtured and educated workers by providing artistic performances, adult education courses, and access to information and ideas through its library and series of speakers. With the Casa del Pueblo, the Socialists succeeded in creating an informal space for workers to gather, socialize, and learn, but the path to more formalized education eluded them.

Given the relative strength of Socialist agitation in other European countries in the 1920s, compared to Spain's sclerotic socialism, Spanish Socialists made a concerted effort to learn how other countries transmitted Socialist values to their respective populations. They sent Spanish

Socialist intellectuals and teachers to study at Socialist institutions in other European countries, and the newspaper *El Socialista* ran a series of columns describing those cultural practices. The most influential of these centers on Spanish Socialist intellectuals was the Brussels-based L'Ecole Ouvrière Superieure (EOS), successor of the Centrale d'Education Ouvrière (CEO), a school that had originally been created to educate workers, giving them the tools to engage in successful class warfare. In 1921, with the support of Socialist cooperatives, private donations, and nominal registration fees, the EOS opened its doors, operating much like a traditional boarding school or university with its lecture halls, offices, library, showers, cafeterias, and dorms.[51] The relative success of the EOS encouraged Spanish Socialists to try and create a similar organization. Prominent Socialists such as Julián Besteiro and Rodolfo Llopis, who led key positions during the Second Republic, studied the EOS's pedagogical methods and wrote about them in pedagogical and Socialist journals. In fact, after his visit to the EOS in 1926, Llopis wanted to set up a workers' university in Madrid modeled on the EOS and hoped to name it the Fundación Pablo Iglesias; given the numerous political and economic constraints, this university did not come into being.[52]

Spanish Socialists took their inspiration from these models during the 1920s and, as we shall see, from the pedagogical models spawned after the Russian Revolution. Given numerous factors, such as the scarce resources held by Socialist syndicates, the paucity of Socialist intellectuals prepared in pedagogy, and the fragmentation of Spain as a whole, among other things, the Socialists did not have the organization or the resources to create such expansive institutions. Instead, they had to wait until the inauguration of the Second Republic to put some of their ideas into action.

Probably the most dominant influence on Socialist intellectuals who wanted to educate the masses, was the Institución Libre de Enseñanza. Fernando de los Ríos, Julián Besteiro, and Rodolfo Llopis, all influential intellectuals of the PSOE, looked to the methods spawned by the ILE for the comprehensive regeneration of Spain into a Socialist state. Although the founders of the ILE established their school as a basis for the gradual, peaceful regeneration of the Spanish nation, leading Socialist intellectuals embraced the ILE's reformist pedagogy for revolutionary purposes. Leading Socialist intellectuals, who would later play important roles during the Second Republic, especially in education, had been associated to some degree or another with the ILE, as either students or teachers, and sometimes both. Their experiences with the institution led them to believe that the lessons taught at the ILE could be spread to the masses, leading to a literate and educated populace who would be willing to transform Spain into a Socialist nation. Socialist intellectuals and pedagogues would draw on their experiences of the Casa del Pueblo, the ILE, and the educational and cultural movements propagated by Socialists outside of Spain to engage in a full assault against what they viewed as a decrepit and dying culture in need of a revitalizing force.

## RADICAL REPUBLICANS

Socialists and anarchists were not the only ones trying to revitalize Spanish culture with the help of the working classes. The final group in the troika ready to befriend and transform the working classes were the various republican parties, although the most persistent and successful of these were the Radical Republicans. Although they were technically a subset of the liberals, the Republicans merit special attention for their attempts to bring the liberal democratic agenda to the masses from the turn of the century onward.[53]

Spanish Republicans viewed themselves as inheritors of the Enlightenment and the French Revolution. They espoused reason and science as the harbingers of progress, and they worked to bring Spain in step with what they saw as other more scientifically and politically advanced countries in Europe. Like the liberals who spawned them, the Republicans wanted Spaniards to fulfill their role as active citizens of a democratic nation, not passive subjects of the state. At the very least, this meant getting Spaniards to slough off their Catholic prejudices. Republicans sought to create mechanisms for Spaniards to divert their loyalty from the church to the nation, and the only way to succeed was to create an educated citizenry who could make informed decisions about the future of Spain. In this sense, they took their cues from the architects of the Third Republic in France who tried to solidify Republican principles and loyalty to the state by creating a national educational system, intricate railroad networks, and other such signs of an infrastructure.[54] After the failure of the First Republic and the subsequent Restoration System in Spain, Republicans underwent a period of retrenchment. By the late 1880s, republicanism resurged, but it was split over tactics and goals, ranging from those groups who wanted liberal reforms within the context of a constitutional monarchy to those, such as the Radical Republicans, who would stand for no less than a revolutionary overthrow of the monarchy and the installation of a republic. But while Spanish Republicans sought to incorporate the working classes into the political system through educational and cultural means, their desire to eliminate the "Catholic scourge" often took the form of virulent anticlericalism, which was best exemplified by Tragic Week in 1909 and, later, the May convent burnings in 1931. The Radical Republicans' ability to whip up anticlerical sentiment among the working classes further alienated and polarized the traditional oligarchs who would resist all attempts at Republican reforms.

Republicans fell in step with other reform- and revolutionary-oriented groups who called for the regeneration of Spain via education. But unlike the anarchists and Socialists who provided at least informal education of the working classes through ateneos and the Casas del Pueblo, the Republicans had a weaker track record for putting their principles into practice.[55] Although many Republicans had ties to the Institución Libre de Enseñanza and hoped to bring the ideals of the ILE to a mass audience, they did not have the means to diffuse their educational and cultural projects on a mass scale. Of all the republican groups, the Radical Republicans were the most successful at diffusing their political and educational principles through a small network of schools. Beginning in 1903, the Radical Republican schools had the most success in Barcelona, especially since they received some municipal subsidies. By 1909, they had created about fifty schools for primary and adult education.[56]

But after the events of 1909, Radical Republicans kept a lower profile and spent less energy on promoting schools. On the whole, the Radical Republicans were less successful than their anarchist and Socialist counterparts in educating and politicizing the working classes. Only when the Republicans joined the Socialists during the Second Republic could they begin their process of national unification through educational and cultural projects. In the meantime, other groups tried to undermine the Republican efforts to coalesce the Spanish nation.

## CATALAN NATIONALISM

If the Spanish state did not have enough problems trying to keep the center holding after attacks by anarchists, Socialists, and Republicans, for the latter part of the nineteenth century through the Civil War, it had to contend with yet one more challenge to its centralizing authority: centrifugal nationalism. As the Restoration System began disintegrating and as Spain endured the shame of "El Desastre" of 1898, regional nationalisms—most notably in Catalonia and the Basque Country—began to emerge as nationalists pushed for varying degrees of autonomy within the Spanish state.[57]

Catalan nationalism provides an interesting contrast with Spanish nationalism because in many ways Catalan nationalists were more successful than the Spanish state in attaining cultural hegemony. Catalan nationalism started off as a cultural movement, but leaders of the nationalist project thought that the Catalans required some form of political autonomy to enable Catalan culture to be accepted on its own terms and not those of the Spanish state. In contrast, Spaniards had the political state but not the cultural unity. This may be one reason cultural programs become so important during the Second Republic. The Republican–Socialist coalition sought cultural unification to cement political unification.

From the mid-nineteenth century on, Catalan nationalism followed the path commonly trod by central and eastern Europe during this same period. As some scholars have remarked, nationalist activists often began their pursuit in the cultural realm, trying to recover a "lost" or suppressed literature, language, or history without necessarily focusing on any political solution to the national problem. The next phase entailed converting that cultural awakening to a political one, with the eventual goal of political autonomy or even independence. The final phase required mobilizing the masses to embrace the nationalist ideal.[58] Catalanism stayed remarkably close to this course from the 1840s on. What began as a cultural renaissance in the 1840s, ended as a full-blown attack against the Spanish state and a call for political autonomy and, eventually, independence as the means to carry on that culture.

Although many scholars of Catalan history debate the starting point of Catalan nationalism, most tend to agree that the source of nationalist sentiment was cultural and that it emerged in the nineteenth century, concurrently with nationalist movements in other parts of Europe.[59] Echoing the nationalist cries of German Romantics, Catalan intellectuals and artists—mostly from Barcelona—set out to recapture their cultural legacy, which they believed had scaled brilliant heights during the Middle Ages but which the Spanish kingdom with its repressive, centralizing mania, gradually eroded, leaving the Catalan people and their culture mere shadows of their former glory. Under this impetus was born the literary revival known as the *Renaixença* (Renaissance) in the 1840s to 1880s.

Much of the Renaixença centered around the Catalan language: on using it, disseminating it, and glorifying it. For only through language, these Romantic nationalists argued, could the true spirit of the people reveal itself. What began as a desire to see Catalan in print, to (re)create an autochthonous literature, later emerged as a full flowering of Catalan poetry, theater, architecture, painting, and sculpture. Many point to the Jocs Florals (Floral Games) of 1859 as the beginning of cultural nationalism. Taking its name from the eponymous medieval Catalan literary contests, in its modern form, the Jocs Florals showcased the Catalan language and engaged in Catalan myth-making, embroidering poems with abundant references to the fair hills and streams of Catalonia. But because there was no standardized grammar or orthography for written Catalan up to this point, the written language bore the defects of archaism. The gap between the medieval language of the poems and the spoken language of everyday life still needed to be bridged. There was a willing audience for this literary self-celebration, even if the poetry jangled the ears a bit.

The literary revival of the Renaixença continued well through the 1880s. Those who took part harked back to Catalonia's halcyon years of cultural, political, and economic power—the Middle Ages—and in the backward glances of their literary contests they were reinventing traditions suited to the modern world. Although the bulk of creativity centered in Barcelona, the Renaixença gained the support of a diverse coalition of Barcelona's professional and industrial classes and rural elites and craftsmen. Like the many Romantic revivals that came out of industrialized areas in the nineteenth century, Catalan cultural nationalism emphasized a preindustrial world, very different from the one confronting Catalan, and especially Barcelona elites.[60] The rural elites who watched industrialization erode their traditional ways of living supported the revival because it lauded and solidified a set of conservative values that seemed to be going by the wayside, while urban elites could look to the revival as a nostalgic snapshot of a preindustrial past that no longer held currency in bustling Barcelona.[61] And all took refuge in this past as a shield against both the centralizing forces of Madrid and the emerging proletarian forces of industrial Barcelona.[62]

But language alone did not a culture make. Although written Catalan had lost some of its archaic edge by the 1870s and Catalan-language magazines and daily newspapers could now be found in Barcelona, the written word was still rife with orthographic confusion and the audience for the literature remained relatively limited. In the 1880s to about 1906, the next generation of Catalan literary and artistic figures who would contribute to the movement known as *Modernisme* (modernism) wanted to broaden the appeal of Catalan literature and other forms of Catalan culture to a wider European audience. They no longer felt the need or the desire to engage in a cultural debate with Spanish cultural elites, choosing instead to view themselves as part of a wider European culture to which Spaniards could not belong. The Catalan poet Joan Maragall summed up this sentiment best when he said that Catalonia needed to "Europeanize itself, severing more or less slowly the cord that bound it to death."[63] Ironically enough, they shared with the most progressive elements of Spanish society the wish to "Europeanize" themselves as a means of cultural regeneration. Less conservative and more politically savvy than their Renaixença counterparts, this generation of modernists began to link language, culture, and politics closely together. In other words, they began to argue that the Catalan language needed a greater Catalan culture and audience to adorn. And Catalan culture could not be achieved without attaining at least a modicum of political autonomy. Therefore, Catalan intellectuals and artists began lobbying for the use of Catalan as an official language and for Catalan instruction in their schools. For the modernists, political autonomy could render cultural autonomy.[64]

Political nationalism soon followed cultural nationalism, although it was often difficult to separate the two. One of the first theoreticians of political Catalanism was Valentí Almirall, whose first daily Catalan-language newspaper, *Diari Català*, helped standardize written Catalan. Fed on the mother's milk of federal republicanism, Almirall found in its platform of local autonomy the springboard for national autonomy under the rubric of republicanism. Although others had brushed the subject before, not until the publication of Almirall's *Lo catalanisme* (1886) did the call for political nationalism for Catalonia become overt. Summarizing previous concerns he had articulated at past Catalan congresses, Almirall called for the Catalan elites to unite under the banner of Catalanism and to sever their ties to Spanish political parties, especially since the central government was threatening to repeal the Catalan civil code. He appealed not only to their cultural pride but also to their pocketbooks. Pointing out the Spanish government's resistance to economic protectionism for Catalonia despite its importance as the industrial engine for the rest of Spain, he challenged the legitimacy of Spanish rule over Catalan affairs of state and economy, and this disgust with Spain would only increase after 1898. Almirall fanned the flames of nationalist desire by conjuring up the memories of a once fiercely independent Catalonia cowed by sinister forces of the Spanish military, and he appropriated these memories as cautionary tales for contemporary Catalans.[65]

Before writing this seminal text for Catalan nationalism, Almirall organized the First Catalanist Congress in 1880 and tried to open up his federalist umbrella to a group of Catalan poets and historians, but most were too conservative to take shelter there. Despite their political disagreements, they did hammer out two concrete provisions: a defense of Catalan law and the foundation of the Centre Català, a short-lived political and cultural organization. At the Second Catalan Congress (1883), organizers from the Centre Català initiated a series of proposals to merge Catalan nationalist political and cultural goals. They condemned any affiliation with Spanish political parties, passed motions making Catalan an official language alongside Castilian, and called for economic protectionism and the creation of a central government for Catalonia.[66]

But Almirall's brand of Catalanism, namely his federalism, did not curry favor with many Catalanists, whose ideas leaned in a much more conservative direction. These traditionalist Catalans best exemplified by modernist architects Lluis Domènich i Montaner and Puig i Cadalfach and future politicians Enric Prat de la Riba and Francesc Cambó tended to frown on extending political rights to the working classes and wanted their Catalanism tied more closely to Catholicism. Almirall's weakened federalism also alienated the more radical federalists. They felt that Catalanism as it was being formulated could not attract the working classes, who were loyal to the anarchists and later to the Radical Republicans.[67]

By the 1890s, the left- and right-wing forces of political Catalanism fractured considerably, but a power vacuum on the left propelled the agenda of the more unified right-wing Catalanism to the head of Catalan politics. The disaster of 1898 also helped bring Catalan nationalist concerns to the forefront. Because 60 percent of Catalan exports went to Cuba, the Cuban industrial elites saw the Spanish loss of this most important colony as a severe blow to the Catalan industrial economy, and they looked on the defeat as another example of Spanish ineptitude. Disgusted with the Spanish government's bungling of the war, Catalan nationalists clamored more insistently for autonomy, feeling that only an autonomous government would protect the interests of Catalan industry.

Arising from this disaffection with Spanish policies, the Lliga Regionalista de Catalunya formed in 1901 under the leadership of the millionaire industrial financier Cambó. This was the first Catalanist political party, and it represented the interests of the conservative Catalan establishment until the Second Republic. Although the Lliga Regionalista would win key municipal elections throughout the early part of the century, it and other Catalanist parties that were beginning to emerge faced great competition from the Radical Republicans headed by Lerroux, especially in Barcelona. The Radical Republicans siphoned off great numbers of working-class and middle-class voters, leaving the Lliga Regionalista bereft of the centrist representatives it needed and the more left-wing Catalanist parties devoid of working-class support to create an autonomous government.

But it was not in politics where the Catalan nationalists made the greatest inroads. Rather, it was in culture. In fact, no matter what side of the political fence they sat on, Catalanist politicians all agreed that political autonomy was necessary for cultural autonomy. While the leaders of the modernist movement had tried for years to disseminate the Catalan culture and language to a greater audience, it was intellectuals and artists centered around the new cultural movement known as *noucentisme* who would use existing and new administrative structures to disseminate culture to the masses. The noucentisme movement began operating in 1906, after the Lliga Regionalista entered Barcelona's provincial government.[68]

The first step in cultural consolidation came with the founding of the Estudis Universitaris Catalans (EUC; Catalan University Studies) in 1906. Set up as an alternative to the Spanish universities, the EUC offered university-level courses in Catalan history, language, law, and literature. By providing an alternative education, Catalan nationalists could groom a new set of leaders for the future. One year later, the city council of Barcelona with the cooperation of noucentista intellectuals, founded the Institut d'Estudis Catalans (IEC; Institute of Catalan Studies), a kind of think-tank, whereby intellectuals could study and write about all elements of Catalan culture (although the main branches tended to center around science, philology, and architecture). Through the auspices of the IEC, for example, the linguist Pompeii Fabra crafted a series of linguistic reforms that culminated in the "Orthographic Norms" published in 1913, a "Catalan Grammar" in 1918, and a "General Dictionary of the Catalan Language" in 1932.[69] By systematizing the written language, the opportunities to spread Catalan culture increased.

But the biggest boon to Catalan cultural dissemination came after the establishment of the Mancomunitat, a body for local self-government, in 1914. Created by a royal decree, the Mancomunitat united the four historic Catalan provinces under one administrative system, setting up the mechanisms for eventual self-rule. The administrative functions of the Mancomunitat served to strengthen the infrastructure of Catalonia, and many intellectuals of the noucentisme movement helped put that infrastructure into place. In its short lifetime, the Mancomunitat created a series of public works projects and cultural institutions that were designed to strengthen cultural and institutional links between the center of culture, Barcelona, and the Catalan hinterlands. Not only did it fund very practical projects such as road building, but it also spent money on Catalan education, and, more important, on creating the National Library of Catalunya in 1914 to encourage research. To complement the cultural research conducted by the National Library, a series of neighborhood popular libraries were established to disseminate Catalan culture to the provincial inhabitants. Elites from the center, Barcelona, would form the cultural tastes for the periphery—that is, any place outside of Barcelona.[70] In the eleven years of the Mancomunitat's existence (1914–1925), Catalan intellectuals and politicians created the cultural infrastructure and the political raison d'être for Catalan nationalism, although it was a Catalan nationalism that still excluded the working classes from their program. By the time the Second Republic arrived, many Catalan nationalists had stopped calling for autonomy and started demanding independence.

Both Catalanist cultural and political demands were temporarily silenced by the dictatorship of Primo de Rivera in 1923. Unwilling to tolerate the turbulence that had wracked Spain since 1917, and blaming Catalan nationalists for contributing to the problem, Primo immediately began divesting Catalans of their cultural heritage. He banned the Catalan flag, the use of Catalan in official places, and the *sardana*, the official dance of Catalonia. By 1925 he disbanded the Mancomunitat, pushing the Catalanist movement underground. Despite these proscriptions, cultural and political Catalanism had made serious inroads during the years of the Mancomunitat. In fact, even left-wing Catalanism began to gain supporters among the working classes, although popular Catalanism would make even greater strides during the Republic. During the dictatorship, Catalan nationalists allied themselves with Republicans, so that when the opportunity arose in 1931 to seize power, the political and cultural infrastructure was ready to take on the demands of self-government. But Catalan nationalists would have to wait until after the Primo regime discredited itself in the eyes of almost all political groups in Spain before Catalan nationalism would emerge even stronger. In the meantime, Primo and his followers had their own ideas about how to strengthen the Spanish nation.

## RIGHT-WING IDEOLOGY

Primo's rule (1923–1930) serves as a focal point for understanding the polemical turn that Spain would take during the Second Republic. Under his leadership, a core group of right-wing ideologues with a well-formulated, dynamic theory of government emerged, ready to build a new, indomitable Spain on the basis of a retrograde nationalism. Although delineating the various strains of modern right-wing thought in Spain is as troublesome as untying the proverbial Gordian knot, one thread connected the disparate right-wing groups, and that was their hatred of liberal democracy. Their sense that society had fallen into secularized decay linked all of these groups ideologically, but their conception of the ideal state and how to attain this state differed markedly.

The term *radical right* incorporated two major trends of right-wing thinking: the Carlists and a branch of the Alfonsine Monarchists who formed the group Renovación Española (Spanish Renewal) and contributed to the radical right intellectual journal, *Acción Española*. Both groups believed that liberal democracy should be destroyed—violently, if necessary—and that a Catholic monarchy should run the state according to corporatist principles. The Carlists, who took their name from the pretender to the throne, Prince Carlos V, the younger brother of Fernando VII (1784–1833), comprised the oldest of the right-wing groups. They were the protagonists in three civil wars during the nineteenth century, fiercely objecting to liberal and constitutional monarchies.[71] Their protest was quelled in the last of the Carlist wars, 1870–1875, but they would reemerge as a threat to the Second Republic.

Concentrated in the areas of Navarre and León, the Carlists derived their support from the Catholic Church, clerics, "middling peasant proprietors and tenant farmers," and various members of the *rentier* and artisinate classes.[72] They were held together by a faith in counterrevolution and neotraditionalism, rejecting any form of liberalism in favor of a strong Catholic monarchy based on the Carlist royal line. Unlike other Spanish right-wing groups, the Carlists opposed a strong centralized government, favoring, instead, government devolution. Like other right-wing groups during the Second Republic, the Carlists supported an authoritarian monarchy buttressed by corporate structures that would ensure group harmony. They also advocated the primacy of the church in government administration, education, and culture.

The Carlists shared the radical right stage with many Alfonsine monarchists, who would continue to remain loyal to Alfonso XIII after his overthrow in 1931. Many of the Alfonsine monarchists had held powerful positions in the Primo de Rivera regime, and they shared some ideological links with the Carlists, such as the belief in a religious monarchy and a corporatist state, along with the need for an insurrection against the liberal government. Taking their cue from their French counterpart, Action Française, the Alfonsine radical right hoped to crush Spanish liberalism and replace it with a Catholic empire reminiscent of Spain during the sixteenth century. Unlike the Carlist devolutionists, the Alfonsines wanted to establish an authoritarian, Catholic monarchy that would act as a centralizing force to create a strong nationalist sentiment and forge a new empire based on the strength of Catholicism. Their ideologues tried both to reignite imperial legends and to invent new ones to create a national unity forged with the "doctrine and sword."[73]

The Alfonsists of *Acción Española* thought the state should be a corporate structure led by an elite. Leaders of the party had no desire to harness the revolutionary power of the masses. The righteous forces of the well-trained elite would overthrow liberal democracy and impose a new order on the ignorant masses of Spain. The accionistas disdained the Enlightenment tradition, blaming it for producing the moribund liberal state that had sunk Europe into the throes of decadence and despair.

One of the core doctrines of *Acción Española* revolved around the concept of *Hispanidad,* a term worked over and codified by the intellectual Ramiro de Maeztu in his work *Defensa de la Hispanidad.* Maeztu blamed Spain's fall from grace on the people of eighteenth-century Spain who became too enamored of foreign ideas. He said that Spaniards effaced their true identity in a desperate attempt to become cosmopolitan. Spaniards needed to turn inward and redirect their energies to cultivating the roots of the Spanish *raza,* people from Spain, Portugal, and Central and South America. The raza was linked historically by the great Spanish empire of the Catholic monarchs and religiously by Catholicism. According to Maeztu, the crisis of Hispanidad was fundamentally one of religion: "There was a day in which an influential group of cultivated Spaniards stopped believing that the principles which were necessary to inspire their government were at the same time those of its religion.... By transplanting these spiritual ideas to America, they necessarily destroyed the fundamental ideals of the Spanish Empire."[74] There was hope for Spain, however, if Spaniards embraced Hispanidad. By doing this, Spaniards would vindicate Spanish culture and civilization by not turning their backs on the values that made Spain truly great: an empire based on a strong, centralized Catholic state, the language and literature of Castile, and a return to tradition.

The "conservative right" would emerge during the Second Republic as a coalition of Catholic parties with a mass following, known as CEDA (Confederación Española de Derechas Autónomas) Those who supported the agenda of the conservative right included Angel Herrera, editor of the rightist Catholic newspaper, El Debate, and Gil Robles, leader of CEDA during the Second Republic. Like the members of Renovación Española, those belonging to the conservative right supported the Alfonsine monarchy. Although they opposed the Republic from the start, they chose to follow the path of "accidentalism," a doctrine set out by Leo XIII, which proclaimed that the form of government was incidental. Instead, Catholics had to operate within whatever form of government was available to them to ensure that the rights of Catholics would not be impugned.

One last group that emerged during the Republic and that many would place on the right ideologically, were the Spanish Fascists known as the Falange Española (Spanish Phalanx). Like other European Fascists, the Falange did not strictly fit the traditional model of a right-wing organization.[75] They criticized many of the same issues of liberalism and capitalism as the left, but their revolutionary politics stressed the nation over the proletariat, and corporate harmony over class conflict. The Falange Española tried to tap into the masses' frustration with the excesses of capitalism, such as high unemployment, poor working conditions, and extreme disparities of wealth between management and labor. They also were more forward-looking than other right-wing movements in Spain, especially in their embrace of technology. The Spanish Fascists differed from their Italian counterparts, however, in that they stressed the need to incorporate Catholicism into their revolutionary, nationalist ideology. Spain was not Spain without Catholicism. As a political organization, the Falange Española would not play a major role until the end of the Second Republic, and that is mainly because the party was not founded until October 1933. But people who later became members of this party did play a crucial role as cultural critics of the Republic.

The various right-wing groups wanted to create an organic, corporatist state in which conflicts could not exist because the very structure of the state was supposed to ensure its harmonious efficiency. The radical and conservative right saw the organic state as one that could be reached only by looking backward to the structures that existed in Spain during the fifteenth and sixteenth centuries. Their vision of the ideal state differed greatly from that of liberal nationalists; their disagreement over this ideal state intensified during the Primo de Rivera regime and reached its highest pitch during the Second Republic.

Primo and his followers began early in his tenure to set up a centralized party that would establish a set of principles to guide Spain in its regeneration. By 1924, this group was known as the Unión Patriótica (UP; Patriotic Union), and although it was never formally called a party, it functioned as the primary disseminator of Primo's party doctrines. The UP was founded on the principles of antiliberalism, antiparliamentarianism, antiindividualism, and anti-Bolshevism; it preached a unitary state achieved through the fusion of church and monarch: "These great realities were the triad of the U.P.'s programme: Nation, Church, and King, *in that order.*"[76]

The disseminators of the UP's program included such figures as Ramiro de Maeztu, José Pemartín, José María Pemán, Vicente Gay, and José de Yanguas, all men who played important roles in spreading counterrevolutionary messages during the Second Republic. Most of these men refined their political skills under Primo's tenure, but they were unable to institutionalize their programs after Primo's popularity steadily declined in the final years of the decade.[77]

By the end of Primo's regime, all of the groups discussed in this chapter—except the right—pressured the central government for radical change. Whether they called for alternative nationalisms or rejected nationalism altogether, they all agreed that Primo, the monarchy, and the corruption that went with them had to go. With the April 1931 elections, the popular vote decided to pursue a Republican–Socialist course for a while, but it would soon become evident that the programs enacted by this coalition would not palliate the concerns of the many groups clamoring for change. As we shall see, Spain's identity was up for grabs.

# CHAPTER 2

# "If These People Had Received but a Refrain of Poetry"

## Creating Consent through Culture

### ROLE OF CULTURE IN THE NEW REPUBLIC

Spain's turn toward democracy in 1931 bucked contemporary European trends. While other European countries steered conservative courses or experimented with fascism, and even the Soviet Union reined in its revolution, the Spanish government rejected its reactionary past and implemented a revolutionary agenda. Spanish voters had rejected the monarchy and (surprisingly) ushered in a republic, and the Republican–Socialist coalition believed it had a mandate to wipe away the misdeeds of monarchs, military men, and legislators by forging a new nation based on the principles of liberty and equality. A host of problems awaited the coalition, however, including inequitable land distribution; a worldwide depression; and religious, class, and regional conflicts. Given the fractious state they inherited, coalition members hoped to consolidate their rule as quickly as possible.

Most historians of this period agree that the greatest problem facing the new Republic was land reform,[1] and I would concur with this assessment. Despite these grave economic and social problems, Republicans and Socialists nevertheless expended much energy trying to integrate previously neglected members of Spain into their vision of the nation through cultural projects. Many members of the Cortes, raised on catechisms from the Institución Libre de Enseñanza (ILE) (see chapter 1 for greater detail), believed that once the spirit was nourished, economic success would follow. Their task lay in creating a citizenry that identified itself as Spanish, and to achieve this goal they tried to shape a national identity that was held together by the glue of culture. For example, they thought that if they exposed the people to a set of common cultural artifacts—such as Cervantes' *Don Quixote* and Velazquez's "Las Meninas"—then social and economic barriers between urban and rural dwellers would melt away, linking the "backward" people in rural areas to the "progressive" people of the city. As former Minister of Public Instruction Fernando de los Ríos said when looking back to the cultural achievements of the Republic and, more specifically, about the programs known as the Misiones Pedagógicas: "We were trying to revive in the mind of the peasant the cultural values of which his ancestors had been the creators. We were attempting to make him conscious of his history, awakening in him a feeling for true 'Spanishness'—and Spanishness, properly conceived, means no less and no more than an awareness of the ideals and aspirations of the Spanish people. This we are endeavoring to do ... by putting the peasant in contact with the great creative works of Spanish collective consciousness."[2] This common culture—which, not surprisingly, emphasized urban and Castilian values—would bridge the fissures caused by differences in class, religion, and region and would serve as an important conduit for integrating the masses into Spain's new political and social structure.[3] But it would do more, too. According to Spanish leaders, this common culture would modernize and, therefore, Europeanize Spain, leading Spain to rival other western European nations in power and influence. Instead of creating an empire based on conquest, as they had done during Spain's Golden Age, Spaniards would create an empire of ideas to lead postwar Europe out of its cultural despair.

But figuring out how to achieve cultural unification and deciding whose culture would be promulgated proved difficult for a coalition that included Republicans, Socialists, and Catalanists. The very diversity of their political backgrounds led these groups to search for various methods to achieve cultural and national unity, or, in the case of some Catalans, to reject unity altogether. So, as inheritors of a country teeming with problems, the new coalition appropriated foreign and domestic models for help in building the new Spain. The Russian and Mexican revolutions, still fresh in everyone's memory, provided guidelines for instituting radical change in Spain, a place that faced similar economic and social problems. But, because the coalition contained both revolutionaries and reformers, it would face difficulties choosing which programs to implement. As we shall see, the coalition's leaders looked to these revolutions and to other regimes such as the Third Republic in France and even Nazi Germany as examples of how to consolidate a nation using cultural and educational programs. We must keep in mind, however, that, unlike the majority of the aforementioned countries, Spain tried its cultural reforms within the context of a fragile democracy, while the others, except France, began theirs under varying forms of dictatorship. But the new Republican regime also cultivated indigenous cultural ideas, especially those stemming from the ILE, such as Manuel Cossío's Misiones Pedagógicas. Any cultural program that appeared successful was ripe for the coalition's picking. The cultural programs discussed in this and subsequent chapters were designed to classify, codify, and preserve aspects of Spanish culture that some Spanish leaders feared would be lost to future generations. These projects were intended to promote progress by preserving particular versions of Spain's past and by serving as a link between the city and the country.

## INTELLECTUALS DEBATE THE ROLE OF CULTURE

The idea that culture could be a force for Spain's regeneration did not suddenly appear out of nowhere. As we have seen, this idea began incubating in the nineteenth century and reached a fever pitch after 1898. As far back as the Krausists—and continuing through the institution of the ILE and the writings of regenerationists such as Joaquín Costa—liberal, leftist, and anarchist intellectuals fastened onto culture as a panacea for Spain's numerous problems. But until the inception of the Republic, the intellectuals who espoused regenerationist ideas had not held the reins of power. Now they planned to implement a series of changes that were designed to consolidate their rule, namely by extirpating the influence of Catholic culture and replacing it with Republican and Socialist ideas about culture.

Most Republican and Socialist intellectuals agreed that democracy, national unity, and progress could be attained only by forging a common culture. As Marcelino Domingo, a Republican and the first Minister of Public Instruction in the Second Republic said: "The restoration of a democracy can be achieved by violence; its consolidation is only through culture. Where there is culture lacking, the democratic system perverts, sterilizes, and disfigures itself, or falls, not by external pressure but by internal consumption."[4] In fact, from the Republic's inception, its leaders perceived that creating an educational/cultural infrastructure was necessary to the Republic's and Spain's survival. In a memo dated August 10,

1931, to Marcelino Domingo, the then-ambassador to Germany, Americo Castro, wrote about founding a popular library in the village of Justás in Galicia. He urged the establishment of this library as "the surest means for extending culture and guaranteeing national unity."[5]

The eminent doctor, biologist, and supporter of the Republic's cultural reforms, Gregorio Marañón also saw that the Republican government viewed Spain's problem as a "problem of culture." For him, the greatest sin of the former Primo de Rivera regime was the way it had ignored or hampered Spain's intellectual development. Now Spain had the opportunity to regain what Marañón saw as its former stature as a cultural emissary. "In the future," he wrote, the world "will not be conquered by arms, but by ideas."[6] For Marañón and other intellectuals like him who bore witness to the horrors unleashed by World War I, war was no longer a possibility for effecting change. Spain no longer had the option of relying on individuals to conserve the "Iberian spirit." Instead, the state needed "to take charge of advancing the movement of our ideas, of our science, of our immortal and uninterrupted ability to create new forms of beauty."[7]

The Socialist members of the government shared these views. The successor to Marcelino Domingo as Minister of Public Instruction, Fernando de los Ríos (nephew of Krausist Francisco Giner de los Ríos) constantly promoted the Republic's cultural projects. In a speech to a conference organized by the Comité de Cooperación Intelectual de Madrid and in language reminiscent of Ortega y Gasset, de los Ríos spoke of two kinds of cultural crises. One is a crisis of "cultural collapse" or "cultural decay," whereby a once-great culture declines into mediocrity. The other is an "ascensional" crisis in which a group of people, who had been denied cultural sustenance for years, suddenly become aware of the benefits that culture can bring them. They begin to long for spiritual growth but do not have the means to attain it. Spain, he contended, was in the midst of a crisis of cultural ascension; Spaniards wished to become a cultural powerhouse, but they were not yet spiritually developed enough to attain their goals. Referring to the intellectuals of 1898, especially Joaquín Costa, de los Ríos said that this generation "told us that Spain could be transformed only by cultural work. Exactly."[8] But he found this past generation's definition of culture—science, religion, technical studies, vital instincts, and ethical norms—too broad to tackle. Instead, to achieve Spain's transformation, he asserted, the state had to make certain priorities its focus, namely what de los Ríos called "the most vivacious emotions of the Spanish soul," the "love of the aesthetic and profound, the cardinal emotion of respect that the Spaniard always has for the ethical, for the austere."[9] Sounding very much like a Krausist and an institucionista in his emphasis on aesthetic and ethical values, de los Ríos contended that the state had to take responsibility for cultivating these two cultural values, which, in his opinion, had permeated Spanish history.

According to these intellectuals and policy shapers, Spain's historical destiny lay in its role as the cultural vanguard of the new Europe. The advocates of this cultural resurgence peppered their speeches with references to Spain's glories of the sixteenth century, glancing nostalgically at its role as the "civilizer" of the New World, and they emphasized the need for *all* Spanish citizens to take part in this new cultural construction. The head of the Republic, Manuel Azaña, believed the Republic was a national project, but he chose not to define the nation by its geographical boundaries or its social makeup; instead, he measured his nation's strength by its "profundity"—its ability to serve as "the instrument to restore all the civilizing powers of the Spanish people." The Republic would "resuscitate the civilizing spirit of the Spanish race" in much the same way as Lazarus had risen from the dead. Calling on fellow citizens to watch over both the culture and future of the Republic, Azaña strove to see a return to Spain's place as "the cradle of civilization that is not a mere imitation [of that past] ... rather a civilization shaped by the sentiments of our own modern men and obtained by means that modern civilization and culture bring us."[10] For him, the idea of the Republic was a universal one, but for it to have any meaning, it had to be infused with values that were truly Spanish.[11]

Marcelino Domingo also argued that once a cultural base was established and democracy was safely entrenched in the villages where the common people resided, Spain could reach a "historical hierarchy more elevated than that of Castile in the XVI century." He compared this new culturally equipped Spain to Don Quixote "inflaming Europe in an ideal," and he added that while Spain in the nineteenth century may have been excluded from the "unity of civilization" found in Europe, Spain's democratic institutions would be "the axis of the new unity of civilization by which Europe [would] be saved."[12]

This diffusion of culture and consolidation faced considerable problems in a country riven by regionalism and, more important, fettered by highly uneven economic development and an illiteracy rate that hovered somewhere around 32 percent.[13] Like other European governments, the Spanish Republican government tried to strengthen its rule by building a national school system that would educate those previously excluded and root out centuries of Catholic influence. As Rodolfo Llopis, the Socialist Director of Primary Education said: "The school has always been the ideological arm of all revolutions. The school must convert the subjects of the Bourbon monarchy into citizens of the Republic.... The revolution will not be [successful] if it does not penetrate the citizens' consciences, changing them into genuine servants of the new regime."[14] Although government officials strove to build a network of schools, they also chose more informal routes for educating their citizens and forging national unity. In fact, the Republican government sent emissaries to the Soviet Union, Mexico, and Germany to study their educational systems with the purpose of applying these foreign ideas to the Spanish school system.[15] Even well after the Republican government had begun to establish cultural programs in the Spanish countryside, they continued to study other nations' cultural programs. They did not let the politics of other nations deter them in their quest for cultural unification. In a letter dated March 16, 1933, the Socialist Luis Araquistáin, then ambassador to Germany, wrote to the Minister of Primary Education, Luis de Zulueta, to encourage the Republic to study the Nazis' new Ministry of Propaganda and Enlightenment of the Volk, headed by Goebbels, "independent of the political ends of this organization." He added, "It is not necessary to stress the importance of this [German] department for consolidating a new regime—and from that its worthiness as a method for the Spanish Republic."[16] But for the most part, the Republican–Socialist coalition studied the achievements of the Russian and Mexican revolutions.

## FOREIGN MODELS: RUSSIA AND MEXICO

Although Republican and Socialist intellectuals often aligned themselves culturally with western Europe—that is, they viewed themselves as inheritors and propagators of the Enlightenment and its exaggerated offspring, positivism—they shared a cultural and economic legacy more akin to Soviet Russia and revolutionary Mexico than to France's Third Republic. Like the Soviet Union and Mexico, Spain had to deal with the problems of land reform, economic disparities between urban and rural areas, rampant illiteracy, limited numbers of qualified teachers and technicians, a poor infrastructure, ethnic differences, and a popular religiosity that, according to revolutionaries, impeded progress. Most important for the new regime in Spain, both Mexican and Russian revolutionaries decided to coalesce their revolutions through formal and informal avenues of education.

Before the advent of Spain's Second Republic, the Russian Revolution had already inspired Spanish Socialists to visit the Soviet Union to learn what they could about implementing a revolutionary state.[17] But it was only during the Republic that some of these ideas could actually be applied to Spain, especially in the realm of education and culture.[18] Some Spanish Socialist intellectuals learned how the Soviets used cultural works to incorporate revolutionary ideas into all public arenas and how they attempted to bridge the economic and technological gaps between the coexisting preindustrial Russia and the industrial, revolutionary Soviet Union. As the Soviet director of the Institute of Methods of School Work, Vasilli Shulgin, told Rodolfo Llopis on Llopis's visit to the Soviet Union in the 1920s: "The child is a victim of a series of contradictions.... Villages and cities exist. The class struggle still has not disappeared. People are fully aware that today different ideologies and morals conflict with one another. What influences will a child receive in the midst of so many contradictions?... This chaos is typical of bourgeois pedagogy. It has not completely disappeared here. We have done all we can to minimize it. This is the duty of pedagogy in times of transition.... Our problem is to create a new man who is not bothered by economic obstacles nor ideological chaos. If the chaos begins to diminish ... it is because the contradiction between the village and the city and the abyss that separates manual labor from intellectual labor begins to disappear."[19]

Although Shulgin was discussing conditions in Soviet Russia, he could just as easily have been talking about contemporary Spain, where cosmopolitan city-dwellers visited the cinema, listened to the radio, and participated in political life, while many people in rural areas had no experience with electricity whatsoever, struggled to earn their daily bread, and had minimal contact with the political ideas emanating from the metropolis. But while Russia (and Spain) tackled these economic disparities, they also paid close attention to cultural ones.

As Spanish pedagogues observed, the Bolsheviks doggedly pursued a cultural revolution almost immediately following their political revolution. For example, theaters, newspapers, radios, schools, syndicates, and sports clubs had as their chief goal "a pedagogical end."[20] That is, every institution served to transmit the values of the new Socialist revolution. Llopis learned from the Soviets that formal education was not sufficient for transforming society: "What purpose do the efforts made in schools and universities serve if this work is later corrected, annulled, by the family, the workshop, the street, the newspapers, the theater? This is the most tragic problem created today in educational institutions in the West: the divorce between the school and the family, between the school and life."[21] Formal schooling was merely one avenue for pursuing cultural change, and Llopis and other intellectual activists during the Republic applied some of these Soviet ideas about cultural dissemination to Spain, especially in the realm of theater.

While Spanish Republicans and Socialists may have looked to the Russian Revolution for Bolshevik applications to their own revolutionary agenda in the cultural sphere, they also could look to the Mexican Revolution and the subsequent Mexican Republic to see how to make passive subjects into active citizens who were willing to participate in a new democracy and how to turn various ethnic groups into nationalists. Despite its numerous upheavals between 1910 and the 1930s, the Mexican Revolution tackled numerous problems that Republican Spain shared: land reform, class conflict, a powerful Catholic Church, regional and cultural differences, and a largely illiterate population. Beginning in the 1920s under the guidance of José Vasconcelos, and continuing under Lázaro Cárdenas's rule, Mexican leaders began a most ambitious project: they attempted to establish a vast educational network in Mexico, concentrating especially on incorporating indigenous groups into the Mexican state.[22]

In September 1931, Marcelino Domingo sent an emissary to Mexico to study its educational organization. The report written by the emissary is rich with information. It highlighted what he saw as the four most important elements of the revolutionary educational system: it was nationalist, democratic, social, and active. The report explained the Mexican government's efforts to promote education and incorporate marginalized groups into the nation's bosom, nourishing in them a "knowledge, appreciation, and love of everything Mexican."[23] The report outlines those things that could apply to Spain:

> In completion of the mission that was entrusted to me last month in September, I have tried during my stay in Mexico to study its pedagogical organization, concentrating primarily on those branches of public education that could have the greatest interest for us.
>
> In my judgment those branches are the ones that relate to the rural schools and to the incorporation of the Indian into civilization. On the organization of the former, interesting statistics can be obtained with respect to the education of peasants and villagers, in which you admit great interest. The *misiones culturales* and the general system adopted to conquer

the natives' laziness, bringing culture to their homes, also include teachings and methods that could perhaps be utilized in our educational system in Morocco.[24]

Not only did these lessons apply to the education of students in Spanish Morocco, they also applied to the rural sectors of Spain, especially to the non-Castilian peoples of Galicia and the Basque Country.[25] The language sprinkled throughout the report—"bringing a civilizing influence to the nucleus of peasants and indigenous groups," "social vindication of the masses of the countryside, separated from the rest of the countryside by enormous distances in both the moral and material order," the "incorporation of indigenous tribes to civilization"—sounds very similar to the language used by institucionistas and other groups implementing the Republicans' cultural and educational aims during the Second Republic.[26]

## DOMESTIC APPROACHES: THE MISIONES PEDAGÓGICAS

But Republican and Socialist reformers did not slavishly copy programs they witnessed in other countries. They embarked on their own cultural agendas, sensitive to the particular needs of Spain itself. One of the most ambitious cultural programs, the Misiones Pedagógicas, had its roots in the ILE. The architect of the program, Manuel Cossío, had been suggesting for years that the government sponsor a program to bring the elite culture and education of the cities to the peasants in the countryside: "If society has little direct influence over the countryside, it is necessary to supplement this influence by means of the school." For him, the school did not necessarily mean the schoolhouse but, rather, the school of life outside those walls. Exposing villagers to law, logic, literature, art, and music could close this cultural gap. City children, he argued, had the benefits of theater, concerts, and museums, but rural children did not: "Where can they ever see a statue? Who will tell them that there existed a Shakespeare or a Velázquez? Who will make them feel the beauty of a melody by Mozart, a stanza by Calderón?"[27]

Eager to fill this cultural chasm, Cossío designed a program whereby intellectuals, teachers, university students, and artists would travel around the countryside with an assortment of mobile lending libraries and museums, makeshift theaters, puppet shows, musical concerts, and slide shows. In addition to the assortment of cultural artifacts that they would haul in from Madrid, the misioneros would take responsibility for fostering civic education by explaining the various workings of the state in meetings and public readings. On May 29, 1931, the provisional government's President Niceto Alcalá Zamora and Minister of Public Instruction Marcelino Domingo signed a decree creating the Patronato de las Misiones Pedagógicas to bring rural dwellers "the wind of progress and the means to participate in it, in progress's moral stimuli and its examples of universal advancement. [They wish to bring them these ideas] in such a way that all of the villages of Spain, even the isolated ones, can participate in the advantages and noble pleasures reserved today for urban centers."[28]

The decree emphasized the scant attention given to the educational and cultural needs of the countryside by previous administrations and hinted at the Republicans' hope to end this neglect. It outlined the state's obligation to "raise the cultural and civic level" of its citizenry to enable these new Republicans to become "collaborators of national progress and to help incorporate the undeveloped villages into Spain." Finally, the implementors of the Misiones Pedagógicas desired to encourage the development of "racial virtues of dignity and nobility" that reflect an "exemplary citizenry."[29] Thus, the Patronato de Misiones Pedagógicas set up a mechanism to diffuse culture and education in the countryside and to shape their vision for the new Spain.

Although those who organized and ran the Misiones Pedagógicas advocated a secular and humanistic program, their methods, language, and even their name evoked the Catholic missionaries who tried to bring the light of Catholicism to the "ignorant savages" of the New World. But unlike the message of their Catholic counterparts, their message revolved around culture and reading, not religion: "The communication of widespread culture in all classes is the ultimate goal of the Missions."[30] Religious language permeated the missionaries' prose: "This is what the Missions propose: to awaken the eagerness to read in those who do not feel it."[31] They spoke of "the abyss of spiritual life," which they claimed was even greater than the economic chasm, of the "social penury" and "moral isolation" that existed in the villages, of the "spiritual lights" they would bring to the villagers, of the need to foster communication to "enrich souls," and of the missionary's office as one that was "tough and full of sacrifice." Those who took on this "evangelical work" were supposed to teach the ignorant but, at the same time, "console the sad ... make them happy and amuse them nobly." Taken as a whole, the misioneros viewed themselves as "shock troops" who would usher in a new spiritual era, replacing Catholicism with a secular humanism that created "social justice" and "social solidarity."[32] Their ideology, reminiscent of Krausist philosophy, coupled Enlightenment teaching with spiritual growth.

Although the misioneros drew on religious metaphors to explain their program, their methods for spreading culture mirrored those of the Institución Libre. In the missioneros' eyes, villagers could learn to love reading by listening to recitations of both contemporary and classical Spanish poetry and prose and by gaining access to lending libraries stationed in the village. Films would educate them about life in Spain and abroad and about technological advances and hygiene; plays and choral groups would act as didactic tools for social reform; and, finally, these "culturally bereft" people would soak up the genius of Spanish artists by visiting the Circulating Museum, which displayed replicas of classical Spanish paintings housed in Madrid's Prado and the Museo del Cerralbo.

## GEOGRAPHY OF THE MISIONES

Those who organized the Misiones Pedagógicas stated as one of their primary goals the delivery of urban culture to the countryside by bringing the fruits of progress to people in Spain's most isolated regions. By traveling across the land, the misioneros hoped to create a unified national culture. But isolation is in the eye of the beholder. By looking at maps showing where the misioneros went, we can infer which areas of Spain the organizers of the Misiones in Madrid considered isolated and how they went about building metaphorical roads to supplement the concrete ones.

Isolation implies distance from the center of power, which in this case was Madrid, but distance may be understood in different ways: geographical, geomorphological, economic, and political distance. Although none of these are explicit in the documents of the misioneros, the implementation of their program indicates that similar distinctions must have been made:

- Geographical distance means simply that, spatially, certain regions are farther from Madrid than others.
- Geomorphological distance refers to obstacles in the terrain—mountains or large rivers, and the concomitant lack of roads and railroads—that isolate places from Madrid. For example, although the province of Segovia is spatially closer to Madrid than is Valencia, the Sierra de Guadarrama that lies between Madrid and Segovia increases the isolation of the villages in Segovia.

- Economic distance is defined by the amount of economic interaction between the core and periphery. For example, although Galicia and Catalonia may be equally distant from Madrid spatially, Catalonia's economic interaction with Madrid was much greater because Catalonia was one of the most industrialized regions in Spain.
- Political distance refers to the amount of political influence a region might have with the central government of Madrid or how much of the political culture a region shares with Madrid.

Of the 495 villages the misioneros visited between 1931 and 1934, 216 of them (44 percent) were in the regions of Old Castile and León. New Castile and Galicia follow as the second most popular destinations (142 villages combined, or 29 percent of the total). In comparison, they only called on a total of 66 villages (13 percent of the total) in Catalonia, Valencia, Murcia, and, surprisingly, Andalusia combined, the latter one of the biggest and poorest regions of Spain (see map 1). What seems most evident from the maps is that the misioneros went to areas that were isolated, primarily geomorphologically and secondarily economically isolated. Approximately two-thirds of their destinations were mountain villages, with about half of those in remote areas above 1500 meters (almost 5,000 feet) in elevation. Many more were equally inaccessible by road or railroad and were located in rough coastal terrain. For example, map 2 (Galicia, Asturias, León, and Old Castile) shows that the misioneros visited 46 Galician villages, most of them on the rugged peninsulas of the coast. Although that terrain may not have been as hazardous as terrain in the Pyrenees, the majority of villages were not easily accessible by railroad lines or major roads. Also, Galicia was one of the poorest economic regions of Spain. Eastward, toward Asturias and León, and south to Old Castile, the misioneros primarily visited places around or above 1500 meters. Map 3 reveals comparatively minor interest in the Basque Country, Navarre, Aragon, and Catalonia. Part of the reason may be because the Basque Country and Catalonia, although mountainous in many places, were the most industrialized areas of Spain. But when the misioneros did visit these regions, here too they concentrated their efforts in the mountainous areas and in places not served by major roads. For example, of the twenty Catalonian (Lérida province) villages they visited, half were in the high Pyrenees near the French border. The misioneros rarely set foot in relatively prosperous Valencia or Murcia, as shown in map 4 (Valencia, Murcia, and New Castile), but concentrated more on

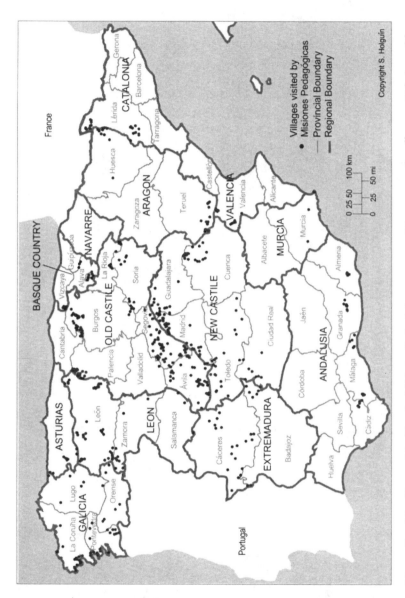

Map 1. Spanish villages visited by the Misiones Pedagógicas, 1931–1934. Map sources for all maps: U.S. Army Map Service, "Spain and Portugal Road Map," 3d ed. (Washington, DC: U.S. Army, 1943), scale: 1:400,000; U.S. Army Map Service, "Railways in Spain and Portugal," 1st ed. (Washington, DC: U.S. Army, 1941), scale: 1:1,500,000; Spanish State Department of Tourism, "Map of Spain, Showing the Main Railway Lines of Interest to the Visitor" (Madrid: Department of Tourism, 1930?), scale approx. 1:2,000,000; El País's Atlas de España (Madrid: El País, 1992). Josephine Adams, cartographer. Copyright S. Holguín.

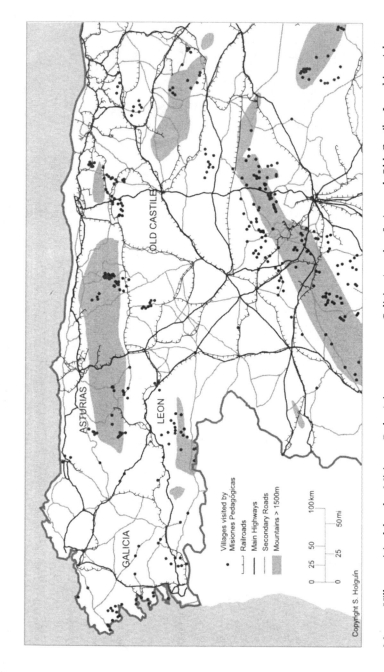

Map 2. Villages visited by the Misiones Pedagógicas, 1931–1934. Galicia, Asturias, León, and Old Castile. Josephine Adams, cartographer. Copyright S. Holguín.

GALICIA

ASTURIAS

LEON

OLD CASTILE

Villages visited by
Misiones Pedagógicas
Railroads
Main Highways
Secondary Roads
Mountains > 1500m

0    25    50         100km
0      25      50mi

Copyright S. Holguín

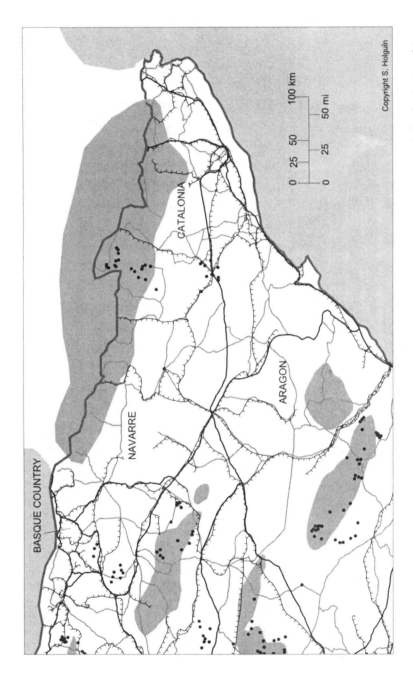

Map 3. Villages visited by the Misiones Pedagógicas, 1931–1934. Basque Country, Navarre, Aragón, and Catalonia. Josephine Adams, cartographer. Copyright S. Holguín.

Copyright S. Holguín

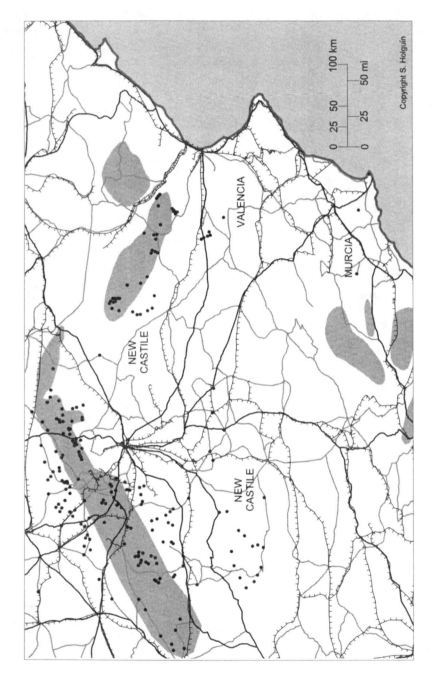

Map 4. Villages visited by the Misiones Pedagógicas, 1931–1934. Valencia, Murcia, and New Castile. Josephine Adams, cartographer. Copyright S. Holguín.

Copyright S. Holguín

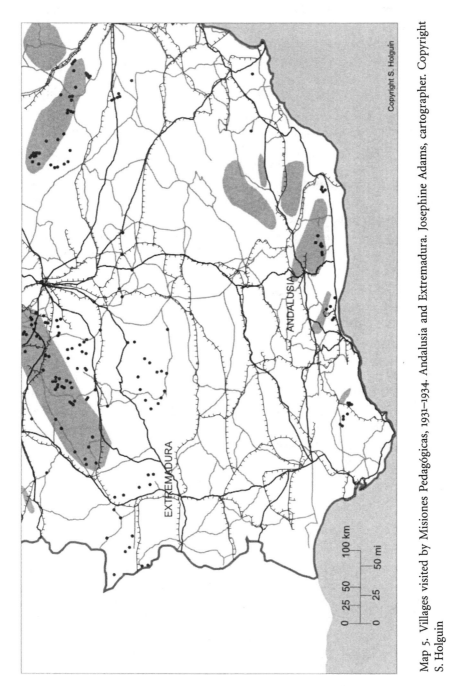

Map 5. Villages visited by Misiones Pedagógicas, 1931–1934. Andalusia and Extremadura. Josephine Adams, cartographer. Copyright S. Holguin

the economically poor sections of New Castile. Map 5 (Andalusia and Extremadura) presents an interesting anomaly. Given the vast areas not served well by railroads and roads, and given that this is where some of the deepest poverty in Spain was located, it is surprising that the misioneros did not visit these regions as much. Numerous accounts of the time comment on the grinding poverty here, which would seem to make these regions likely targets for missionary work. Further research is needed to firmly explain this apparent aberration, but two factors might be tentatively suggested here. One possibility is that because the majority of Andalusians lived in towns and cities instead of in villages, the misioneros did not consider them as isolated as those in the north. Another possibility is that the misioneros' drastically reduced funding after 1934 may have eliminated the financial resources necessary to expand their work here. But, overall, it seems that the misioneros' desires to bridge the "isolation gap" were genuine. Given the poor transportation infrastructure of the 1930s, the misioneros did cover a great deal of ground in almost three years.

## ACTIVITIES OF THE MISIONEROS

Once the misioneros settled into a village, a typical program went as follows: The villagers might see a documentary film about people in a different part of the world; then they would view some popular art, listen to poetry readings, and hear regional music from a gramophone; later, they might watch another movie interspersed with cartoons; misioneros would lecture villagers on a topic such as "the concept of equality as seen through the Spanish Constitution," and then the villagers might watch some more films (perhaps something by Charlie Chaplin this time). The misioneros would give rural Spaniards a two- to four-day crash course in Spain's greatest achievements, and before they left the village for good, they installed a library and gave villagers a gramophone, records, and reproductions of famous Spanish paintings as mementos to cherish.[33] Over the years the Misiones Pedagógicas included in their repertoire a traveling theater and museum.

The first mission took place on December 16–23, 1931, in the Segovian village of Ayllón. The misioneros began—as they did when they reached any town—by entering the village with great fanfare and gathering its inhabitants in the town plaza. Once everyone assembled, one of the misioneros read a speech written by Cossío explaining the reasons for their visit. Trying to soothe the villagers' possible fears, Cossío's words told them that the misioneros had no intention of taking anything from them; in fact, the misioneros hoped to shower them with cultural gifts. Cossío called their project a "traveling school," but unlike typical Spanish schools, this one had no textbooks and no desire to punish its students. He stated explicitly that the Republican government sent the misioneros to find people in the most unreachable places and to educate them, thus linking the fate of the countryside with that of the city and, by extension, the Republic. He also said that although the misioneros came to teach the people, the first goal was to entertain them.

Entertainment came by way of the unfamiliar technology of film and phonographs. Through film the misioneros hoped to capture the interest of the villagers while teaching them about life in other parts of the world, and through phonographs they tried to make them appreciate their own cultural contributions by demonstrating the variety of Spanish regional music and poetry. According to Fernando de los Ríos's account of the mission in Ayllón—whose interest in promoting the program cannot be separated from his enthusiasm in describing the Misiones—when the misioneros played a song from that region, the villagers understood that this was their song being exalted by the people from the city: "And all of the days when the Mission met, the first thing that the people demanded was that which they called 'our song.' Why did this popular song create such a profound impression on them? It was the way that something that they had been indifferent to or taken for granted had been dignified; it was the way they found 'the popular' truly praised and dignified. It was, in short, the echo of an essentially educational act; they felt the lyrical intimacy of their village life ennobled."[34]

Despite the discussions of the noble qualities of local culture, the programs presented to the villagers tended to emphasize Castilian culture: the misioneros taught them the history of El Cid; the Castilian paintings of El Greco, Velázquez, and Goya; and the Castilian poetry of Santa Teresa de Avila, San Juan de la Cruz, and Antonio Machado. In fact, the misioneros constantly tried to balance displays of Castilian culture with regionally produced culture, but they tended to fall back on Castilian works as the embodiments of the truly Spanish spirit.

While the Misiones were designed for all those who had been denied an education, Cossío emphasized their importance for adults, those who had spent most of their lives working hard but receiving little spiritual and intellectual sustenance. They lacked the opportunities of urban dwellers to partake in leisured pursuits. The Republic, therefore, hoped to "to try an experiment, to see if it is possible to begin, at least, to undo a similar injustice."[35] Once again, Cossío portrayed the Republic as a beneficent emissary bringing social justice to the long-neglected populace and linked the fate of rural dwellers to the central government. In fact, Cossío's language sounds very similar to that used to describe the Mexican Misiones Culturales: "The Misiones Culturales have been created to bring about the social vindication of the masses of the countryside, separated from the rest of the Mexicans by great moral and material distances."[36]

After outlining the goals of the Misiones Pedagógicas, the misionero then explained that the villagers were about to learn "what the land and those areas where we have not been are like; what Spain, above all, our nation, our Patria, is like: its mountains, its plains, its rivers, its great cities..What Spaniards were like in other times, how they lived, what great feats they accomplished."[37] By evoking what Anthony Smith calls "poetic spaces," the misioneros attempted to create a nationalism that Spain sorely lacked.[38] If they could convey the variegated landscape of Spain as one unit—"nuestra Patria"—and convince the villagers that the history of Spain was everybody's history, they might be able to break the bonds of regional loyalty and channel that loyalty to the Spanish state.

Cossío's earlier writings reflect this attitude. He stressed that a historian-educator should begin teaching children history by exposing them to cultural artifacts such as churches, monuments, and paintings. This method of teaching history, he believed, changed the focus from political history to what we might today call social history. It concentrated on common people rather than on the actions of a few politicians and awakened "the idea (without saying so) that all that there is, is done *by all*, and that the true subject of history is not the *hero*, but the *entire people*, whose joint work produces civilization."[39] By describing how "Spaniards were in other times and what great works they achieved," Cossio and the other misioneros hoped that if they could convince the rural populace that they were just as much a part of Spanish history and culture as the politicians and city dwellers, the villagers might be more willing to cooperate in the reforms of the new government.[40]

To ensure this loyalty, the misioneros coupled the display of Spanish cultural works with lessons in citizenship. As stipulated by decree, the misioneros lectured the populace on "democratic principles" already established (theoretically, at least) in modern towns, and they explained the various mechanisms of the state and the citizens' role within that state.[41] Cossío focused on the state's benevolence, on its desire to see people familiar with their "rights and obligations" as citizens because, in keeping with the Republican ambition to establish a working democracy, they needed to know that "the people, that is to say, you, are the origin of all power."[42] The misioneros discussed the constitution and drew out the history of liberal ideas in Spain by concentrating on Riego, the officer who led a pronunciamiento in 1820 to restore the liberal constitution of 1812 and who was immortalized as a hero of liberalism in the "Hymn of Riego," the unofficial national anthem of the Second Republic. This not-so-subtle history of liberalism provided the villagers with a liberal trajectory that ultimately led them to the Second Republic.

Ultimately, however, the misioneros' chief goal was to awaken everyone's desire to read, which they hoped to achieve by setting up small libraries in Spain's most remote villages. In a country not then known for its educational rigor, a literate populace could facilitate Spain's modernization and Europeanization. It was not enough for the population to be literate; it had to truly love literature—only then would there be "a new Spain."[43] By equating reading with Spanish regeneration, the Republican misioneros echoed the cries of nineteenth-century Spanish Krausists and regenerationists and established themselves as inheritors of this creed to forge Spain into a powerful nation.

Some were even convinced that this program of national unification could work to bring back into the fold those who had once been Spanish, namely the Diaspora Jews. In the same speech in which he outlined the cultural projects already advanced and those about to be advanced by the Republic, Fernando de los Ríos hinted at the possiblity of sending Spanish teachers to Sofia, Bucharest, Salonika, and Constantinople to set up some version of the Misiones Pedagógicas. Considering that Spain was trying to set up a viable government in the midst of a worldwide depression, one wonders how certain officials could even consider spending money on this type of foreign venture. De los Ríos explained

> Because there are millions of ancient Sephardic Jews who continue to speak in Spanish, who continue to emotionally understand what Spanish culture represents. In some of these cities ... their numbers rise above 50,000. And we're going to search for them in a purely imperialistic manner, but it does not resemble anything like ancient imperialism. We are not going for lands or bodies. We are going to reconquer for Spanish culture the consciences of those who still live within the breast of this culture.[44]

Figure 1. Village visited by the Misiones Pedagógicas. This dilapidated housing and the contrasting dress between the middle-class men on the left and the villagers on the right illustrate the urban–rural gap. Photo by permission of the Biblioteca Nacional, Madrid.

Figure 2. The misioneros build a stage in the town square, while villagers look on. Photo by permission of the Biblioteca Nacional, Madrid.

Figure 3. Close-up of misioneros constructing a stage. Photo by permission of the Biblioteca Nacional, Madrid.

Figure 4. Watching a performance by the Misiones Pedagógicas. The founder of the Misiones Pedagógicas, Manuel Cossío, is the white-bearded man sitting left center. Photo by permission of the Biblioteca Nacional, Madrid.

Figure 5. A rural audience views a performance of the Misiones Pedagógicas in the open air. Photo by permission of the Biblioteca Nacional, Madrid.

Figure 6. Peasants watch a film put on by the Misiones Pedagógicas in the open air. Photo by permission of the Biblioteca Nacional, Madrid.

Figure 7. Peasants gathered in a classroom, captivated by a film. Photo by permission of the Biblioteca Nacional, Madrid.

Figure 8. People of all ages congregate to see films. Photo by permission of the Biblioteca Nacional, Madrid.

Figure 9. With a mixture of amusement and skepticism, peasants watch the members of the Misiones Pedagógicas. Photo by permission of the Biblioteca Nacional, Madrid.

Figure 10. A misionero playing the gramophone for villagers. Photo by permission of the Biblioteca Nacional, Madrid.

Figure 11. A misionero showing children how a generator works. Photos by permission of the Biblioteca Nacional, Madrid.

## RESPONSES TO THE MISIONES PEDAGÓGICAS

Reactions to the Misiones were mixed. Proponents of the Misiones saw the villagers as childlike and innocent, Lockean "blank slates" eager to receive the values imprinted on them by the liberal/socialist state. Once educated, they could participate in the transformation of Spanish society. The traditional and radical right, however, perceived the peasantry as essentially uneducable and, therefore, unable to participate in government affairs. Peasants remained where they belonged in the social and political hierarchy, and any attempt to remove the peasantry from their God-given place would disturb the organic whole of Spanish society. In some ways, the various criticisms of the Misiones Pedagógicas serve as a prism for examining left- and right-wing attitudes toward the peasantry and toward Spain itself.

Many journalists favoring the Republican agenda had only good things to say about the Misiones and other projects. Some people applauded the Republicans' efforts to carry out serious educational reform in a novel way.[45] Others saw the work of the Misiones as crucial for the creation and survival of the state, encouraging state functionaries to continue to travel around the countryside with "particular diligence." The journalist J. de Izaro employed examples from seventeenth-century Spanish history to warn Spaniards about the hazards of not maintaining contact with the hinterlands: "Spain lost Portugal, thought Cánovas, because the Austrian monarchs [Hapsburgs] didn't spend their summers in Portugal. Many things are lost by not going to them, by not engaging their conversation and company. It is necessary to console these lonely Spaniards placed at the ends of Europe's paths."[46] De Izaro understood that the tenuous connections between the center and periphery had to be renewed constantly through ritualistic or symbolic visits by the central authority.[47] In fact, if one looks at the maps in this chapter, one notices that the misioneros tried specifically to target people who were not served by major roads or railroad lines. In this way, they created metaphorical roads to the periphery.[48]

De Izaro also shared in the misioneros' belief that cultural artifacts could transmit the values and history of a national culture. Paintings, for example, acted not only as objects for art criticism "but also as a representation of history, religion, mythology, or fable."[49] Taking this reasoning one step further, an anonymous writer in *El Socialista*, describing the cultural projects planned by Fernando de los Ríos and his entourage, argued for the necessity of the Misiones in preventing "tragedies such as that at Castilblanco," where villagers murdered a member of the Civil Guard. This would not have happened, he said, "if these people had received but a refrain of poetry; for then this would humanize them and open new horizons to men."[50] In ushering in the new era, Spain had to battle harmful ideologies with aesthetics, not armaments.

Some who sided with the Republic in general opposed the ideas and methods of the Republican leaders to impose cultural unification. As early as October 1931, the Barcelona newspaper *La Vanguardia* printed an article by "Gaziel,"[51] lambasting Castilian intellectuals for claiming that "Spain is dead." The author, puzzled by this idea, asked, "Is all of Spain truly dead?" "No," he concluded, it is the "traditional Spain, the exclusively Castilianized Spain, the uniform, rigid Spain represented by the glorious spirit of Castile." He recognized that Castilian intellectuals would find it difficult to acknowledge that they could no longer identify Spain as solely Castilian, that Spain included a landscape and a history of diverse peoples. He bombarded the reader with a barrage of names and phrases usually associated with Spanish history—"The tragic sensibility of life, the flavorful and interminable meditations about Quixote.... The mystics, Avila, Toledo, El Escorial, El Greco, the classic theater, the picaresque novel, the conquistadors, the tercios of Flanders, Covadonga, and the Cid"—and then he condemned those who tried to associate the values reflected in these names and deeds as somehow representative of the values of all of Spain.[52] Gaziel called into question the Catalans' choice of a republican form of government, because this government was as stubborn as the monarchy about maintaining Castilian cultural hegemony. But by the very nature in which the republican government was formed, he contended, it had opened the door to a new, diverse Spain that could not be closed by those who wanted to maintain Spanish (read: Castilian) tradition. He ended his diatribe against the Castilianizers with a cheer to diversity, and he sounded the death knell for One True Spain: "Spain is dead. Long live the Spains!"[53]

The journalist Francisco de Cossío criticized the arrogance of Madrid's cultural elite for thinking that the countryside needed Madrid's civilizing influence. Instead, they should have been asking what cultural wares the countryside had to offer Madrid. Because of industrialization and modernization, some aspects of city life, such as radio, had overrun the local culture of rural areas, culture that was represented by folkloric tales, dances, and regional artwork. The countryside did not need to be exposed to such things as jazz or the radio because they were having a difficult enough time maintaining the culture they already had.[54]

Of course, the right wing completely opposed the cultural programs of the institucionista-influenced misioneros, condemning them as Socialist propaganda and ungodly cosmopolitanism. In the traditionalist Catholic newspaper, *El Debate*, for example, an anonymous writer who never really identified what the misioneros were actually doing denounced the Misiones Pedagógicas as a rude group performing "lascivious dances, movements, and exhibitions," giving the author the impression "of having penetrated a Zulu village." After dismissing the misioneros' work, he castigated their efforts by stating that any European capital could emulate what the misioneros had done. But they had not. "Why not? Because in more cultured countries, there are authorities who do not tolerate such grotesque attacks on public morality; they have a conscience and collective education that rejects such attacks with disgust and disdain." Consistent with the ideology propounded by the staff of *El Debate*, the writer believed that those who sponsored the Misiones were determined to undermine the fundamental morals and values of Spanish society. Instead of staging shows for the people, the government should avoid the showy, immoral excesses displayed by the Misiones Pedagógicas and focus on a "mission of healthy pedagogy" that would not cost the nation a peseta. (The author declined to explain how this "healthy pedagogy" would be paid for.) [55]

In debates over the budget for the Ministry of Public Instruction and Culture during the entire span of the Republic, purveyors of right-wing thought moved to have the funding for the Misiones and other cultural projects cut off for a variety of reasons: peasants needed economic aid, not movie shows; the ignorant masses were being converted into left-wing revolutionaries ready to destroy the imperial, Catholic fabric of Spanish society; peasants lacked the mental capacity to understand the array of ideas passing their way. In the early years of the Republic, for example, Representative Terrero stunned the Cortes by comparing the fate of university professors and teachers who sought to educate the rural populace to military men stationed in backwater outposts: "They have a saying in the army that when soldiers are divided into small groups and go to places of scarce importance, they lose their technical skill. . . . When they create so many centers in modest, tiny villages that lack a university or cultural life, it is not the professors who civilize the villagers; it is the villagers who make brutes out of the professors." [56] The harshest criticism came from Representative Gómez Roji, a Carlist from Burgos, who said that Acción Católica had conducted its own brand of Misiones Pedagógicas. Instead of being the eager recipients of knowledge that the misioneros had portrayed them to be, the rural villagers were, instead, ungrateful people unwilling to accept the help that Acción Católica had given them.[57]

Others chastized Fernando de los Ríos—then Minister of Culture—and his allies for romanticizing the villagers' plight. Representative Riera argued that de los Ríos believed the Spanish pueblo was highly sentimental. In contrast, Riera contended: "When people are hungry, they do not see things through the vantage point of emotions or sentiments; rather, they view them under the sorrow of great pain, determined by two fundamental problems within the Spanish Republic: the economic problem, of urgent solution, of rapid resolution, and the cultural problem, [which needs] a slower, more serene, more rhythmic resolution."[58]

De los Ríos countered some criticisms by appealing to nationalism. Angry that the Cortes was arguing over what he thought to be a paltry four million pesetas for the Misiones Pedagógicas, he implored the Cortes to consider installing radios—if they could not afford to pay for films—in remote villages as an aid to the Misiones. Once again alluding to the perceived informational gap between urban and rural areas, De los Ríos stated that the radio, with its ability to broadcast lectures on a whole range of subjects, provided a way to "connect [the villagers] to the nation." The only way to create a "state of national conscience" was through this medium, and the Republic desperately needed this instrument of the state.[59]

As the years went by, the complaints against the Misiones Pedagógicas and other programs instigated by the Republicans increased. Peasants were portrayed by certain factions as even more dim-witted and unworthy of receiving the money spent on them. People accused the Misiones of moral bankruptcy because they did not base their teachings on Catholic precepts. Pedro Sáinz Rodríguez, a right-wing intellectual who eventually became Franco's Minister of Education, argued that he could not support a cultural program that lacked a religious base. Citing the works of José Ortega y Gasset, Karl Jaspers, and Walter Rathenau, he contended that the problem facing all of Europe was that "Spain has lost its morals, and it is necessary to find a new morality, one that no philosopher has yet been able to elaborate. Because a morality for the great masses, a collective type of morality, can only have one foundation: the religious education of the people and of the masses."[60] If the work of the Misiones continued in what he thought to be its stridently secular vein, he could not vote to support it because it would be using "culture as a sectarian instrument of denationalization and decatholicization of Spaniards."[61]

These remarks summarize the position taken by such groups as Acción Española, of which Sáinz Rodríguez was a member. Acción Española based their worldview and their perception of Spain on the idea that European civilization was decadent and facing a Spenglerian decline. Any attempt on Spain's part to copy the programs or methods of other European countries would result in anarchy and moral turpitude. At its core, Spain was Catholic. Removing the Catholic base from Spanish culture and education was tantamount to ripping apart the Spanish nation and tearing out the soul of the Spanish people.

The positions taken by hardliners ossified as the years passed. No matter what their political stripe, everybody perceived that Spain was in the midst of a terrible crisis that could be resolved only by unifying the country and stirring up patriotic enthusiasm. The ideology under which Spaniards were supposed to unify, however, was still under contention. Cultural programs became the nexus through which ideologues fought over Spain's "one true identity." For example, theater and film became the forum for multivalent interpretations by various groups contending for power. And various forms of literature became a battleground for molding the identity of Spanish society. The succeeding chapters will demonstrate how the disagreements among radicals, reformists, and traditionalists played out in these various cultural fronts.

CHAPTER 3

———

# Theater as Secularized Religion

## *Return to the Golden Age*

HAD SPAIN LOST ITS MORAL FIBER, AS THE RIGHT CLAIMED, BY ABANDON-
ing its Catholic center and searching north of the Pyrenees for solutions
to its internal problems? While the mostly anticlerical left would fault the
right for placing an inordinate amount of faith in the power of a strong
Catholic state to reinvigorate Spain, it did not completely ignore the
possibility that Spaniards could foster and cement national unity through
a tradition that was peculiarly theirs: the Spanish theater.

The culture-shapers of the incipient Second Republic, trained in the
Krausist tradition and those of the Institución Libre de Enseñanza, saw in
the Spanish theater, especially the Golden Age theater of the seventeenth
century, the means to create a long-lost community and to mediate the
tensions between those who wanted to see Spain more Europeanized
and those who wanted to see it made more Spanish. From the onset of
the Republic, certain policy makers encouraged the creation of theatrical
troupes to roam the countryside and bring the classic Spanish drama to
the culturally neglected peasantry. The two most important of those were
the Coro y Teatro del Pueblo (Choir and Theater of the People) of the
Misiones Pedagógicas and Federico García Lorca and Eduardo Ugarte's
La Barraca (The Hut).

Those who believed in the theater's restorative powers did so because
of the way they interpreted its effect on audiences of the distant past.
Through a modern lens, they peered into Spain's dramatic past and saw a
theater that could bring together vastly varied elements of society through
spectacle, religious fervor, and poetic language. Sensing that modernity

had fractured all elements of commonality and community among the peasantry and the urban dwellers, Republicans looked to old forms to reestablish that community and to reconnect the nation with its past, and thus to lay the groundwork for building the future. They attempted to refashion drama of the sixteenth and seventeenth centuries by extracting the mysticism and pageantry of the religious drama and combining them with the thematic elements of the secular drama. Though never mentioning Richard Wagner by name, those who strove to restore drama and, by extension, community to the people were implementing a Wagneresque spectacle replete with music, dancing, pageantry, and allegory, minus the religious underpinnings. A few theorists of the right also saw great possibilities for Spanish regeneration by reprising Golden Age theater, but they wished to keep the religious aspects of these plays intact. Some also called for the creation of new dramas that would deal with modern themes and modern audiences—much like Soviet theater—but that still maintained the religious sensibilities of Golden Age drama. Unlike the various dramatists of the left, who were able to test their ideas on the stage during the Republic, dramatists of the right did not put their ideas into practice until the Civil War and the years that followed.

## CRITICISMS OF SPANISH THEATER
## BEFORE THE SECOND REPUBLIC

The idea of reinvigorating the theater began at the turn of the century, and the call came not merely from the literary community but also from Socialist and anarchist intellectuals. Literary critics of the late nineteenth and early twentieth centuries agreed that Spanish theater was in crisis. Citing the rise of an urban bourgeoisie that spent its money on popular entertainments such as light opera and the cabaret, critics of the theater and some playwrights themselves bemoaned the mediocrity of contemporary Spanish drama, claiming that it appealed to the lowest common denominator. Benito Pérez Galdós, for example, wrote that the contemporary theatrical scene was dominated by a morality that was "entirely artificial and incidental, like a society that lives with fictions and conventions."[1] Whereas the rest of Europe boasted such compelling modernists as Ibsen, Chekhov, Shaw, and Pirandello, Spaniards had produced "an inexhaustible succession of monstrously fecund popular playwrights who had the knack of giving audiences exactly what they wanted."[2] Serious writers such as Azorín and Valle Inclán wrote thought-provoking plays, but their works garnered little commercial success and were rarely produced.

The anarchists were some of the most vocal critics of contemporary theater at the end of the nineteenth century. They complained about both commercialization, which produced pabulum, and exhorbitant ticket prices, which excluded the majority of people from seeing any productions. Anarchist critics wanted to take theater out of the hands of producers who judged plays on their revenue potential and place it in the hands of those to whom it belonged: the workers.

Like the institucionistas and the Socialists, the anarchists credited the theater with the power to educate. Because the majority of laborers were illiterate, anarchists thought that this form of education could be used to disseminate anarchist ideas. As one person wrote in the anarchist magazine *El Productor* after seeing a performance of Ibsen's *An Enemy of the People,* "This is even better than a meeting to propagate our ideas."[3]

But unlike the Republicans and Socialists during the Republic who would revive the classic Spanish drama, many anarchists at the end of the nineteenth century saw little relevance in past theater because they believed it could not offer solutions to contemporary problems, especially those caused by capitalism. They preferred instead to concentrate on contemporary theater—more specifically, on the "drama of social action"—which revealed such problems as the disasters engendered by unequal labor relations, prostitution, inequality in marriage, and sexually transmitted diseases.

To promote their ideas, they began to do what the Republicans would do in the 1930s: they brought the plays to the workers themselves. Lily Litvak claims that identification of the theater with the people and the blossoming of anarchist theater reached its greatest heights at the turn of the century, surpassing any theatrical experiments carried out during the Republic or even the Civil War. Anarchists created traveling theater troupes and brought this drama of social action to villages and urban areas that did not usually have access to the theater. Workers performed the plays, and much of the time they did not charge admission since they equated drama with education. And when one considers the context within which workers viewed these plays, the educational aspects of drama become clearer. Laborers would not just go and see a drama; they might also attend conferences, hear talks about an array of subjects, listen to music and poetry, and sing revolutionary songs in the same place on the same day. Thus, the theater was only one of many events designed to educate workers.[4]

For many of the same reasons as the anarchists, Socialists also saw the theater as an educational vehicle. But Socialists were more divided about what kind of theater workers should see. Some wanted an independent Socialist drama "to cultivate the workers' spirit, to entertain them, that is to say, to make them good Socialists." Others wanted the drama to be judged on its own artistic merits, regardless of the politics (or lack thereof) embedded in the play. Others took a position somewhere in between, preferring that the drama display a literary bent while satisfying the politics of socialism.[5]

Despite the anarchists' and Socialists' inroads in bringing some theater to workers, they still could not overcome the hegemony of the commercial theater. As late as 1930 the Socialist intellectual, critic, and soon-to-be ambassador to Germany, Luis Araquistáin, lamented the *embourgeoisement* of the Spanish theater. How, he asked, did the seventeenth century produce such dramatic geniuses as Lope de Vega and Calderón de la Barca, dramatists who wrote highly stylized verse and tackled themes that may have been too complex for popular audiences of their day, yet still manage to please both aristocratic and popular audiences? Had increased literacy marked a decline in the Spanish audience and the Spanish drama?

Golden Age drama, he contended, recruited its audience from both the aristocracy and the popular orders; therefore, the writing had to appeal to both. On the one hand, the dramatic themes dealt with complex—and perhaps abstruse—theological, political, and psychological problems that satisfied the "elevated culture" of "the ruling classes." The popular orders, on the other hand, attended, as they had for centuries, the "histrionic spectacle" of the theater as a "religious unction," born, as they were, "out of religion and nurtured in its shadow." Unlike contemporary audiences of judges and technicians who attended the drama with a critical eye, popular audiences of the seventeenth century "went to the theater to learn and to be moved with childish ingenuousness and the deep respect that literary inventions awaken in young consciences." Their "childlike" minds, Araquistáin argued, predisposed the popular audiences to welcome whatever the dramatist put in front of them. The audience's diversity, therefore, enabled the dramatist to experiment with new forms and new themes. The decline of drama at the turn of the nineteenth century had little to do with the decline of the spectators' tastes; rather, the audience that now frequented the theater was radically different; this audience, the bourgeoisie, had not existed three centuries ago. And repeating the claims made by anarchists, Araquistáin argued that only those with financial means—the bourgeoisie—could attend the theater regularly. This limited audience, then, had limited tastes. Contemporary theater, according to Araquistáin, served the audience what it wanted.[6]

But if Spain was pursuing the same economic path as the rest of industrializing Europe, why did Spanish audiences prove less willing than its European counterparts to tolerate experimental theater? Many blamed the government itself for this mediocrity, contending that a federal subsidy or nationalization of the theater would enable talented playwrights and untried authors to perform their works without bearing the cross of commercial success. At the same time, theatrical productions could be aimed at more "worthy" audiences than those that were currently attending the theater. These calls for nationalization of the Spanish theater grew increasingly loud during the end of the century, as many critics concluded that the decline of Spanish theater was a reflection of Spain's own general decline and an example of the encroachment of mass tastes. But more important, I believe, Spaniards who cared about the state of Spanish drama viewed it as a means to educate and possibly to shape a mass psychology. While anarchists would call for a drama that would shape a revolutionary culture, the Republican–Socialist coalition at the beginning of the Second Republic would fight for a national theater to rescue Spaniards from their degenerate state and to fashion a national identity. Even some members of the right shared the sentiments of the left, and they called (belatedly) for a new theater that would promote national regeneration.

The idea that drama could instill national identity did not surface suddenly with the advent of the Second Republic. The roots took hold during the nineteenth century with the teachings of Krausists such as Francisco Giner de los Ríos and Rafael Altamira de Crevea, who transmitted their ideas to pedagogues of the Institución Libre de Enseñanza, who then passed them on to pedagogues active in other institutions in Madrid, such as the Residencia de Estudiantes.

For people such as Francisco Giner de los Ríos, theater was history; it remained the only hope for understanding a nation's spirit and conveying it to the people: "It is useless to ask history what the Athenian of Pericles' time, or the Spaniard of Philip II's, was like. History will give us detailed information about everything but that. The image that history will give us of those periods lacks only one thing: life. And it is precisely life that we capture instantly in a drama by Sophocles or a comedy by Lope. Hence literature is nothing other than the first and foremost way to understand past history."[7] Giner de los Ríos's statement begs some essential questions, however. Which elements in the drama are particular to a specific national identity, and which dramas embody the national spirit? Why does history suck the passion out of ideas, while literature brings them to life? For Giner de los Ríos and his cohorts, Spain's essential spirit came out of the Golden Age drama of the sixteenth and seventeenth centuries, and it was this article of faith that Krausists transmitted to the students in the Institución Libre de Enseñanza and the Residencia de Estudiantes, the training grounds for many of the officials of the Second Republic.

Rafael Altamira y Crevea, a Krausist and a historian, saw Spanish drama as a force for moral instruction and spiritual reform. In 1925, for example, he spoke to the Royal Society of Literature of the United Kingdom about using Spanish drama to promote moral education. Recognizing the fears that dwelled within a generation that had just survived the Great War and which was looking for solutions to quell the European-wide despair, Altamira stated: "Thinking people … are coming to realize that the only efficacious solution of the present crisis lies with spiritual and not with material forces."[8] Like a true Krausist, he envisioned a world that could be transformed by aesthetics, and, like many disillusioned members of the interwar generation, he abhorred the destruction wrought by modern weaponry, viewing it as an outgrowth of excessive nationalism. Downplaying the forces of nationalism, he argued that spiritual regeneration would have to be achieved through international rather than national efforts, efforts that promoted ethical values over material and national ones.

Although he advocated internationalism, at the same time Altamira took a nationalistic approach to solving the European malaise. He urged the study of Spanish literature and Spanish theater, in particular, because he thought it provided the "world at large a moral value which can contribute to that work of the reconstruction of ideals which is so urgent." Altamira did not identify which specific ideals had vanished, but he and others believed that they had been destroyed by the brutality of war. The Spanish drama's value lay in its depictions of "the concept of human life, the relations between human beings, and the mainsprings of emotion of will." According to Altamira, Spanish drama—as opposed to other national dramas—tended to impart morality by focusing on "the most important ethical problems," solving them "from a high moral point of view," esteeming justice over law, and reflecting a "serene and optimistic outlook on life."[9] Like other critics, Altamira chose predominantly Golden Age literature to illustrate the ethical values held by Spaniards. He cited Calderón's *The Mayor of Zalamea* as a treatise condemning military excess and corruption in the billets, and Lope de Vega's *Fuenteovejuna* as a battle cry for "popular justice and equal responsibility." In fact, Lope's works represented to him "the most genuine expression of the basic characteristics of our national psychology."[10]

By the Second Republic, the debate over the relationship between the Spanish theater and the regeneration of Spain had been raging for decades. During Primo de Rivera's dictatorship cultural critics intensified this debate. Some called for an "intellectual dictatorship"[11] along the lines of theater in Moscow; others embraced the Italian Fascist theater, and still others advocated a more decentralized theater along the lines of Austria and Germany.[12] The debate did not end with the advent of the Second Republic, of course; instead, it moved out of the realm of newspapers and into that of practical politics: theater became a means to coalesce "the Spanish identity."

## IDEAS CONSIDERED DURING THE REPUBLIC

When people sympathetic to the Republic first began to consider how they might use drama to forge a national identity, they faced the task of presenting complicated verse to the masses without destroying its literary or political integrity. Some social critics and playwrights thought that drama should be highly political and should be presented in "proletarian theaters." Writers such as Cezar D'Río advocated forming a Teatro y Coro del Pueblo as a way of gearing drama toward the popular classes. Claiming that although Spanish drama often lacked originality compared to other nations' dramas, he contended that Spanish drama had the advantage of creating "strong characters" that are "uprightly human" and who "penetrate the deepest sensibilities below a form of sincere art." Theater was one of the clearest ways to achieve social education, but not if it required the audience to work arduously to "redeem or purify an idea from under so many vestments." He called for an end to literature that served scholarly elites and wanted to replace it with a theater that addressed the masses. Such a theater, one with well-directed appeal and well-channeled energy, one in which "the deepest problems that affect the world are expounded with success, would be an extremely useful and necessary platform for the education and direction of these masses, whose hopes sometimes appear restricted or far-fetched."[13] According to D'Rio and others who shared his views, now was the time to create this theater for the masses.

Many groups on the left who were not overtly connected to Republican officials did try to organize a new theater for the masses. Playwrights such as María Teresa León and Rafael Alberti, inspired by the "theater of urgency" that was being practiced by Bertolt Brecht and Erwin Piscator in Germany's Weimar Republic, wanted to create a theater that would give the masses a political education and that would be a collaborative effort between authors, audiences, designers, and directors. In this new theater, the spectators were expected to be actively involved in interacting with the players on the stage. As we shall see later, Alberti played with the idea of the theater of urgency by putting revolutionary messages in traditional Spanish theatrical forms. But while groups such as Alberti and León's worked to create political consciousness in the masses during the Second Republic, they did not receive subsidies from the government.[14]

The Republican coalition decided that the best method for transforming the populace lay in performing works from the classic theater of Spain, namely, theater from the sixteenth and seventeenth centuries. Almost immediately, the Republican government subsidized two major theatrical projects: the Teatro del Pueblo, a component of the Misiones Pedagógicas, and La Barraca, a student-run traveling theater troupe directed by Federico García Lorca and Eduardo Ugarte. By encouraging these two theatrical troupes over others, the culture-shapers of the Republic attempted to re-create their vision of a Golden Age when plays were designed and performed for "the people."

Those sympathetic to the Republic's aims and most closely involved with the day-to-day politics of the early Republic continued to believe that somehow the theater had been taken from those to whom it originally belonged. They felt that it had to be restored to the people as a way to forge the bond that Spaniards shared in some mythical past and to transmit the true Spanish values that were embedded in the Spanish national character. An editorial praising the work of La Barraca demonstrated that many believed that "the theater is without a doubt one of the best ways to give unity to a mass, to a people. A theatrical representation worth its salt contributes more ... to create a common consciousness than numerous meetings."[15]

## EVOLUTION OF RELIGIOUS AND SECULAR DRAMA

Spanish Golden Age theater attracted a spectrum of reformers from the far left to the far right. For those allied with the Republic, it provided a way to recapture what they perceived to be a loss of community by combining the mysticism and pageantry of religious drama with the thematic elements of secular drama. Leftist social and political reformers of the twentieth century, then, would ostensibly be able to transform the religious fervor of drama and channel it into secular pursuits.

Like many dramatic forms in Europe, much Spanish drama began in the religious realm, commemorating the miracles of the Nativity, the Passion, and the Resurrection. In Spain, an offshoot of these dramas was born out of the Corpus Christi festival, which evolved during the thirteenth and fourteenth centuries to honor the sanctity of the eucharist ritual and to display the sacred host. While villagers all over Europe honored the eucharist by staging processionals, Castilians and Andalusians developed the *auto sacramental* (often called simply the *auto*), a didactic one-act play that represented the theological and doctrinal underpinnings of the eucharist.[16] In Castile and Andalusia, the eucharistic drama, performed by the clergy, began in the local cathedral or church and later moved to the public plaza. Because the auto had to render the representation of transubstantiation to keep the thematic unity of Corpus Christi, it would seem that playwrights would be limited in what they could write. But they transcended these boundaries by borrowing from a variety of narratives and stock characters found in the body of literature. Authors easily adapted characters and plots from the Bible, Greek and Roman histories, medieval tales, folklore, and contemporary literature.[17]

The allegorical representations helped simplify some of the abstract and abstruse themes that could confuse even the most learned theologians. Today's critics often wonder how the auto managed to interest popular audiences when their themes became increasingly wedded to obscure questions of religious dogma. The answer is that it was the form, not the content, that attracted the public. For example, the event was lavish: the costumes, were worn only once, despite their intricate detail and costly expense. The sets, too, displayed a splendor accorded to the sacrament. Finally, the visual aspects of the drama were brought to their full pageantry by the inclusion of dances, songs, ballads, and short one-act plays. The auto functioned as a religious ceremony laden with the sensuality that only a religious pageant can bring. It impressed the public with its theatricality and religiosity, while the spectacle highlighted the grandeur of the religious theme.[18] The auto fused "the artistic and religious feelings of the people, in the same manner as the liturgy was able to do."[19] Republican reformers hoped to elicit from Spanish secular drama a similar collective raw emotion that transcended social classes.

In fact, although he was not associated with the Republican projects until the Civil War, the Communist playwright Alberti experimented with the auto. In his *Farsa de los Reyes Magos* (The Farce of the Three Wise Men), he used the form of the auto to write a stylized social commentary on contemporary Spain. In one fragment known as "El Espantapájaros" (The scarecrow), which he wrote as a puppet show, the contemporary allegorical figures were a proprietor, a priest, and a scarecrow with a different face and body on front and back—one side is a scrappily dressed Bolshevik, and the other is a fat, bourgeois governor. The Bolshevik scarecrow scares the priest and proprietor and asks them for money. They both claim to have no money. Then he asks for their clothing. They begin to throw their clothes at the Bolshevik scarecrow when, all of a sudden, the scarecrow (manipulated by a worker and student) turns around and is now dressed like a fat *Señor*. The proprietor and the priest greet this gentleman with respect and complain about how they have been mistreated by the scarecrow on this, of all nights, the Epiphany. The gentleman scarecrow then asks them for money. They are willing to give him some, but not as much as he wants. He then turns around again to reveal the Bolshevik, who threatens to kill them. After begging for help against the Bolshevik, the panicked proprietor calls to the gentleman and says, "Three million duros, my capital, my plantations, Your Excellency, if you'll help us." The Bolshevik scarecrow frightens them again, and they flee, thus ending the morality tale.[20] Through his modern rendition of the auto and by depicting the modern landowner and priest as mean-spirited skinflints, Alberti kept the allegorical didacticism but stripped it of all religious significance. In fact, he used the religious style for clearly anticlerical purposes.

While some Spaniards revived the auto sacramental in the 1920s and 1930s, intellectuals and artists sympathetic to the aims of the Republic concentrated most heavily on bringing the secular dramas of the sixteenth and seventeenth centuries—the *comedia, entremés,* and *paso* (comedy, short farce between acts, and skit)—to the Spanish peasantry, probably because these forms did not have the religious content of the auto, which was an important consideration for a largely anticlerical regime such as that of the early Republic. But although they often rejected the form of the auto, as we shall see, they were intent on harnessing its mysticism.

Distinct from religious drama, the Spanish comedia—a general three-act play interspersed with short set pieces, dances, and songs—evolved from the Italian commedia dell'arte. Secular drama emerged slowly in

Spain. During the fifteenth and early sixteenth centuries, groups of three or four strolling players traveled through the various villages and performed their short skits in the public plazas on makeshift stages. The carts on which the players traveled across the countryside were known as the *farándula,* a term that would later be employed by García Lorca to describe his dramatic enterprise. Later, these strolling players would combine into a more professional organization known as the *compañía.*[21] To house the compañía in a location suitable to display the actors' talents to the villages and urban centers, towns built *corrales,* the skeleton of a stage that would eventually become a playhouse. All levels of society attended the corrales, and rank determined where one would sit or stand. Between acts, the companies performed *entremeses* or *pasos,* short comedic skits—usually no longer than ten minutes—accompanied by music and dancing that had little to do with the action of the drama and which usually relied on such stock characters as the student, the yokel, and the soldier. Much like the comedic interludes in Shakespearean tragedy, the entremeses with their slapstick and bawdy humor entertained the Spanish peasants.[22]

Spanish Golden Age drama reached its apogee in the seventeenth century with the works of Lope de Vega and Calderón de la Barca. Tackling such issues as peasant revolts, military corruption, and royal excesses, Lope, for example, struggled with questions of honor, asking whether peasants could fight to retain their honor, when it was supposedly only the nobility who had any honor to defend. Both playwrights also addressed many of the social issues affecting a nation that was beginning its long decline. Their ideas appealed to both intellect and passions, thus enabling the authors to cast their nets to diverse and appreciative audiences. In fact, Américo Castro, the widely esteemed literary scholar and historian active in the cultural programs of the Second Republic, once described Lope's theater as "an immense national deed of epic proportions, a variegated compendium of popular songs and sayings, a compilation of poetic, erudite, and vulgar material both national and foreign." He claimed that Lope invented the genre of the comedia, while those who followed him really added nothing new to it: "In this way the theater stands before us an immense collective poem in which everyone demanded his right to participate."[23]

The idea that Golden Age theater was a "collective poem" thought to be able to unify a group of people from different social strata might explain why reformers of the Second Republic favored programs that were designed to expose the most isolated Spaniards to these particular works.

The Republican coalition felt that it needed to persuade the populace that they shared traditions and cultural values. Only then could citizens begin restoring Spain to its (long-lost) rank among the great nations. Inherent in this theory, too, was that Spaniards must find their identity in the past, in the pre-modern world, where the forces of the marketplace did not interfere with the supposed harmonious social relations among all Spaniards.[24]

## CORO Y TEATRO DEL PUEBLO

On May 15, 1932, six months after the Misiones Pedagógicas began to travel around the Spanish countryside, the Coro y Teatro del Pueblo put on its first performance in the public plaza of Esquivias, in the province of Toledo. The troupe chose this place specifically because it was the home of Cervantes' girlfriend, Catalina Salazar.[25] Modeling themselves, at least at first, after the Carreta de Angulo el Malo, the theatrical troupe in Cervantes' *Don Quixote*, the misioneros hoped to create a theater that was "merry, ambulatory, easy to assemble," and spare in its use of materials and decorations. The productions were supposed to educate the peasantry "without dogmatic intention, with the simple didacticism of good proverbs."[26] With the goal of bringing the theater to the people and emulating the theatrical spirit of the seventeenth century, the misioneros performed the plays outdoors, usually in public plazas.

The makeshift stages and sets of the misioneros resembled those of the sixteenth- and seventeenth-century corrales. The stage itself measured four by six meters; it was bisected by an arch that held a curtain and was flanked by two doors. Sets and backdrops consisting of collapsible and corrugated panels filled out the stage, while light frames and small iron tubes held the curtain in place. Trucks transported these various parts along rural roads, and a dozen people could set up the stage in the village plaza in about a half hour.[27]

The fifty volunteers for the Coro y Teatro del Pueblo emerged from Madrid's universities and educational centers. According to the misioneros' writings, the performers were not "servants of some institution of official culture." They could help choose the plays and distribution of parts and were not beholden to any professional organizations.[28] Of course, one could argue that volunteering for a program that was heavily subsidized by the Republican government tied a person to an institution of official culture, but perhaps the voluntary nature of the program and the organizers' willingness to consider the volunteers' ideas helped take the edge off its official character. In fact, one could measure the troupe's success by the number of students who willingly forsook every Sunday and holiday to perform these plays before an unfamiliar rural population.

Unlike the organizers of La Barraca, the misioneros of the Teatro del Pueblo chose to focus on the shorter, more comical works of the Spanish classical theater, preferring to perform entremeses and pasos rather than the three-act comedias. Their reasons were based on their perception of their audiences as simple folk who did not currently have the capacity to understand the more complex dramas. As Alejandro Casona wrote of his own participation as director of the Teatro del Pueblo: "The *comedia* and drama proved to be genres too evolved for [this public]. On the other hand, the farce, proverb, and fable, with their violent games and bitter taste, were the natural expression for them, just as the music of the *romance* chorale, the *cantiga,* and the *serramilla* was."[29] Trying to explain the work of the Teatro del Pueblo to contemporary European audiences, Enrique Díez-Canedo wrote: "This is not theater, it is true; it is popular education by means of the theater. The purpose is to create an audience for the future."[30]

And so the misioneros kept their choices simple. Their repertoire included an eclogue by Juan del Encina; Lope de Rueda's entremeses, "La carátula," "El convidado," and "Las aceitunas"; Cervantes' "Los alcaldes de Daganzo" and "El juez de los divorcios"; and Calderón de la Barca's "El dragoncillo." In the same vein as the Spanish classical theater, the misioneros interspersed their performances with popular songs and ballads from "the purest tradition, taken from our enduring folklore."[31] The two elements—theater and chorus—were inseparable.

The director of the theater's chorus, Eduardo Torner, aided in recreating many of these songs.[32] Torner was best known as Spain's leading musicologist and folklorist who headed the Division of Musicography and Folklore in the Centro de Estudios Históricos, compiling, classifying, and recording traditional folk songs and ballads, and reconstructing the music for ballads from the sixteenth and seventeenth centuries. He believed that Spaniards could not begin to understand the modern music emanating from Europe, and especially from Spain, if they lacked knowledge of traditional music. His passion was to trace the roots of Spanish folk songs and those of elite culture to discover their commonalities and reach some understanding of "the spiritual character of our people," thereby continuing "the glorious tradition of the polyphonists and vihuelistas of the

Figure 12. A performance of the Teatro y Coro del Pueblo. Photo by permission of the Biblioteca Nacional, Madrid.

Figure 13. The Teatro y Coro del Pueblo stage a Golden Age drama. Photo by permission of the Biblioteca Nacional, Madrid.

Figure 14. The Teatro y Coro del Pueblo perform in front of school children. Photo by permission of the Biblioteca Nacional, Madrid.

Figure 15. Members of the Teatro y Coro del Pueblo. Photo by permission of the Biblioteca Nacional, Madrid.

sixteenth century whose works ... [belong] in the most eminent place in the history of European music of that time."[33] He therefore saw no real separation between popular and elite music but argued instead that all Spanish music shared elements of a great organic whole.

In this spirit, Torner and his chorus sang and danced the many regional songs that he had collected in his studies, "giving back" the songs that belonged to the people and that linked them to the common musical culture of the Spanish elite. He opposed the Castilianization of music and lyrics that had occurred in playhouses throughout the major Spanish cities and, instead, insisted on re-creating and performing songs in their original regional tongues.[34] Therefore, the choral performances of regional songs not only celebrated regionalism but also revealed the tensions between centralized and regionalized culture so present in the Misiones Pedagógicas and, by extension, the policies of the Second Republic. The plays themselves may have been Castilian, but the songs that accompanied them often came from outside Castile. And although no one argued this explicitly, I believe that the entire theatrical experience reconciled many elements, making the whole greater than the sum of its parts and incorporating the periphery into the center. At the end of the performance misioneros handed out the song lyrics, and sometimes the musical score, to the peasant audience, thus codifying and officially legitimating folk songs that had once been passed down the generations through oral tradition.

The misioneros chose this particular repertoire for its "elemental spirit, its innocent humor, and its easy comprehensibility," feeling that these qualities somehow reflected the needs of their audience. They shied away from presenting an accurate historical reconstruction of the classic theater, fearing perhaps, that a too-precise replica of the performances could suck the life out of a vibrant literature, enshrining the form and killing the spirit of the drama. Trying to provide an explanation for the apparent success of the Teatro del Pueblo, one misionero stated: "If the theater of the Misiones is born and lives in the same way that our primitive *farándula* was born and lived, and is nurtured by these same repertoires, it is only because it is directed at a public with similar tastes, sensibilities, emotional reactions and language as the public of the ancient *corrales,* the humble people of the towns and villages."[35] Here the misionero explicitly linked the present rural populations to those who lived three centuries before, blurring the lines of time and making no real distinction between past and present, much like Miguel de Unamuno's characterization of the Castilian peasants as the true *castizos*, the veritable heart of Spain, whose hands toil endlessly while events unfold around them unnoticed. The peasant was the *longue durée*, embodying Spain's steadfast ideals for an eternity.[36]

Describing the antics of the characters represented in the entremeses—a clown's fear at seeing a ghost; a knock 'em, drag 'em fight over the selling price of olives that have not yet been planted; a conversation between a rustic and a courtesan—a misionero asked, "Have [the entremeses] lost any mere fraction of their healthy comedy, of their realist topicality?" In essence, were these not the same people who laughed at these characters hundreds of years ago?[37] In this vein, the misioneros chose entremeses that they thought would resonate with their rural audiences.

For example, in Cervantes' entremés, "El juez de los divorcios" ("The Judge of the Divorce Court"), various couples come into the courtroom, airing the dirty laundry of their marriages, hoping that the judge will grant them a divorce. Most couples do not get their request. By the end of the skit, a couple who had been in the judge's court weeks earlier invite the judge to their house to thank him for saving their marriage, and musicians sing:

A man and his wife may disagree
but decent folk, of course,
*know reconcilement, even the worst,*
*is better than divorce.*[38]

The misioneros did not necessarily advocate the advice given at the end of this skit, but the descriptions of violent husbands and shrewish wives bound together for life by the laws of Catholicism and the state probably resonated with some of the couples who viewed this skit. Even though the Republic had allowed divorce in 1932, most of these rural audiences would not have had the means to get one.

The misioneros also adapted more complex works for their audiences, but they tried to simplify the texts as much as possible. Given that Cervantes' *Don Quixote* was (and still is) a national treasure, Manuel Cossío wanted the misioneros to perform a chapter of it, and he put Alejandro Casona in charge of adapting the material. Out of this request came Casona's *Sancho Panza en la ínsula* (Sancho Panza on the island), a short dramatization of the chapter in which Sancho Panza becomes governor of an island. This work serves to introduce rural audiences to a snippet of

*Don Quixote* and to demonstrate that there are literary characters very similar to themselves who are given a measure of dignity even while they are being laughed at. In Cervantes' chapter and Casona's adaptation of it, the simple country bumpkin, Sancho Panza, is unknowingly part of a joke in which he is allowed to be governor of an island for a short while. Casona's sketch opens with the following dialogue:

CHRONICLER: Is it possible that our Dukes have chosen this rustic with boots and saddlebags, with the looks of a laborer and a two-week-old beard to govern us?

MAYORDOMO: Indeed, the Dukes have brought him here. But you have to know that this is nothing more than a famous joke. This Governor that is arriving here is none other than the great Sancho Panza, the simple, air-headed rustic.

CHRONICLER: The sidekick of that extraordinary madman they call Don Quixote of La Mancha?[39]

Already the audience receives important information: This joke is well-known, the character is famous for being the sidekick of some legendary madman named Don Quixote, and the new governor looks much like them.

At first, Sancho looks ridiculous; for example, his first demand as governor is to ask the Mayordomo to look after his donkey as if it were his daughter or wife. But as the sketch continues, Sancho sounds more and more like someone who is capable of ruling the island. He rejects the title Don Sancho, since it masks his lowly birth. Later the Mayordomo tells Sancho that all governors are asked to solve a tricky question, and the people judge this new governor by his reponse:

MAYORDOMO: This is the case, sir, that at the entrance to this village there is a bridge, and halfway across the bridge is a gallows. And the order is that all who pass the bridge are asked where they are going. If the person answers truthfully, he is allowed to pass freely, but if he lies, he must be hanged then and there. All right, this morning a man arrived at the bridge, and when the guards asked where he was going, he answered, "I'm going to die on these gallows." And here is the serious part, Mr. Governor: there is no way to comply with the law. Because if he is set free, he will have been let go having told a lie, and if he is hanged, he will have told the truth. What is your sentence?[40]

At first Sancho says that he would kill half the man and save the other half, but since it is impossible to do that, he would set the man free. He concludes that the law itself is excessive, and that he would rather err on the side of mercy than on that of punishment. He is then lauded by the Mayordomo, who says: "If all of your judgments are like this one, we can feel secure being in your hands."[41]

By the end of the sketch, the audience has been exposed to a fragment of the national classsic, *Don Quixote,* and they are made aware that a character like them—rural, poor, and illiterate—has dignity and greatness about him. As Antonio Machado noted to Casona and Cossío, Sancho's judgments "have this natural sense of justice inseparable from the popular consciousness."[42] So, in presenting *Sancho Panza en la ínsula,* the misioneros attempted to introduce in a meaningful way the characters of the classic work from Castile to the campesinos in rural Spain. And by focusing on a character much like the people who saw the performances, the misioneros sought to humanize their audiences.


## LA BARRACA

What began as a single-handed project to reacquaint the peasantry with their dramatic past received reinforcement from the young avant-garde poet and playwright from Granada, Federico García Lorca.[43] This talent began making a name for himself in Madrid's Residencia de Estudiantes and in Spanish literary circles in the 1920s. He also wished to renew Spain's creative energies and encourage the formation of a new Spain at the onset of the Republic. A friend of fellow Granadian Fernando de los Ríos, García Lorca belonged to the circle of people with ties to the Institución Libre de Enseñanza and subscribed to its requisite philosophical underpinnings. Though not himself a student of the ILE, García Lorca lived intermittently at the Residencia de Estudiantes between 1918 and 1928, where he found himself the companion of Luis Buñuel, Salvador Dalí, and others, and listened to lectures by such Spanish intellectuals and men of letters as Torner, Unamuno, Ortega, and Valle Inclán. He may not have been academically inclined, but he did incorporate many of the principles that evolved out of nineteenth-century Krausism, as well as the artistic interests propounded by the growing Spanish avant-garde. Additionally, many of his artistic interests and influences grew out of his childhood years in Granada, where he learned the folklore of local gypsies.

By the beginning of the Republic, García Lorca already had an established reputation as a poet and playwright. Like many of his contemporaries, he detested the commercial, lifeless state of the Spanish theater,

once calling it "a theater made by pigs for pigs."[44] He dreamed of revitalizing the Spanish theater. On the night of November 1, 1931, after having
seen a production of José Zorrilla's *Don Juan Tenorio* that infuriated him
by its tepid, unimaginative direction and production, he rushed into the
room of his friend, Carlos Morla Lynch, talking excitedly about a new
project. He wanted to save the Spanish theater from its wretched state
by re-creating the old institution of the farándula. His theater troupe,
which he would call "La Barraca" would be a traveling theater that could
be assembled or disassembled in a short time. Performing the classic
works of Calderón and Lope de Vega, García Lorca's La Barraca would
bring Spain's true theater to the people to whom it originally belonged,
the peasantry.[45] His intentions seemed similar to those of the directors of
the Misiones Pedagógicas, and in many ways they were. But in addition to
educating, exposing, and uniting the countryside to its past, he hoped to
reinvigorate the aesthetic qualities of the theater itself.

Originally, he had grand plans for La Barraca. In an interview in March
1932, Lorca enthusiastically outlined his master plan. He conceived of two
Barracas: a permanent one would be stationed in Madrid, preferably in an
open space such as a park, where actors would perform plays while the
students studied during the winter; the other one, a Barraca "on wheels,"
would perform in the outskirts of Madrid and through La Mancha on
weekends and holidays. During the summer the Barraca troupe would
tour all of Spain. Ideally, Lorca said, "Students will do all the work—students in Architecture will make the barracas and go along with us in the
caravan to do the stage setting and the assembling, students in Philosophy
will collaborate with the group of poets on the executive committee."[46] In
fact, the whole enterprise had a collaborative air, one that mirrored the
newly installed Republican ideal of working harmoniously to rebuild a
new Spain.

But Lorca's vision for La Barraca went beyond simple mechanics. He
had an educational, spiritual, and aesthetic vision for Spain: "The Spanish
theater is especially adapted to educational purposes here in Spain. It used
to be the most important means of popular instruction, popular exchange
of ideas. In the days of Lope de Rueda it was just a theater on wheels, as
we are planning now. It went into all the villages and gave all the famous
old plays which foreigners find so marvelous, and which are so badly
neglected in Spain. Outside of Madrid today the theatre, which is in its
very essence a part of the life of the people, is almost dead, and the
people suffer accordingly, as they would if they had lost eyes or ears or

sense of taste. We are going to give it back to them in the terms in which they used to know it, with the very plays they used to love."[47] By conjuring the spirit of Lope de Rueda, Lorca could meld audiences of the past with those of the present, forging an inextricable link between the playwrights of yesteryear and those of his day. Historical events or lapses of taste within the drama could be overcome by the strong thematic undercurrents of the classic Spanish drama, themes that had as much relevance in Lorca's time as they had in the seventeenth century.

In addition to presenting classic Spanish dramas, Lorca also envisioned producing contemporary plays—avant-garde theater—that he would make comprehensible by explaining "simply" the particular dramas ahead of time and by streamlining the presentation. Thus he hoped to expose new viewers to the contemporary experimental theater that he found so interesting. To demonstrate the plasticity of the classic drama, he planned to perform the same play on two consecutive nights to see which version received the better response. The first night the play might be "old-fashioned, realistic, the second simplified, stylized, as new as the latest experiment and as old as the most ancient technique of stage setting and gesture."[48] The audience could then choose which version they preferred. Again, the drama of the past could inform the audience of the present, and the present audience, director, and performers could reinterpret the past.

At the end of this interview Lorca once again linked his aims to those of the Republic, focusing on the drama's pedagogical possibilities "of restoring [to the people] their own theater."[49] He reiterated this theme in an interview with Madrid's leading newspaper, El Sol. Bringing the theater to the people was an educational project, one that he called a "great political idea" and an "idea of great national politics," and he insisted on delivering new interpretations to classic theater so that the theater's "pedagogical efficacy is not lost."[50] The rebirth of the Spanish drama could occur only in the soil touched by the bustling activities of real people: "We will take Good and Evil, God and Faith into the towns of Spain again, stop our caravan, and set them to play their parts in the old Roman theatre in Mérida, in the Alhambra, in those plazas all over Spain that are the center of the people's life, those plazas that see markets and bull-fights, that are marked by a lantern or cross."[51] Thus he sought to revive the allegorical figures of the auto sacramental in the crucible of Spain's past monuments. The theater might be Roman; the Alhambra, Muslim; and the plazas, a conglomeration of regional styles—but the audience would always be Spanish.

Though Lorca had to pare down the scope of his production during the following months—he would not, as he had hoped, take La Barraca to Paris, America, or Japan[52]—the spirit of his enterprise remained true to his original conception. In February 1932, he received, through the influence of his friend Fernando de los Ríos, a subsidy of 100,000 pesetas from the Spanish government to carry out his plans.

In collaboration with Eduardo Ugarte, Lorca began recruiting apostles for his mission. Avant-garde painter Benjamín Palencia helped the enterprise by designing posters describing the project and placing them on walls where university students would see them. Avant-garde painters and designers such as Palencia, José Caballero, Ponce de León, and Santiago Ontañón worked on program, set, and costume designs. Lorca said of them: "As scenographers, I have the collaboration of the best painters of the Spanish school from Paris, of those who learned the most modern language of line under the tutelage of Picasso."[53] Additionally, poets such as Antonio Machado and Luis Cernuda read their Castilian poetry to village audiences. These collaborators received no remuneration for their work.

To emphasize the ties between Lorca's middle-class performers and the working class and peasantry, he designed the uniforms of La Barraca—the blue *mono*—to look like the garb of workers. The uniform led one interviewer to comment: "What? An Andalusian poet dressed in the 'mono' of the proletariat? For the Constitution says that we are a Republic of workers. Here is a poet who wants to obey the precepts of the Constitution. He appears [like] a mechanic, a chauffeur, a factory worker, with his dark blue suit made of ordinary cloth, so that all that he lacks is the addition of a hammer sticking out of his pocket. The singer of the poignant gypsies has been transformed into a machinist or some such thing."[54] On the uniform itself was the emblem of La Barraca, a wheel with twelve spokes, representing the wheels of the traveling theater, with dramatic masks superimposed on it. While the uniform represented an attempt to unify the various classes of contemporary Spain, the logo revealed Lorca's desire to link the present performances with the drama of Lope de Rueda.

Lorca had spoken earlier about presenting "modern" experimental theater, but the bulk of his repertoire consisted of dramas and entremeses by Lope, Calderón, and Cervantes. Why, always, the glance backward? While I have already touched on some of his reasons, Lorca provides more clues in interviews he gave to various newspapers: "People have asked why we don't represent modern works. For the simple reason that in Spain

Figure 16. Eduardo Ugarte *(left)* and Federico García Lorca *(right)*, creators of La Barraca, dressed in the *mono* of the proletariat. Photo by permission of the Fundación Federico García Lorca, Madrid.

Figure 17. Members of La Barraca, February–March 1933. Seated *(from left)*: Eduardo Ródena, Jacinto Higueras, Aurelio Romeu, and Pepe Obradors. Standing *(from left)*: Edmundo Rodríguez Huescar, Doña Pilar, Modesto Higueras, Conchita Polo, Ambrosio Zamazares, Federico García Lorca, Julia Rodríguez Mata, José García García, Eduardo Ugarte, Carmen García Lascoity, Carmen Galán, José María Moraz, Diego Tarancón, Diego Marín, and Rafael Rodríguez Rampún. Photo by permission of the Fundación Federico García Lorca, Madrid.

Figure 18. La Barraca's truck traveling the roads of Spain. Photo by permission of the Fundación Federico García Lorca, Madrid.

Figure 19. The set from *La guarda cuidadosa* is taken out of the truck. Almazán, 1932. Photo by permission of the Fundación Federico García Lorca, Madrid.

Figure 20. Members of La Barraca. Among them are Jacinto Higueras and Enrique Díez-Canedo assembling the stage set. Almazán, July 1932. Photo by permission of the Fundación Federico García Lorca, Madrid.

there exists practically no modern theater; the things that are represented are usually propaganda pieces and bad at that.... Our modern theater— modern and ancient—that is to say, eternal, like the sea—is that of Calderón and Cervantes, that of Lope and Gil Vicente."[55] Like his European modernist contemporaries, Lorca saw an eternal quality in the symbols and tales of the past and wanted to reinvigorate them with a modern sensibility.

He had other reasons as well. The theater of Calderón and Cervantes, he told audiences who were about to view the performances of La Barraca, represented the range of experiences and the particular spirit of the Spanish people, along with the universal spirit of drama in general. Cervantes and Calderón symbolized the theater of "Earth and Heaven," respectively. From Cervantes' ironic distillation of all of the "burning sexuality of his epoch" to Calderón's auto sacramentales, one could find "the entire scope of the scene and all the theatrical possibilities that there have been or will ever be." The theater of Cervantes invented a blueprint for farce, traces of which could be found in Pirandello, whereas Calderón's

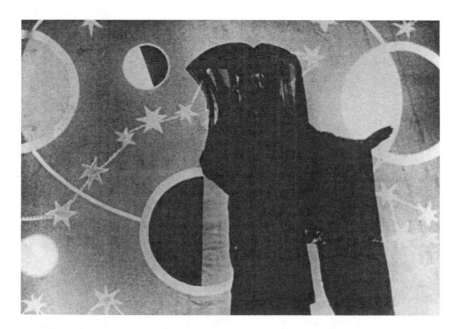

Figure 21. Federico García Lorca playing the role of the Shadow in the auto sacramental *Life Is a Dream*. Photo by permission of the Fundación Federico García Lorca, Madrid.

*El Mágico Prodigioso* led one to Faust. Once again, we see how Lorca linked the Spanish drama to the great European tradition, and through these associations he underlined the tension between particularism and universality inherent in modernism/modernity and in the "Spanish problem" itself. Then, in what seems to be a strange commentary, Lorca said that through *El Mágico Prodigioso* one also comes to "the great drama, the best drama that is represented thousands of times everyday, to the best theatrical tragedy that exists in the world: I refer to the Santo Sacrificio of the Mass."[56]

Lorca's discussion takes us full circle to the religious qualities of the theater or, perhaps, to the theatrical qualities of religion. Just as Luis Araquistáin had written of the ancient peoples' reaction to the "histrionic spectacle" of the theater, Lorca equated religious spectacles and dramatic renderings as spectacles capable—if done correctly—of generating profound emotion in their viewers. In some strange way, the modern drama had to re-create the passion of the Mass before it could move the masses. It had to be popular with "the aristocracy of the blood, spirit, and style," but "marinated and always nourished by popular vitality."[57] According to Lorca, even contemporary renditions of the classics had lost their soul and drained the souls of spectators along the way. He and his troupe were ready to restore the vitality the classics so sorely needed. Only by taking the plays "from the depths of the libraries," snatching them from scholars, and returning them "to the sunlight and the free air of the villages" could they accomplish this task.[58]

We can find a clear example of how La Barraca strove to revitalize Spanish drama in their rendition of Lope de Vega's *Fuenteovejuna*. Although written around 1619, *Fuenteovejuna* is set in the fifteenth century, during the reign of Ferdinand and Isabel. The plot revolves around the small village of Fuenteovejuna, where the overlord, Comendador Fernán Gómez, has returned from battle. An abusive overlord, he raises the peasants' ire by bedding every available and unavailable peasant girl, whether or not she or her family acquiesces. The subplot reveals another aspect of his dishonorable character: he joins forces with the young Maestre de Calatrava to conspire against Ferdinand and Isabel and bring their dominions to the king of Portugal.

Once in the village, the comendador focuses on his latest object of desire, Laurencia, who tries every means possible to escape his clutches and, generally, manages to succeed. During one encounter when Laurencia appears doomed to be raped, her betrothed, Frondoso, comes to her rescue by challenging the comendador's authority and thus enabling Laurencia to escape. For his defiant behavior, Frondoso becomes an outlaw, hunted mercilessly by the vengeful comendador and his retainers. The villagers manage to keep Frondoso hidden, and when it seems as if Fernán Gómez has departed for battle, Frondoso and Laurencia get married in the plaza of Fuenteovejuna. During the ceremony, however, the comendador surprises the wedding party, imprisons Frondoso, escapes with Laurencia, and, as we soon discover, rapes her. None of the villagers does anything to stop Fernán Gómez, as they feel powerless within their station and against his force of arms.

In the final act, the villagers of Fuenteovejuna meet to discuss what can be done about the comendador's abuses. Laurencia, unrecognized because of her torn and bloodied clothing, interrupts the meeting, calling all of the men cowards for allowing such dishonor to fall upon them. She incites them to action, calling for the death of Fernán Gómez and his men. The villagers kill him. After his death they all agree that if questioned by the authorities about who committed the murder, they would say "Fuenteovejuna." All of the villagers are tortured by a judge under the employ of Ferdinand and Isabel, but no one reveals the secret, preferring instead to protect the community by bravely declaring that "Fuenteovejuna" killed him. The frustrated officials drag the villagers to the court of Ferdinand and Isabel to state their case. Although the king and queen frown on such lawless behavior, the royal pair choose to forgive the villagers rather than put every single member to death. By killing Fernán Gómez, the people rid Fuenteovejuna and themselves of someone who harmed both the village and the crown. The villagers then swear allegiance to the crown and to Castile. By the end of the play, the social order and honor are restored to Fuenteovejuna, and the crown of Castile remains united and strong.

The social tensions within this play reverberated clearly to those people who had their eyes open during the Republic. Instead of bending to the will of the comendador, the peasant had to kowtow to the commands of the *cacique*. The peasants were still isolated from the power structure and still lacked the means and the knowledge to challenge their "superiors." Lorca and his troupe knew that people would draw parallels between the action in *Fuenteovejuna* and the life of the peasant in contemporary Spain. As one *barraco* who played the role of the comendador, Luis Sáenz de la Calzada, said of Lorca's version: "The action of *Fuenteovejuna* occurs during the reign of the Catholic monarchs, but Federico set it during the

1930s. Alberto, the extraordinary sculptor, who did the decorations for the work, was able to put all of Castile inside the play ... place by place, piece by piece ... and the characters wore the actual costumes, that is to say, costumes corresponding to those worn by peasants in 1932."[59]

Not only were the costumes contemporaneous, but Lorca also expunged from his text the entire subplot of the Catholic monarchs.[60] He justified such ruthless cuts in many ways. For example, he claimed that in *Fuenteovejuna* the cuts serve to eliminate the "political drama" in order to concentrate on the "social drama."[61] This emphasis on the social drama illustrates nicely the tension between the reformist and revolutionary strands of the Republican–Socialist coalition. Lorca contended that he had brought the life back to the original drama by excising the parts that dragged down the action. But, of course, one could also surmise that he viewed the monarchy as irrelevant to the lives of everyday folk, just as Alfonso XIII had been made irrelevant by his exile during the first days of the Republic. Luis Sáenz de la Calzada provided another explanation for Lorca's editorial liberties. Like Lorca, Sáenz de la Calzada believed that the cuts made in *Fuenteovejuna* and other such classics were a legitimate device to seize the spectator's "emotional fiber." But he also felt that by removing complete scenes that obscured or eliminated the specific temporal aspects of the drama, Lorca made the work more universal. This change did not detract from the drama, however, because "in this way ... the rural drama that has been cosubstantial with Spain was laid bare, surely since the Neolithic Age. And the people understood it as such; they applauded not only the interpretation, direction, the scenic play of decorations and figurines, etc., but also because it made obvious, like a wound, something that, unconsciously known, the peasant carries with him in his mental mechanisms, in each drop of his blood and in the black seas of his daily sweat."[62]

Once again, and like many observers before him, Sáenz de la Calzada equated the essence of Spain with its seemingly unchanging rural elements and the rural drama as the embodiment of that essence. In fact, one reviewer of La Barraca's performance of *Fuenteovejuna* remarked on the play's "dramatic intensity," calling it "the drama that most faithfully reflects the last centuries of Spanish life" and a "drama for all times and for all oppressed people."[63]

But it took more than words recited with vitality to resuscitate the Spanish drama and bring unity to a people. Lorca believed that the other fine arts, such as music and dance, were essential to the organic unity of the play, to the interplay of passion and intellect. His experience organizing a competition and festival of *cante jondo* ("deep song," or traditional flamenco music) with composer Manuel de Falla[64] and his exposure to the revival of folkloric music by Eduardo Torner in the Residencia de Estudiantes probably contributed to his dramatic Weltanschauung. Lorca invented and choreographed a dance that he called "El baile de las agachadas" for the wedding scene of *Fuenteovejuna,* using music he had culled from the years when Torner had worked at the Residencia. Attempting historical accuracy, Lorca chose to incorporate music from the fifteenth and sixteenth centuries into his renditions of Golden Age drama.[65]

Lorca applied his ideas about music to the auto sacramental as well, insisting that an auto was "incomplete" if the performance did not incorporate music. Therefore: "There, hidden, are some *vihuelas* [ancient guitars] and adolescent singers that, in the necessary moments, let their voices, their *loas,* and their *réplicas* be heard, in the manner of the chorus of a Greek tragedy and the way they usually played in the time of

Figure 22. Performance of *Fuenteovejuna* by La Barraca in Ciudad Real, February 1936. Performers in this scene include Julián Risoto, Carmen Risoto, Orgaz, Carmen García Antón, Jacinto Higueras, Diego Tarancón, Carmen Torres?, Salinas, Teresina Risoto, Carmen Galán *(white shawl),* María del Carmen García Lasgoity, Manuel Puga, and Joaquín Sánchez Covisa. Photo by permission of the Fundación Federico García Lorca, Madrid.

Calderón in the atriums of temples. It is a short and simple music, in the nature of an ecclesiastical song, such as is today performed in the "seises" of the Sevillian Cathedral."[66] Lorca and his supporters also posited that the "remote air" of the music in the auto reminds one of "those centuries in which one same faith congregated in one sole preoccupation to all of the components of society, gentlemen and plebes, old and young."[67]

Lorca's entire discussion gravitated toward the creation of community through the musical ambiance in the drama. He linked the drama across time, beginning with the Greeks and ending with the present performances of past liturgical dances in the Cathedral of Seville. In ways reminiscent of Nietzsche and Wagner, by referring to the chorus in the Greek tragedy and the plaintive nature of the music that had once united all members of the community in faith, Lorca ascribed to the drama a mystical quality that was capable of uniting a disparate audience.[68]

With both theatrical and theoretical baggage intact and thirty performers and technicians to aid him, Lorca took La Barraca on the road on July 10, 1932, performing first in Burgo de Osma, about one hundred twenty-five miles north of Madrid, and then in various villages in the province of Soria. When La Barraca performed in a village, the troupe followed a relatively uniform formula. Usually they began with an entremés that lasted about fifteen minutes and then performed a larger work such as *Fuenteovejuna* or *El burlador de Sevilla*.[69] La Barraca also geared its performances to varying audiences, emphasizing, for example, Cervantes' entremeses for more "popular" audiences, while choosing the auto sacramental *La vida es sueño* for more "restricted," educated, ones.[70]

But before they presented their plays, Lorca generally read a speech describing the mission of La Barraca: "The students of the University of Madrid, helped by the Government of the Republic and especially by the Minister [of Public Instruction] Don Fernando de los Ríos, are creating for the first time in Spain a theater with the creative heat of a nucleus of young artists now standing out with a luminous profile in today's life of the nation." Thus, Lorca linked the work of his theater directly to that of the Republic, and he emphasized the youthful, dynamic qualities of the performers, equating them with the creativity of the youthful Republic. Next, he spoke of the need to revitalize the theater and bring it to remote parts of Spain. At other times he gave a lecture on history or literary criticism. All of this La Barraca did with "absolute impartiality and for the joy of being able to collaborate to the extent of our power with this beautiful hour of the new Spain."[71]

## RESPONSES TO THE TRAVELING THEATERS

By the end of 1932 and the beginning of 1933, both Federico García Lorca's La Barraca and Alejandro Casona and Eduardo Torner's Teatro y Coro del Pueblo of the Misiones Pedagógicas had begun to infiltrate the more remote regions of Spain, sharing the Castilian drama with illiterate peasants. And although both groups received the spiritual and financial blessing of Republican leaders during the first half of the Republic, interviews and memoirs of some of the participants hint at a rivalry, albeit a friendly one, between the two groups. Casona, for example, said that La Barraca went to "little towns" that had remnants of "decent" theater, interpreting Lope well with a modern sensibility, whereas the Misiones Pedagógicas brought "the theater to the illiterate peasants who did not know what the theater was and, therefore, [it was something] they saw for the first time." "For this reason," he claimed, their repertoire had to be simplified with "short works with music and little dances. The difficult part was to create this repertoire that had not existed."[72] In contrast, La Barraca troupe member Luis Sáenz de la Calzada writes of Lorca's enterprise as "authentic theater, with a defined mission that it fulfilled completely." The Misiones Pedagógicas, although similar to La Barraca, were, "as [the] name clearly indicates, more pedagogical than artistic."[73]

Overblown rhetoric aside, La Barraca and the Coro y Teatro del Pueblo had more in common and shared more resources than some of its members cared to admit. For example, two actors from the Misiones Pedagógicas, Mario Etcheverri and Julián Orgaz, performed in La Barraca's rendition of Juan del Encina's *Egloga de Plácida y Victoriano*,[74] while the Coro y Teatro del Pueblo received "folkloric contributions" from García Lorca.[75] In fact, the majority of performers for both groups came from students at the University of Madrid.

Both groups shared similar visions about Spain and its people. They presented to rural Spain elite culture in the form of classic drama melded with folkloric songs and dances, and so hoped to incorporate all Spaniards into the fold of Republican Spain, a Spain with Castile as its heart. The centerpieces of the performances were dramas and entremeses of Castilian origin, whereas the songs and dances often originated from regions outside Castile; therefore, these dramatic renderings mirrored, whether consciously or not, the Republican political vision of a strong Castile uniting a regionalized nation, a Spanish *cocido* (stew) containing many different elements but maintaining a wholeness all the same.

Additionally, both groups had their roots in the Institución Libre de Enseñanza with its vision of a Spain regenerated through education.

It is difficult to gauge how effectively La Barraca and the Coro y Teatro del Pueblo fostered a sense of community in rural areas because the programs were designed specifically for a largely illiterate audience. Therefore, we have to rely on the writings of those who directed or performed in the troupes and those who wrote about the performances in the popular press. While this information tells us little about audience reception, it tells us plenty about those who favored or rejected these programs, and, ultimately, it offers us a prism through which to look at the politics of the Second Republic.

Lorca, for example, stressed the "cordiality" of the peasantry and their ability to understand the productions, "more perhaps than in the capitals." While he realized that the peasant may not have understood Calderón's symbolism, Lorca was confident that they could "intuit the magical quality of his verses."[76] In fact, he professed a greater faith in popular audiences composed of workers and the "simple people of the villages" than in the middle and upper classes—those "who have nothing inside." He thought that popular audiences intuited the greatness of the Spanish theater, while the bourgeoisie muttered empty phrases such as "their work is not bad," not realizing that they were viewing "high art."[77] García Lorca and his performers never denied that they sometimes faced hostility from their audiences, but they attempted to convince readers that they generally won the hostile audiences over by the artistry and professionalism of their performances.

Similarly, those who worked for the Misiones Pedagógicas also stressed the warm reception by rural audiences. The *Memoria of the Misiones Pedagógicas* described audiences bewitched by the drama and music, appreciative of the attention they finally received by the people from the city. Pictures of the rural audiences show faces captivated by the spectacle, smiling faces awaiting the next dance, the next song, the next entremés. Alejandro Casona remarked that of all the projects carried out by the Misiones Pedagógicas, the theater "dazzled" the people most.[78] But sometimes these audiences living in regions known to be anti-Republican met the misioneros with hostility. If we take the misioneros' words at face value, then these hostile audiences, too, could be won over by their infectious spirit. Casona recalled how at the beginning of a performance of Calderón's "El dragoncillo" a peasant with a "contemptuous attitude" had begun, as the curtain rose, to roll a cigarette: "He had stuck the smoking papers to his lip and forty minutes passed in a second. When the performance ended, he felt a type of surprise" at having passed the time so quickly.[79]

The participants were not the only ones carried away by the ideals embedded in these programs. Journalists, politicians, artists, and intellectuals favorable to the Republic also wrote positive reviews of the work accomplished by La Barraca and the Misiones Pedagógicas, imposing on the productions their hopes for and conceptions of the Spanish state and its people. Many of these writers perpetuated the idea that theater in general, and seventeenth-century theater in particular, both unified the populace and reflected the "true Spanish essence." For example, a review of La Barraca's first performance in front of an audience of government officials spurred the theater critic and La Barraca performer Enrique Díez-Canedo to write that the theater "is a means to create spirit, diffusing ... the work of our great dramatists, in whom is embodied and lives the Spanish soul."[80] (Obviously, this article was written with an element of self-interest!) Another journalist noted that even if the uneducated populace could not understand all of the subtleties present in the dramatic works, they would "discover from this fictional life that conserves, despite the centuries, the profound aroma of the race and the eternal footprint of the spirit."[81] The playwright and brother-in-law of Manuel Azaña, Cipriano Rivas Cherif, pinpointed Calderón as the one who embodied the "true national character" because he was able to integrate in his plays the strong union between the Catholic Church and the Hapsburg monarchy, a Spanish unity that had not been matched since then. In fact, he argued, the German Romantics were attracted to Calderón's works precisely because of his ability to portray an "authentic representation of a national theater, of myths, abstractions, and symbols placed for really dramatic contributions."[82] And, finally, paying a compliment both to La Barraca's performance and the popular audiences, an unnamed journalist wrote that this urban contact with a rural audience "vitalizes the Spanish theater and newly provides them with the authentically national content that was lost with the masters of the seventeenth century."[83]

These performances of classic theater supposedly worked so well because the plays still spoke to the "unchanging" and "simple" rural audiences by re-creating the emotions of a religious spectacle. And because the popular audiences remained unchanged—as many claimed—from the last three centuries, they were still very impressionable and, therefore, highly educable. "The villager is like a child," said Unamuno after viewing a performance of La Barraca, "He wants to be told the story he already knows from memory." These classic plays performed by the likes of La Barraca, he implied, stimulated the collective memory and acted as a salve to the common people. Socialist and Communist workers and peasants filled the theater to see La Barraca "in the same way that in certain places they attend the processions of Good Friday." They all partook of the theater's mysticism and, as Unamuno contended, these performances functioned not only pedagogically, but also politically.[84]

Others also noticed the political, pedagogical, and religious aspects of these performances. After viewing a performance of the Misiones Pedagógicas in Ríofrío, outside of Madrid, theater critic A. Hernández-Cata asked whether, as some have questioned, the Misiones Pedagógicas could effectively act as a pedagogical tool for shaping the people. He believed wholeheartedly that they worked to initiate the common people in the Spanish tradition, but he suggested that they could widen their scope even more by including "modern apologues" to show audiences that "art is not solely a mirror of the past. With skill, the aesthetic revelation remains to serve ethical and political propaganda."[85]

There were also people who disapproved of these theatrical projects. Besides those who directly tried to sabotage the performances by shouting, booing, and hissing (actions attributed to "professional agitators" and "Catholic students"),[86] others used the pen to discredit the work of La Barraca and the Misiones Pedagógicas. The editorialists of the conservative Catholic newspaper *El Debate*, for example, disliked any of the cultural programs sponsored by the first Republican government solely because these programs emanated from the Republic. They almost automatically viewed the works as anticlerical and antitraditional.[87] They also attacked La Barraca for taking away jobs from professional actors because the actors in La Barraca received no remuneration for their performances, thus undercutting the salaries that professional actors could make.[88] After the troupe performed in Sanabria, a particularly scathing review of La Barraca came out of a Catholic, CEDA-affiliated newspaper in Oviedo. The entire review pointed out the class differences between the performers—those who wore the blue monos "that [did] not belong to them"—and the bedraggled, starving villagers. He ridiculed the performers for having the nerve to ride up in their cars pretending to know what's best for this neglected peasantry. He fired off a diatribe: "You, if you're hungry, look: It's La Barraca, ambassador of art. Fill your stomach with verses.... You, the thirsty one, leave water alone. Drink this old wine in new wineskins.

What? It doesn't take away your thirst? Not even if they're brought disguised as *comedias* and *autos* and *entremeses* and dramas.... Ragged ones: your rags are nothing. An illusion that you forge. Look at the *farándula*: they're dressed in the velvet of Flanders. Skirts shine from silk and mix with the petticoats embroidered with lace on fine linen from Holland. Don't think of your rags: dress in fantasies of Farse."[89]

These comments, vituperative as they were, rang with some truth. Some might ask how the misioneros and barracos could have been so oblivious to the material conditions of the peasantry. Alejandro Casona asked the same questions about his own involvement in the Misiones Pedagógicas. After visiting the village of San Martín de Castañeda in 1934, he was shocked by the depth of misery etched on the residents' faces. Noting the starvation, illness, goiter, and a host of other ailments, he thought: "Fifty-something happy and healthy students who arrive with their *romances*, songs and comedies.... The unexpected shock with that brutal reality painfully shocked us all. They needed bread, medicine ... and all we had were songs and poems in the missional pouch that day."[90] The misioneros tried to contend, at least in part, with the indigence that confronted them by setting up a more rigorous social and political mission in Sanabria. They imported doctors, social workers, and agriculturalists from the city to try to make the area of Sanabria less inhospitable, but this type of program was not a regular practice of the Misiones.

Even if the Misiones had decided to step up economic aid to these villages, their opportunities to do so would have been squelched after the November 1933 elections. After these elections, the Socialists lost half of their seats, and the CEDA, a conservative federation of Catholic parties, helped by an alliance with Lerroux's Radicals, gained a majority in the Spanish Cortes—although the cabinet itself was headed by Lerroux. Because anything associated with the previous coalition was tainted in the CEDA's eyes as rabidly anticlerical, this new coalition substantially cut funding for both La Barraca and the Misiones Pedagógicas. For example, in 1933 the Misiones received 700,000 pesetas from the central government; the budget in June 1934 was cut to 650,000 pesetas; by 1935, the subsidy for the Misiones Pedagógicas was eliminated altogether.[91] Nevertheless, La Barraca and the Coro y Teatro del Pueblo managed to influence the lives of countless Spaniards who had been virtually ignored for centuries by the central government. La Barraca performed in sixty-four places in all, and the Coro y Teatro del Pueblo ventured through one hundred seventy-nine areas by the end of 1934.[92]

## THEORISTS ON THE RIGHT

One could argue that the right lacked the numerous theorists of the drama that were available to the left during the Republic, and that the right did not write plays for educational and propagandistic purposes until the Civil War. But at least a couple of critics existed before the war, even if plays with a right-wing bent were not performed until the late 1930s. Like theorists from the left, those from the right who actually addressed the subject of theater concurred with the left's assessment that the Spanish theater had declined over the last century and needed to be revitalized. Like the left, the right saw value in returning to the Golden Age dramatists for inspiration, but instead of emphasizing solely the populist appeal of writers such as Calderón and Lope de Vega, the right extracted from these playwrights messages about nationalism, imperialism, religion, and hierarchy. The new theater needed to stress these values to help bring Spaniards back to the national fold.

Ernesto Giménez Caballero was the most famous of these critics, and his work *Arte y Estado,* which covers painting, architecture, theater, and film, has even been referred to as "the official handbook of aesthetics under Franco."[93] As the founder and editor of the avant-garde literary journal *La Gaceta Literaria* (1927–1932), Giménez Caballero was a literary figure in his own right. He was also a member of the editorial board of the radical right's journal *Acción Española* and a dedicated partisan of the Falange.[94] Unlike many followers of the right who had no use for anything that originated from the Soviet Union, Giménez Caballero admired how the Soviets had created a cultural revolution and rallied the masses through such avenues as the Proletkult movement. Like García Lorca and some of the members of the Misiones Pedagógicas, Giménez Caballero sensed that the theater's power came in the form of religious spectacle. For example, he described a festival at Moscow's Winter Palace in 1920 where eight thousand spectators showed up to celebrate "The Triumph of Production." He told his readers: "Think of those allegorical processions that Russia organizes for its masses in the public squares before they perform a *social auto,* and you will see how closely they resemble those liturgical processions of our Calderonian and Austrian [Hapsburg] Madrid." He thought that the theater needed to return to its mysterious, religious roots, for "this was the origin of Tragedy: the blood, the sacrifice of a God or a Hero." Like Lorca, he perceived the Catholic Mass to be the greatest drama, where the priest "*represents* the passion of the Savior, taking communion with the blood and wine in front of all men." He continued: "Russia understood the need to return to the *mysterious, symbolic* performance. Just as our Calderón understood when he made the Eucharist powerful in his sublime *autos sacramentales*."⁹⁵ In this declaration we have come full circle to Calderón again, with the right reclaiming the religious aspects of the drama, in contrast to the left extracting its social ones.

To out-Russia Russia, Giménez Caballero dreamt of a Fascist theater that would "abandon and surpass" Soviet theater at the same point that the Catholic Church "abandoned the evangelical vagaries of a golden age, of a paradise, where only the humble masses, the proletariat could fit. At the point of *Hierarchy*. In the return of the *Hero*, the *Protagonist*, the *Saint*, the *Savior*, over a background of the masses and the herd."⁹⁶ In particularly Nietzschean language, Giménez Caballero called for the theater to return to strong characters—saviors, if you will—to lead the masses on a mystical journey.

Other lesser-known Fascist critics also chimed in on the state of Spanish theater. In the student-run Fascist newspaper, *Haz,* one columnist lambasted the Republic for contributing to the national decline of the theater. The author did not shed tears for the death of this theater, for he saw the inevitable birth of a Fascist theater from the remains of the moribund one. This new "youthful" theater was not going to be "those historical reconstructions at the service of a party ... Nor Isabel of Castile ... nor Cisneros warding off the Socialists, nor saints at the service of *El Debate.*" In other words, the themes that the old-guard conservatives pushed could not serve the new Fascist generation. Instead, the new theater would be "a political theater: of masses, not of members of Parliament. And a social theater: not of pampered children, but of individuals who suffer the anguish of rough, unsocial, humanity."⁹⁷

Despite the direct jab at the many intellectuals who served in the first government of the Republic and who subsidized such programs as La Barraca, this Fascist author's political theater sounded very much like what the left had proposed, but he deviated from the left in the lessons that he believed Golden Age Spanish theater should impart: "And when it is necessary to revive the majesty of our classics, it will be done giving them a totalitarian, national, Catholic, and imperial significance, instead of the way they now use our imperial Spaniard, Lope de Vega, in the Teatro Municipal, where the brother-in-law of Azaña [Cipriano Rivas Cherif] turns the work upside down to create a false propaganda separated from the popular and just sentiments that the drama possesses."[98] For this columnist and for Ernesto Giménez Caballero, the new Fascist theater would take on many of the characteristics of fascism itself. That is, the theater would represent the triumphs of the nation; the themes would emphasize a heroic figure who could sway the masses while at the same time respect the anguish the masses often suffered. It would be youthful, mystical, and political, but not backward looking in its politics. The past was a storehouse of myths that one could use to bring forth a new vibrant society that was both harmonious and hierarchical. But the right would not try these ideas until the Civil War, and they would not reach their zenith until the Franco regime.

The left, however, as we have seen, began their theatrical experiments under the favorable shelter of the Republican–Socialist coalition. By attempting to revitalize the theater, the organizers of La Barraca and the Teatro del Pueblo hoped to salvage and re-create a community that they believed had been lost on Spain's bumpy road to modernity. And in some ways, one could look at these attempts as backward-looking enterprises determined to slow the process of modernity and return people to simpler times and more modest entertainments.

In many rural areas, where the trappings of modernity were nowhere in sight, the use of traditional, slower-paced forms of entertainment and education might have worked to foster the sense of community and nationhood that Republicans and Socialists were trying to achieve. But in the cities, where people lived an increasingly fast-paced, impersonal, industrialized, rationalized life, the revitalization of the theater might not have been the boon that Republicans hoped for. How could such an ancient art form speak to the urban masses? Many argued that it could not. An increasing number of theater critics sounded the death knell for theater, as the new art form—the cinema—stole young, urban audiences away from theaters and lured them into the dark movie halls where rapid-fire images flickered across enormous white screens. If the Republican–Socialist coalition hoped to include the rising urban masses into the national community, they had to use modern technology—namely, film—in the same way that they attempted to use theater in rural Spain.

# CHAPTER 4

# Taming the Seventh Art

## Battle for Cultural Unity
## on the Cinematographic Front

IF THEATER EMBODIED TRADITION, THEN FILM SPOKE THE LANGUAGE OF the future. Theater, generally the purview of an educated elite, had to make room for the entertainment that thrilled the urban masses throughout the industrial world. Once exposed to the seemingly realistic images and fast-paced motion captured on a piece of celluloid, most people would succumb to its charms. Still a relatively new art form, film had the potential to revolutionize society.

During the 1920s and 1930s, when critics lambasted Spanish theater directors for airing lackluster productions that only accelerated the decline of Spanish theater, they also pointed to the cinema as the greatest threat to its survival. Film provided a new aesthetic for a modern, urban audience with increased leisure time. Reformist Republicans and Socialists took these critics' statements to mean that the theater needed to be revitalized, and—as we have seen—they embarked on renovating the theatrical tradition. Instead, they should have asked: What was it in particular that attracted audiences to movie houses? Did movies create a more intimate community than the theater? But because they were more familiar with the theatrical genre than with the cinematographic one, reformers of the Second Republic failed to generate as all-encompassing a theory for the production and distribution of film as they had for the theater. Therefore, they never figured out how film could serve the national interest.

The inability of the early Republicans to harness film's potential may have been a function of their educational background and political ideology. Because many Republican leaders inherited their intellectual tools via Krausism and the Institución Libre de Enseñanza, they may not have comprehended other uses for film. They employed it mostly as a documentary tool to interest citizens in "higher" forms of culture, such as literature and theater. Their use of movies really extended only to the school system and those projects promoted by the Misiones Pedagógicas. The Republicans' limited conception of film and—as we will see later—their fear of social revolution, prevented them from sharing the view of others outside the liberal sphere of politics: namely, that film should revolutionize the masses.

Therefore, the debate over film and its potential to capture the loyalty of the masses and define the Spanish character really occurred outside the sphere of liberal politics. It took place instead in partisan film journals and was conducted primarily by disciples of the extreme left and right, by some who feared the cultural hegemony of Hollywood, and by others who embraced the supremacy of the Soviet Union. Film, then, often became the chosen tool of the political extremes to break down and challenge what they saw as a tired liberalism and replace it with a wholly new vision for Spain's future. For critics from the radical left, film could be used to beget the long-needed social revolution in Spain, to instigate a Socialist or anarchist revolution. For some members of the radical right, film could reinscribe Catholic and imperial values under the auspices of a stronger nation modeled on the newly rising Fascist states.

## FILM BEFORE THE SECOND REPUBLIC (1896 TO 1931)

Like all Europeans and Americans, Spaniards in the first few decades of the twentieth century confronted a cultural landscape that had been utterly transformed by the invention of film. By the 1920s, the cinema—especially American cinema—was the urban entertainment of Europe par excellence. Here, at last, was an art form that toppled the hierarchies of official, avant-garde, and popular culture.[1] Film's novelty—its ability to reach mass audiences cheaply and quickly, to blur cultural, social, and national boundaries, and to pander to the irrational in its spectators—threatened elites on both sides of the Atlantic. Not only did guardians of European culture fear the social changes wrought by this form of mass entertainment (What would become of a nation that encouraged people of different social classes or unchaperoned youths of different sexes to sit in the dark in undifferentiated rows?), they were also appalled by what they saw as the domination of crass American values over long-standing, refined European ones. To overcome the onslaught of American vulgarity, European elites clamored for self-sufficient film industries that would reflect their respective national values and identities.[2] Spain was no different in this regard.

The first films premiered in Paris in 1895, and Madrid got its first glimpse of the medium on May 15, 1896. Because film was a latecomer to the world of the arts, many people who matured before film's early bloom failed to see what all the fuss was about. While the masses clamored for more entertainment, some Spanish intellectuals of the cohort often categorized as the Generation of 1898 scorned film, seeing it as a destructive power that was damaging an already decayed theater and undermining what little literacy existed in Spain.

The philosopher-intellectual Unamuno, for example, decried the elevation of film into an art. He was "substantially bothered" by silent movies, which "disassociated the word from the gesture." What upset him most about this new medium was the tendency for filmmakers to conflate film and literature, to meld "highbrow" art forms with "lowbrow" ones. Not all literature, according to Unamuno, was "filmable," nor should it have been. Using a series of puns on the words *película* (film) and *pelleja* (skin), he argued against the use of the word *filmar* (to film) and wanted to substitute *pelicular* (to make movies) instead, claiming that "to make a movie out of a work of literature is to flay or skin it." Literature had no place in films; movies may have fulfilled a purpose as "a recourse for deaf people who do not know how to read," but they were a pernicious force that would "damage the talent of the men of letters who want to dedicate themselves to inventing pantomimes."[3]

Another of Unamuno's contemporaries, Ramiro de Maeztu, who would later be a follower of the radical right, saw danger and immorality in the cinema, for film, at least silent film, was a mesmerizing medium that compelled the hordes to act in uncivilized fashions. Because film reduced the world to image and movement rather than sound or thought, he argued, it excited in people only emotion, and negative emotion at that. Film "presents us with the human figure surrendered to [special] effects, without the word to subjugate them, to humanize them." It produces in people an affection for "ambition, greed, sexuality, blood." Without the mediation of dialogue or soliloquies, an audience watching a filmed version of *Hamlet* might think of him as a "crazy assassin."[4] Words were the force that reined in passion.

Both Unamuno and Maeztu believed that words, and literature specifically, mediated the human condition, and it was a view that many Spanish Republicans would also share. Their arguments against film stemmed from a belief in literature's redemptive ability and from their prejudice that an audience should be literate. In some ways their views exemplify a tendency among European intellectuals in the late nineteenth and early twentieth centuries to perceive a great divide between mass and elite culture and, in some instances, to widen this split.[5] What they did not see, but what later generations in Spain and elsewhere in Europe and the United States discovered, was film's ability to tap into the irrational and emotive side of human existence. Therefore, political ideologues began to employ film to inculcate new or already-existing national myths in a much larger population.

Despite Unamuno and Maeztu's complaints, the cinema was here to stay, and Spaniards consumed films as fast as studios could produce them.[6] Until World War I, France dominated the film industry, controlling the technology and worldwide distribution of film. The Italian, Swedish, and Danish film industries also blossomed during the early years. While other European nations and the United States began almost immediately to adapt Lumière's technology and make it their own, Spain's film industry sputtered along, having to be content with distributing foreign films or producing a minimal number of Spanish ones that slavishly copied storylines and stylistic flourishes imported from Italy and France. The only really original films that Spaniards did make were *zarzuelas*—a Spanish genre of light opera—touristic travelogues, and filmed plays, none of which was highly exportable to other nations.[7]

If the Spanish masses lapped up movies, then why was the Spanish film industry so slow to respond to their enthusiasm and tap into a ready-made market? The reasons are numerous.[8] One of the most obvious is Spain's uneven economic development. While Barcelona and Bilbao thrived as industrial powerhouses, the rest of Spain was slow to industrialize and suffered from a variety of economic ills. Add to this mixture Spain's recent humiliating defeat in the Spanish-American War (1898), and the concomitant political, economic, and social upheaval wrought by the defeat, and one begins to understand why subsidizing a national film industry might not be the government's first priority.

And then there were the Catalans. Catalan industrialists—those most able to afford to shape the film industry—invested little in it, not realizing that soon the cinema would be a lucrative enterprise. Pronouncements by the conservative Catholic Church also bore down on the Catalans. Almost from film's inception, the Catholic Church in general and the Spanish clergy in particular railed against film's immorality, both for its themes and for the new social relations it was engendering. Pressure from the clergy helped to get the first film censorship law on the books on November 27, 1912.[9] Since the Catalan industrialists were closely allied with the clergy, the social pressure to stay away from this industry was great. Finally, Catalan nationalism, in both its political and cultural manifestations favored developing an autonomous Catalan industry over merging with a national, Spanish one.

All these factors help explain why the Spanish film industry lagged behind those in much of Europe and the United States in the early years of film. The Spanish film industry did slowly begin to come into its own, especially during World War I, when it could take up the slack left by the European film industries of the warring nations. But this slight advantage disappeared at the end of the war, when European film studios began retooling and restructuring their industries. But the end of the war did not signal a crisis in the film industry for Spain alone; the once-ascendant French and Italian film industries, for example, found themselves surpassed in technology, distribution, and sales by the seemingly relentless American studios. By the end of the war, the United States became the number one producer and distributor of films, with Germany following closely behind.[10]

With the advent of sound in 1927, the weaker economies of Europe suffered even greater losses at the box office. Spain was also hard hit by this new invention because it could afford neither the technology necessary to make talking films nor the expense of retooling movie houses to provide audiences with sound. Spain, like other European countries, found itself struggling to compete with the Hollywood industries that were churning out cheap films by the score and exporting them around the world.[11] Not only did American film studios corner the market in making and exporting English-language films, they also began dominating the making of foreign-language films after 1929 by setting up American studios to make non-English-language films in Joinville-le-Point, a suburb near Paris, and hiring the most talented actors in neighboring nations to act in Hollywood productions, thereby increasing American revenues in foreign countries.[12]

Europeans panicked—and not just because the Americans were siphoning away precious film revenues; more important, after the advent of talking pictures, Europeans increasingly worried that the Americanization of film was eroding their national identities and infiltrating the souls of the European masses with mindless action, crass commercialism, loose morals, class mixing, and all manner of vice that smacked of modernity. Europeans responded in two ways: they sought economic protections for their national film industries, and they began calling for films that reflected their national values and traditions.[13]

Spain was no different. Although slow to nurture its film industry, by 1928, even the Spanish government began to see the cinema as a force to be reckoned with.[14] Aware of both the Hollywood infiltration in Spaniards' lives and the propagandistic power of film, the Primo de Rivera government began taking a more active role in the promotion of the Spanish film industry and the exclusion of "objectionable" foreign films.[15] The dictator's brother, José Primo de Rivera, called on Fernando Viola (a lawyer, silent-screen actor, and sometime-director) to stop the tide of "immoral" films—the majority from the United States—that flooded Spanish cities. Viola suggested that the government devise ways to nurture and protect the fledgling Spanish film industry. He suggested four major plans: (1) censor films according to the audience's age; (2) create Spanish newsreels (the Spanish equivalent of *Movietone News*); (3) offer economic protection to the Spanish film industry; and (4) create a Congreso Hispanoamericano de Cinematografía (Spanish American Congress of Cinematography; CHC) to unite all Latin American nations' film industries and fell the Hollywood giant.

With the cooperation of Ibero-American educators and film aficionados of varying political stripes, Viola eventually succeeded in organizing the CHC, on October 12, 1931, significantly, the Día de la Raza, or Columbus Day—which was precisely the time when Spain was undergoing the transition from a military dictatorship and monarchy to the Second Republic. The conference goers proposed a series of protectionist measures to encourage homegrown films that highlighted themes thought to be particularly Spanish or Latin American, and to prevent foreign, American morals from slipping across their borders.[16]

In the end, the majority of the proposals generated by the CHC never materialized. The Confederación Iberoamericana de Cinematografía (Iberian American Cinematography Confederation), which was created at the end of the congress, functioned in name only. The great cinematographic unity of Iberia and its Latin American brothers against the hordes of Hollywood heathens was never to be. Perhaps the group's heterogeneity prevented such visions from being realized, or perhaps the new Republic lacked the finances and the ideological commitment to the previous political regime to realize the congress's proposals. Whatever the reasons, the new Republican government shied away from instituting the all-encompassing reforms proposed by the CHC. Instead, the Republic focused only on those suggestions that called for enacting protectionist laws and subsidizing educational films. And far more than in the Primo regime, Republican officials and their allies promoted educational film as a means to transform Spanish society.

## REPUBLICANS HARNESS THE SILVER SCREEN: FILM AS DOCUMENTARY

As we have already seen, the Republican–Socialist coalition first set about to gut, and then reform, the educational system by eliminating any remnants of the clergy and building a network of new schools, and they displayed a keen interest in allying themselves with progressive, secular educators. These educators, in turn, needed the Republic's financial backing to institute the educational reforms that previous regimes could not. While they sought classrooms and books and laboratories, teachers on the cutting edge requested films to disseminate information. Film, they thought, offered a panacea for Spain's endemic educational failures. And Republican officials, at least in the first few years of the Republic, obliged these educators in their quest to bring film to a rural Spain that was largely untouched by literacy.

Educators and social reformers placed their faith in film to heal all manner of wounds, from illiteracy to criminality to poverty to war. Some even claimed that talking film's influence on the contemporary world could be compared to the effects "the discovery of America" had on the "Old World."[17] Perhaps educational cinema's greatest advocate was F. Blanco Castilla, who held the title of Inspector of Primary Education during the Republic. He credited film's success in the classroom with its ability to engage a person's emotions and thus increase the person's ability to remember a film's particular lesson. Film "convinces more" because "it reproduces more than any other instrument ... the phenomena of real life, and real life *in movement*." It had the power to transform a person completely: "He who frequents the cinema acquires agility, boldness, confidence, and optimism," and it could "cultivate and exalt the great ideas of justice and fraternity."[18] What separated film from other pedagogical devices, he noted, was its accessibility to all levels of intellect or education. Film democratized education in a way that books could not and served as a strong source of information in a largely illiterate country.

Blanco Castilla thought that film, if used to its greatest potential, could popularize science, change morality, improve hygiene, teach agricultural techniques, organize work scientifically, promote worker safety, stave off absenteeism, foster literacy, develop civic education, and increase national prosperity. More important, however, he believed that if each village were provided with a film projector, Spaniards would see "congregated in the school these poor people who would not be brought there by any other means. Later they will approach the teacher, the book, the newspaper, civilization."[19] Film, then, would open the door to further education. His statement resonated with liberal, regenerationist principles, including the belief that education was an evolutionary process whereby an individual, once literate, approached the boundaries of civilization. Celluloid would act as the catalyst for the organic progression toward an increasingly moral world.

Given educators' strong support for creating and disseminating educational films to their students (and to the population at large), what types of movies did they envision to best achieve their goals? For Blanco Castilla, educational films needed to gear themselves to the "mentality of the worker and peasant." They had to be simple, clear, and short, and if they were to maintain the viewer's interest, they could not "lack ingredients such as interest, humor, [and] emotion."[20] For Luis Gómez Mesa, a film critic and member of the CHC, good film was "documentary" in that it facilitated people's understanding of such things as physical and cultural differences within various lands.[21] The pedagogue Lorenzo Luzuriaga thought that educational films served three purposes: to entertain, to instruct, and to "illustrate" and "propagate" particular ideas to a group of people. But he warned against falling into the trap of making films overly didactic and rendering them indistinguishable from the treacly "morality books" that were forced down children's throats.[22] Finally, more radical reformers recommended that the Republicans look to the Soviet Union, a country that before the Revolution had literacy rates as low as Spain's, to see how its citizens incorporated film into their daily lives.[23]

The Republican-sponsored Misiones Pedagógicas immediately accepted the challenge to bring film to the poorer regions of Spain. Although many areas lacked such facilities as electricity to run the film projectors, the missionaries pushed forward with the project (bringing their own generators) because they saw it as the "most powerful" educational resource they had.[24] They invested film with the authority to "show [Spaniards their] own unknown land, the cities that were the home of history, far-away places, the development of human force, from primitive manual labor to modern machinery, the natural phenomena that surround them, and the deserts and volcanoes, the most unexpected and remote climates and vegetation."[25] The films' contents varied widely, ranging from agriculture, geography, history, natural science, and hygiene to cartoons and feature-length comedies.[26]

But one is struck by the number of films that dealt with geography. It is difficult to know if these numbers reflect the misioneros' general interest in spreading geographical knowledge to villagers or the types of film available to them. Certainly, geography was an important component of many regenerationists' programs. They believed that teaching Spaniards about their own geography would tie them to the patria. Geography also represented science, and scientific knowledge forged the path to modernization.[27] If, as the misioneros claimed throughout their reports, they sought to broaden the horizons of the forgotten villagers and link their aspirations with those of people in urban areas, then perhaps using films that showed a vast array of geographical regions suited their needs perfectly. Generally, however, the films fell into two categories: those that instructed and those that entertained. A sampling of the titles conveys their contents: *An Island in the East Indies, Underwater Life, America's Desert, The Whale Hunt,* and *Jumping Beans.*

More interesting than the titles, however, are the comments of a journalist who followed the Misiones Pedagógicas for roughly a week and reported their actions for the *Diario de Almería*. He had nothing but praise for their work, and he described every action with exclamatory phrases. About *Spanish Airmail Lines,* a film shot from an airplane as it travels and delivers mail from Barcelona to Madrid and then to Seville, he said: "It constitutes a perfect and successful study of a great part of our peninsular territory, with stupendous photography [and a] bird's-eye view of the villages and cities of the itinerary."[28] He said the film *Irrigation Systems* highlights the "triumph of the will ... where man's perseverance is capable of modifying nature, to make prosperous and extremely fertile that which, without the great power of the will, would continue to be uncultivated, sterile land."[29]

In many ways, given the journalist's descriptions, the films embodied the lessons that reformist Republicans hoped to transmit. The airplane trip mapped out the territory that was Spain, unfolding its variegated contours and presenting a much larger world to the many people who had not once ventured outside their tiny villages. More important, they belonged to the panoramic Spain on the screen. *Irrigation Systems,* in contrast, appears to have been a film meant both to inspire and to educate. If humanity could modify nature with "perseverance" and "will" (and undoubtedly machines), if it could transform a bleak and barren land into a lush and bountiful expanse, then there remained the hope of prosperity, or at least comfort, for the desperate peasants from, say, Castile or Extremadura, who often could not eke a meager morsel of food from their inhospitable lands.

But the first step involved capturing the attention of this toil-worn population. According to the misioneros, the absolute novelty of film enchanted the peasants. It "entertained" and "dazzled" them so much that some members of the crowd imposed silence on those who tried to talk through the film. Others—some elders of the villages—who had never witnessed even the power of electricity, thought that the films represented the work of witchcraft. Generally, however, the villagers responded positively to this new technology. Although the misioneros wanted to share film—as well as all of the other cultural accoutrements of Spain and the West—with all members of the village, they discounted having any influence whatsoever on the communities' elders and focused their hopes instead on the youth who followed everything with intensity: "Their sensibility is open to everything, they feel closer to what they see, with the hope of traveling in some way through the horizons that are revealed to them."[30] The misioneros claimed that the children were much more open to learning, fascinated not only by the movies themselves, but with how the technology of the projector itself operated. The misioneros' distinction between what the old and young could gain from the films illustrates this long-held Krausist/institucionista belief that Spain could be transformed only by educating people at an early age, before they became too rigid and unwilling to listen to ideas outside their scope of knowledge and belief system.

Curiously enough, the misioneros sometimes had to censor the content of their discussions because of the volatile political situation in a particular region. One misionero notes that one could never really gauge a unified or fixed political sentiment in any one place, only "ignorance mixed with passion." Therefore, they encountered problems when they showed the film *Granada,* one of the few films made specifically for the

Misiones Pedagógicas, in Navas del Madroño (Cáceres). The misioneros explicitly used the film to "talk about the discovery of America and the unity of Spain," but they could not mention the names of Ferdinand and Isabel, the Catholic monarchs responsible for the toppling of Muslim rule in Granada, presumably because the crowd was thoroughly anticlerical.[31]

While films seemed to offer a means to begin the educational process and cultural unification, they were not the panacea longed for by educators such as the misioneros. According to a 1935 account rendered in *El Sol*, when right-wing members of the Cortes attacked the cultural programs launched by the early Republicans, the organizers of the Misiones said that "the principal problem with respect to film has been the scarcity of good films to [enable people] to know Spain."[32] Perhaps the *misioneros* were convinced that Spaniards from all regions would eventually feel linked together as one nation once they were inundated with historical information and a cinematographic view of the Spanish terrain. But, as we can see, the Misiones Pedagógicas lacked the economic means to expand their project.

## LEFT-WING RESPONSES

Not everyone believed that educational film solved the problems endemic to Spain, however. Some argued that without a complete overhaul of the social structure, film could only serve to solidify already-existing social inequalities. Numerous film critics of the left criticized the Republic for not creating the necessary conditions to transform Spanish society. Whether due to narrow-mindedness or fear, or to an impulse toward censorship, the Republicans' tepid approach to film was impeding the inevitable social revolution.

The sometimes rancorous debates among left-wing film critics reflected the even larger divisions among the Republican coalition. Unlike the Republicans, who wanted to see a gradual, progressive transformation of Spanish society using more traditional educational methods, anarchists, Socialists, and Communists pushed for rapid and revolutionary change, even if it meant raising the hackles of their more conservative counterparts. For them, film wielded revolutionary power. Topping the list of people critical of the Republican educational film program was Mateo Santos, an irascible anarchist film critic for *Popular Film*. In one column he debated the merits and shortcomings of bringing educational film to Spain's rustic regions. Although he posited his arguments two months before the advent of the Republic, his opinions, as voiced in film journals, remained consistent throughout the Republican period.

The Spanish schools, he claimed, "cultivate illiteracy," avoid teaching children about "the will" and "civic virtue," and close their minds to the truth. He scoffed at suggestions that Spain adopt a pedagogical system similar to that of the Soviet Union, citing the Spanish regime's antipathy toward anything that smacked of Soviet influence. While praising the Soviet system, Santos dismissed the Spanish government's ability to institute such measures or to show Soviet films: "Their lessons are too alive for a society with a bourgeois structure." Those who supported the distribution of educational films, he suggested, wanted only to teach the underclasses "practical" things such as the best means to cultivate the land. And while he extolled such measures, especially in a land that depended on agriculture for its livelihood, he reminded his readers that "the Spanish peasant is the mortal enemy of modern systems of cultivation." Although peasants toiled on the land daily, it did not belong to them. Instead, the peasant "fears that machinery will make his arms unnecessary." What films should have shown the peasants, but did not, Mateo Santos argued, was that "whoever cultivates the land has the right to possess it." Films that neglected to question the underpinnings of society were not worth promoting. Not surprisingly, he refused to endorse the "pedagogical mission of film."[33]

Mateo Santos and the other critics on the far left wanted film to represent more than just a tool of pedagogy. They envisioned it as a potentially transforming and revolutionary medium, and they held up Soviet film as the quintessential example of what they would have liked to achieve in Spain. Film, they argued, should embody "Marxist principles" and "bring to the screen the intimate tragedy of each home ... it has to serve, more than any other thing, to revive the sacred flame of the proletariat." People should create "films for the masses, social films in which great crowds of the proletariat participate."[34] Mateo Santos called for film that had "blood, muscles, and nerves" and that "reflect[ed] the worries that agitate and disturb humanity." In short, since "film belongs to our century" and is the "art of the masses," it must be "at the service of the people if it wants to complete its historic mission."[35]

Given their entreaties for a cinema that captured the vibrancy and passion of the human spirit, radical film critics would see the fare offered by such groups as the Misiones Pedagógicas as the cotton candy of film. Nor did they have much use for the comedic bits and the "kisses of a femme fatale" that were generated by so many American films.[36] Instead, they looked eastward, to the Soviet Union, where the masters of revolutionary film— Sergei Eisenstein, Dziga Vertov, and the Vasiliev brothers— used their extraordinary filmmaking talents to commemorate and keep alive the notion of revolution.

When the Republicans first took power, leftist film critics thought they had a sympathetic ear among the new leaders and believed that the current government would immediately lift the ban on Russian films that had been imposed by the now-exiled monarchy. They soon discovered that the Republic was just as unwilling to unleash potentially revolutionary films. Critics lambasted Republican officials for their cowardice and questioned the reasoning behind banning exemplary Russian films that could truly transform the masses, while allowing seemingly puerile American films to numb them with tales of love and seduction.[37]

Mateo Santos complained that while the monarchy banned Russian films because they clashed with the ideas of the "reactionary ear," Republicans were now banning these films "under the denomination of [a] 'measure of public order.'"[38] Of course, public order was a problem for Republicans, just as it had been during the First Republic. And perhaps the ban illustrates that Republicans *did* know that films had a powerful effect on the masses and that they were afraid the masses might riot in the streets if they saw them. But Mateo Santos argued that if Republicans only opened their eyes, they would be able to see how well Russian films fit into the Republican agenda of educating the populace. According to him, these films had the potential to "broaden" and "humanize" education, "to become a live and dynamic text, in contrast to the usual dead letter texts that one memorizes but that do not disturb the spirit." Making a not-so-subtle analogy with Spain, he contended that Soviet films documented a new society in the making, a society possibly even more underdeveloped than that of Spain, a society that overcame the obstacles of poverty and endemic illiteracy to become a power to reckon with. By extension, he implied, Spain could achieve the same type of transformation by importing Soviet "educational" films. A film like Eisenstein's *The General Line* (also known as *The Old and the New*), for example, "instructs peasants in the ways of working the land and makes them understand the material advantages of cultivating it collectively."[39]

Rafael Gil, a critic considered to be more moderate than Mateo Santos but still sympathetic to Republican aims,[40] maintained Santos's conviction that Spaniards were often fed the pabulum of film fare. Wanting to strike a balance between what he saw as the opiate-like but entertaining mix of American westerns, comedies, and musicals and the throat-parching dryness of documentary films put out by specialists in universities, Gil beckoned Republican officials to consider importing Soviet films as a way of filling the cinemas and educating the populace at the same time. Spectators went to the cinema primarily to be entertained, he realized. Only as a possible afterthought did they attend to learn something. Therefore, if the Republicans truly wanted to create an educated citizenry, they would have to promote films that hid a cultural message within an entertaining spectacle.

Gil pointed out that scientific films produced by universities failed to reach the commercial movie houses because they were not made for the public but, rather, for "their creators: doctors, chemists, naturalists." Some documentaries did become commercial successes, however—and here he cited Marien Cooper and Ernest Schoedsack as successful documentary producers—because they captured spectacles that entertained the masses.[41] These, the films that captivated large audiences, were the ones that needed to be nurtured by the government. According to Gil, such educational films already existed in the Soviet Union, and "none has the 'aridity' of a textbook." He claimed that all Soviet films "are documentary in the greatest extension of the word" because they "reflect authentic ambiance and customs," "describe past history with complete fidelity," and "orient the masses toward the creation of a future life." He held Dziga Vertov's *History of a Piece of Bread, One Year after the Death of Lenin,* and *A Sixth of the World* as exemplary "documentaries" from which the masses of Spain could learn and be entertained.[42]

Of all the Soviet films the leftist critics would have liked to see freely distributed and shown in Spain, Eisenstein's 1925 cinematographic account of the Russian Revolution of 1905, *Battleship Potemkin,* topped the list. The film's evocative images and powerful pleas for mass solidarity and revolution in the face of brutal exploitation inspired and generated awe and respect in many of its viewers.[43] Surrealist Luis Buñuel called it one of the hardest films to forget and one that influenced him greatly. Describing his reaction to the film after leaving the movie theater, he said: "At the exit— in a street in the Alesia zone—we wanted to put up barricades and the police had to intervene."[44] This was probably the response that leftist film critics hoped spectators would have when they watched the film, and probably the one that Republican officials most feared. In fact, although Republicans had permitted the screening of *Battleship Potemkin* in private film clubs that generally drew membership from the middle and upper-middle classes, they banned the film for general public viewing. In early 1933, the Workers' Syndicate of the Port of Seville wanted to show the film to its workers. Five thousand workers were set to view the film, but the municipal government of Seville obtained an injunction against the film, fearing that public riots like those within the movie would occur on its streets.[45]

Republicans had reason to fear such repercussions. The Casas Viejas affair of January 1933, in which a botched anarchist general strike and insurrection in Andalusia resulted in the brutal murder of twenty villagers by Republican Assault and Civil Guards, illustrated the grave social tensions facing the Republic. Waves of general strikes continued for the next five months.[46] But leftist critics dismissed these concerns out of hand as mere posturing by a so-called democratic "government of workers,"[47] that had one standard for the bourgoisie and another for the working classes. In discussing a continued ban against showing *Battleship Potemkin*, Rafael Gil writes, "As is the custom in these cases, the government that made the village of Casas Viejas famous could not tolerate the projection of this film [to workers]."[48]

Critic Francisco Martínez González read this film differently and added a new twist to the debate over Soviet film. He saw this and other Soviet films not as incitements to revolution but as expositions of problems that already existed—of embodiments of revolutions that had already taken place. Discussing Casas Viejas (yet again!), he compared the "sacrifice of 'Seisdedos'" (who was burned alive in his hut by the Civil Guard) to that of Vakulnichuk, the movie's sailor-hero who instigates the revolution on board his battleship. Martínez González asked his readers whether they knew the story and whether they had "observed the transcendence that this act had for the revolution that was later to occur." Describing the movie's depiction of the violent clashes on the steps of Odessa, he said: "Nobody would have thought that this was the seed of a transformation that they would have to suffer. Moreover, the middle class—this hypocritical middle class, so insensitive to the troubles of the productive people— would consider [these actions] as 'disturbances of the peace,' exactly as they do here today in Spain."[49]

Clearly, then, those who advocated the use of Soviet film in Spain saw the pre-revolutionary conditions in Russia as analogous to those of contemporary Spain, and perceiving that the Soviet system had created a new type of society by employing a heavy hand in the cultural sphere, some of the more radical leftists sought to transform Spanish society in the same manner. As one writer so succinctly put it: "In the schools, in the open air, in all parts, film is propagandistic, a preacher of politics, it is the new school."[50]

This notion of film's "propagandistic" value and its perceived potential for inciting public disorder prevented Republicans from endorsing and allowing Soviet films into the country. This is not to say that the types of films the Republicans encouraged and the ways in which they presented the films were not propagandistic: they were. But the Republicans viewed the purpose of film in a different manner from their more radical counterparts. Having been trained in institutions that followed liberal precepts, the cultural planners of the early Republic saw in film only a tool of pedagogy in the most literal sense, and they could not abide educational lessons that had an overtly ideological basis. Much like the Institución Libre de Enseñanza—the institutional backbone of the Republican intelligentsia—which was founded on the basis of its being "completely free from any religious affiliation, philosophical school, or political party,"[51] the organizers of the Misiones Pedagógicas sought to transmit a seemingly value-neutral education through the conduit of "entertaining" film.[52] By making learning less palpably rigid as some of the peasants might have been accustomed to, they hoped to encourage more Spaniards to learn.

Equally important, the Republican governments faced mounting attacks on their legitimacy by both the left and right. Not wishing to repeat the chaos of the First Republic when, in a space of eleven months, four presidents ruled over an increasingly embattled country, these Republicans sought ways to ameliorate increasing social tensions. Republican cultural emissaries wanted an evolutionary transformation of Spain, not a revolutionary one. That is why the Soviet vision of film could not be included in the Republican framework as it stood.

Similarly, Republicans could not tolerate films that explicitly criticized Spain or its government. Buñuel's documentary, *Las Hurdes: Land without Bread* (1932), sent shock waves through Spanish official circles for its unsparing depiction of the miserable existence of the villagers who lived in the small Extremaduran region of Las Hurdes. The region included fifty-two villages with a total population of around eight thousand people. The film itself combines elements of ethnography with the image of social protest found in many Soviet films of that era. The narration is cold, dispassionate, and, to our contemporary ears, condescending.

The film begins with a written prologue that says: "This is a filmed essay in human geography made in Spain in 1932. Until 1922, when the first road was opened, Las Hurdes was almost unknown to the rest of the world, as well as to the people of Spain. Visitors come to this region against the advice of geographers and explorers alike, for Las Hurdes is a sterile and inhospitable place where man is obliged to fight, hour by hour, for his subsistence." Buñuel catalogues the miseries of Las Hurdes: malnutrition, unfarmable land, dirt, illness, incest, idiocy, and death, always death. With ironic juxtaposition he draws attention to scenes that strike the viewer as being simultaneously horrible and comical. For example, his camera intrudes on a classroom in which a teacher recites maxims to a few bedraggled Hurdano children. Buñuel pans the camera along a wall that displays a print of a finely dressed aristocratic woman. A voiceover says, "What is this ridiculous picture doing here?" and then the viewer sees a child going to the blackboard to write one of the teacher's maxims: "Respect the property of others." Buñuel continues the film along this vein, portraying misery heaped upon more misery, until the final scene of the film shows an old woman of Las Hurdes saying, "There is nothing better to keep you awake than to think always of death, to say an Ave Maria for the sake of the souls of the dead." The camera then pans to some clouds in the sky and the narrator says, "After a stay of two months in Las Hurdes, we left . . ." The end leaves the viewer with little hope for change in Spain.

The film was first shown in 1933 in the Cine Studio Imagen of Madrid. Many of Madrid's intellectual elite attended the premiere, including Dr. Gregorio Marañón, the president of the Patronato of Las Hurdes. Probably at the urging of Marañón, who seemed to have missed the entire point of the film and criticized the work for not showing enough of the beautiful architecture and religious artifacts of the area, the film was banned in Spain for casting too negative a light on the Spanish government. For Republicans such as Marañón, the portrayal of "uncivilized" and "backward" Hurdanos living in conditions that would make beasts of burden shudder, ran counter to the Republicans' self-image of Spain as a modern, progressive, European state. Later, Lerroux extended the ban during his tenure as head of the government and attempted to prevent the film from being shown in foreign countries for fear that the images found in this documentary would be injurious to Spain.[53]

## REACTION OF THE RIGHT

Like the leftists who criticized the Republican government for taking a tame approach toward the promotion and distribution of certain types of film, the right also attacked the government's complacency. Although rightists—and here I would include both the traditional right and the radical right—concurred with the radical leftists over such issues as developing a Spanish film industry, blocking the flow of American films, developing an aesthetic for the masses, and modeling Spanish films on Soviet ones, the reasons behind their criticisms and their visions for the future of Spanish film differed considerably. On the one hand, many steadfast, conservative Catholics wanted to stop the inexorable flow of American films into Spain because they believed that these films—along with the anticlerical statutes passed by the early Republicans—were eviscerating the Catholic values that had been ingrained in Spain for centuries. On the other hand, they sought to promote films that encouraged Catholic, traditional, and nationalistic values in an attempt to preserve these values.

Some members of the radical right, most vocally represented in discussions of film by the literary critic and devoted Falangist Ernesto Giménez Caballero, actively engaged in shaping the genre for revolutionary purposes. While the more radical members of the right also disdained the Hollywood "immorality" seeping into the movie houses of Spain, they did not view themselves simply as film police ready to set up barricades against the onslaught of American films; instead they perceived themselves as wielders of powerful weapons, ready to undertake an aesthetic *reconquista* that could transform the masses and give them a new forum for worshipping the twin pillars of traditional Spain: Catholicism and Empire.

As mentioned earlier, certain leaders under the Primo de Rivera regime and the monarchy of Alfonso XIII, finding many of the films imported into Spain of questionable value, wanted to impose strict censorship. While both the right and left decried the influx of American films, the right did not reject them—as did the left—for supplying audiences with puerile plots and tepid themes but, rather, because they concentrated too much on sex, violence, and greed and induced audiences to forget all manner of morality. Film, in other words, rent the social fabric of Spain.

Catholics, at least in the early years of the Republic, had little recourse to change the state of film production. They could write editorials in conservative Catholic newspapers such as *El Debate* to dissuade audiences from viewing certain films, but they needed political power and money to carry out the type of censorship they deemed necessary for the salvation of the Spanish people. When Lerroux's conservative Catholic–Radical

Republican coalition took power in 1935, the opportunity for some Catholics to promote their agenda seemed quite promising. Film historian Román Gubern contends that with the advent of this conservative regime, influential Catholics pumped money into certain sectors of the Spanish film industry. In May 1935, for example, a group of Catholics "in the orbit" of the political group Acción Española and the conservative Catholic journal *El Debate* formed a production company known as Ediciones Cinematográficas Españolas, S.A. Using the company to advocate films with a traditionalist and Catholic sensibility, its members produced a series of docudramas narrated by Father Laburu, Angel Herrera Oria (editor of *El Debate*), José María Pemán (a founding member of the intellectual Catholic journal, *Acción Española*), and Father Alcocer. The company produced three films in all—*El 113* (1935), *Currito de la Cruz* (1935) and *Lola de Triana* (1936)—but they had to disband with the coming of the Spanish Civil War.[54]

The right-wing Catholic elements of the Lerroux government were also influential in banning a Hollywood film that they felt to be injurious to Spain's honor, Josef von Sternberg's *The Devil Is a Woman (Tu nombre es tentación)*. Starring Marlene Dietrich as the seductive femme fatale, Lola, who toys with the affections of an ex-army captain (Paco) and a Republican outlaw during the turn of the century, the movie trots out every stereotype of the mysterious, exotic Spain, including scenes from Carnival, a cigarette factory à la Carmen, and a Spanish *cueva*. Lola's hot and cold behavior and Paco's (as well as every other man's) puppy-dog attraction to her are merely cartoonish. Despite a seemingly innocent plot, the movie generated great controversy in Spain. As minister of war, Gil Robles sought to ban the film because he said it brought shame to Spaniards by showing a captain acting foolishly and because it denigrated the Civil Guard.[55] Von Sternberg suggests that Gil Robles despised the movie because it portrayed the Civil Guard as ineffectual and unable to maintain order during Carnival. Whatever the reasons for this perverse ban (which continued throughout the Franco years), the Spanish cabinet asked Paramount to stop circulating the film around the world and to burn the negative. Paramount agreed, and the Spanish ambassador to Washington burned a negative of the film, unaware that other copies remained.[56]

More vocal than the government in their protests against "offensive" film, however, were writers in journals such as *Filmor*, a film journal founded by the Catholic Confederation of the Fathers of the Family, whose aim it was to challenge the film establishment by penning editorials and film reviews for its (presumably) Catholic audience. In its first issue of June 20, 1935, the editors outlined their mission to "redeem film": "*Filmor* is born with the determined desire to contribute its grain of sand to the work of cinematographic regeneration. It will condense in its pages the critiques of many films that are shown in Spain." The editors also promised to view the films disinterestedly, but with caution and a great attention to detail. In that way they would analyze each film with "synthetic, serene and impartial judgments." To help their readers decide which films were suitable for viewing, they devised a ratings scale coded both qualitatively and by color:

| | | | |
|---|---|---|---|
| B | For all | B | = White |
| D | Passable, but with some serious defects that can be mended | D | = Yellow |
| F | For mature people only | F | = Blue |
| P | Dangerous, even for mature people | P | = Green |
| M | Dangerous for all | M | = Red |

This scale allowed them to "subject all [of the films] to Christian morals" and "give a vast critique within the obligatory synopsis."[57] For example, the Hollywood film *The Painted Veil* (1934), starring Greta Garbo, rated an "F" and received this review: 'Romantic intrigue outside of marriage that ends with the return of the adulterous woman to her obligations. The thorny dilemmas that come out of such a slippery situation, although presented in this case in a most discreet manner, maintain a shameless tone that is unacceptable. The artistic aspect of this movie also deserves censure for the heaviness of its interminable dialogue and excessive intervention of Greta Garbo, who absorbs and overshadows the work of the artists who surround her. The work itself imparts a moral lesson that people of mature judgment only can appreciate. It is not suitable for the rest of the public."[58]

*Filmor's* editorials frequently addressed the subject of transforming the film industry, although not everybody agreed precisely on the methods. One writer, F. Castello, argued that films encouraged immoral attitudes and behavior in three ways: (1) through the films' plots; (2) through the atmosphere of the movie theater; and (3) through their attacks on religious, social, and family customs. Clearly underlying much of Castello's crusade was his sheer terror of the "New Woman" who often graced the screen. He felt that the cinema had undermined Spain's quiet and modest domestic sphere and replaced it with a metropolis in which no one's role was particularly clear and commerce and sexuality reigned supreme. The "worldly woman" (who presumably now strutted her stuff on the streets of Madrid and Barcelona), the woman who dressed up, wore makeup, smoked, drank, and displayed her charms to passers by, he contended, "ha[d] its origins on the screen." Clearly, film heroines drove thousands of young women to their perdition, women "who aspiring to nothing else but to reach that glory, have crossed the boundaries of all moral laws."[59] He held the cinema responsible for the rise of women in the workforce, a trend he called women's "abandonment of the home."[60] In search of lucre and what it could buy, heroines on the silver screen "fill[ed] offices, shops, universities, and other centers," inspiring real women to form a partnership with Mammon instead of contenting themselves with their "old-fashioned modest life."[61]

For Castello, movie plots minimized the importance of social relations or made light of church doctrines, and they accustomed the public "to see divorce and suicide as natural solutions" to problems. In other words, Castello blamed the movies for having violated social mores, particularly Spanish ones, by "introducing customs, accepting norms, and adapting customs that have generally erased the beautiful characteristics that distinguish the Spanish woman from women in the rest of the world." Castello's fear of the immorality displayed on the screen was exceeded only by his trepidation that the ineffable quality of Spanish womanhood was being subsumed by the cosmopolitan women on celluloid. To combat the bilge emanating from the screen, Castello urged people to boycott any film "whose morality of argument, whose figures and ensemble, [could] be a barrier reef against which consciences continue to be shipwrecked."[62]

Castello's second line of attack was against the theaters. Although movie plots had disastrously threatened the Spanish social fabric, the movie theaters themselves had also jeopardized more than one person's virtue. Theaters, he thought, posed a problem to Christian morality because the darkness and intimate seating inspired people to lose all decency. Castello suggested that the lights in the movie theater be raised enough for people to distinguish one another, thus preventing them from engaging in licentious activities. He called on parents to protect their daughters' virtue by requiring them to have a chaperone at the movies.

Third, Castello focused on the threat posed to social and religious customs. To weaken the hold that the movies had on Spanish youth—a bond that has taken Christians away from their religious obligations such as saying rosaries and novenas—Castello urged parents to "recover the reins of family authority" by "severely prohibiting daily attendance" at the movie houses.[63] As we can see, Castello could not really find any redeeming qualities in film, and so all of his prescriptions seem like the dismal but necessary task of sandbagging an area that is threatened with decimation by raging floods.

Not all writers at *Filmor* took such a reactionary stance against film, however. Felipe Lluch Garín, an industrial engineer who took the work of film criticism seriously, invested movies with much of the same potential for promoting social change as his leftist counterparts had done. He tipped his hat to Russia for having discovered and developed films with a social, political, and moral agenda, and he praised Germany and Italy for imitating the Russian example. He called for Spain to do the same, to develop a national industry that "exalts, demonstrates, and makes attractive the great nobility and beauty that exists in the Spanish Catholic tradition, transforming a simple spectacle into a history lesson, moral teachings, and patriotic stirrings." Film, more than any other medium, he argued, can "create consciences and wills"; movies infused with Catholic sentiments and lessons could transform the collective practices of Spaniards and influence their everyday activities. Once Spain purged itself of the "immoral cinema that is undermining its Catholic roots," a new Spain would emerge. This task could be accomplished only by developing "a new cinema that will be a compendium of the old and eternal virtues of the Spanish tradition."[64] No doubt these virtues included Catholicism and the monarchy.

Despite printing editorials clamoring for change, *Filmor*, with its series of film reviews and ratings, functioned primarily as a source to warn filmgoers against attending films that could be detrimental to their morals. The call to fight fire with fire, to herald the regeneration of Spain's imperial Catholic tradition using modern technology, would come most vociferously from Ernesto Giménez Caballero. Known by many as Gecé, Giménez Caballero showed an early interest in making and promoting films, especially those that reflected well on Spain. In *La Gaceta Literaria* he began featuring film reviews and discussions of film theory written by such luminaries as Luis Buñuel, Salvador Dalí, Rafael Alberti, and Jean Epstein. In 1928 Gecé founded the Cineclub Español in Madrid, Spain's first film society that enabled its members to discuss film and film theory, and to view films of the avant-garde, which were often prohibited to the general public.[65]

His appetite for movies did not change over the years, but his political leanings became increasingly right wing, following the path of German "reactionary modernists."[66] He collaborated in the project of the Congreso de Cinematografía Hispanoamericana and was secretary of the Comité Español de Cinema Educativo, and his ties to the Italian Fascists grew stronger throughout the 1930s.

A prolific writer, Giménez Caballero penned a series of books during the Republic that, among other things, outlined his critiques of the Spanish state and society and provided solutions for Spain's regeneration, solutions that called for a strong, corporate Catholic state.[67] In *Arte y Estado* he drafted a theory for the function of art within the state. All art, for him, functioned to increase the power of the state and to fight off heretical ideas. The arts are "instruments of militias" a "combative force" that can "expand ideas" and "faith." Never one to eschew a colorful metaphor, Gecé declared: "Art is simply a technique of conquest. A technique of war. It is something similar to possessing a woman after desiring her for a long time and impregnating her with one's child."[68]

In his discussion of art and culture he held a special place for film, the newest and most potent forms of art.[69] Not since the development of the book (or more precisely, the printing press), he argued, had there been such a tool that could revolutionize history. Just as the book was "born as a 'liberation of the masses,'" so too was born the cinema, the "prodigal and rebellious son" of the book. Because film acted as an art for the masses, it possessed more power than the book, which reached only "enlightened minorities." Although film production copied the methods of literary production, its transmission, he asserted, improved upon that of the book: "In place of aiming innumerable copies to one intelligence, it directs one 'sole image to many souls.'" In other words, he said, film "recreated the plans and foundations of the Medieval Church. Each movie house constituted a new cathedral, a parish."[70]

In a sense, then, just as the printing press facilitated the spreading of the Protestant Reformation, the invention of film could conceivably be used as a tool of the right's neo-Counter-Reformation to solidify the soon-to-be strengthened Catholic state. He claimed that it was Spain's task to begin implementing a new moral (Catholic) film aesthetic that would transcend both the Occident's "individualistic" and "capitalistic" type of film, as well as the Soviets' films of "absolute masses" and "social subversion."[71] This aesthetic, according to Giménez Caballero, would incorporate all aspects of (Catholic) religiosity. He continued to use the movie-as-cathedral metaphor in his 1943 work, *El cine y la cultura humana* (Film and human culture), a work that built on his ideas from *Arte y estado* but which focused strictly on film and its place in the state. Much like Buñuel, who called a film's power "hypnotic,"[72] Gecé saw it as inebriating and mystical:

> Music, darkness, passions, trips, mystery, turmoil, unusual smells ... have made of films ... demonic and sinful substitutes that, at these hours, in past and more pious times, were sought in the mystical and religious functions of the church....
>
> ... This magic, demonic substratum of film confers upon it a certain religious importance.[73]

According to Giménez Caballero, film's ability to re-create the religious experience and feeling of community made it an especially powerful tool for the state. He believed that film, with the added "kinetic" element lacking in books or theater, truly held the key to communal unity. It prevented Spaniards from having to contend with the "problem of an intellectual interpretation." Film relied on harnessing the spectators' passions, much as the Catholic mass had done for centuries. Therefore, he claimed, "the Spaniard will return to find in film his *castizo* [pure] taste for a 'theater of action' from our secular tradition." He urged (albeit in 1943) religious figures to bring "rolls of film" along with "prayers and crosses" so that Spain (and Europe) could be reborn; for film had taken the place of "the old and universal Latin, the arbitrary Esperanto, the diplomatic French, and the imperialist English" in asserting its universal hegemony.[74] Giménez Caballero, unlike many liberal Republicans, believed that film was the truly revolutionary tool that could shape the masses.

But revolution was a word too dangerous to utter for the moderate coalition in charge of cultural reform in the first tumultuous years and the last few months of the Republic, for revolution disturbed their conception of the state as an entity that needed to be nurtured delicately. Moreover, locked into a nineteenth-century vision of culture as literacy, and literacy as the catalyst for both individual and societal change, they failed to realize that film, a twentieth-century art form, required new methods of representation and new ideas to represent. Stuck on the assumption that film was a document, an unmediated reflection of the outside world, and unwilling to awaken further already explosive social tensions, Republican reformers feared unleashing the propagandistic powers of film. They conceived of culture in liberal terms, predicating their vision of cultural

enlightenment on gradual reform, on changing the system through consensus. Liberal and moderately left Republicans rejected the vision and
fundamental assumptions inherent in the works of Giménez Caballero
and his leftist counterparts. Those radical groups that challenged the
Enlightenment project, those who saw the potential for revolutionary
change within the newly politicized masses, seemed to understand that
film harbored unprecedented methods for conquering this relatively
untapped political bloc. Only when the Republic's continued existence
was threatened by Franco's armies in 1936 did the Republicans attempt to
rally Spaniards and foreigners to their cause using the types of propagandistic films advocated by such film critics as Mateo Santos, and that was
probably because the government was now run by Socialists. Many of the
people who effected the liberal and leftist reforms during the first years
of the Republic had been trained in such places as the Institución Libre
de Enseñanza. Because this institution emphasized a seemingly nonideo-
logical curriculum that substantially focused on the literary tradition as a
means to attain greater understanding of the world, many Republicans
balked at films that were as blatantly ideological or emotionally manipu-
lative as those advocated by the political extremes. Obviously, many felt
uncomfortable working with this new medium. Although Republican
reformers carried with them the best intentions for employing the newest
technological advances for education and "cultural development," they
were still products of the nineteenth century, straddling uncomfortably
the divide between elite and mass culture.

# CHAPTER 5

---

# Cult of Reading

## *Literacy and Regeneration*

AS WE SAW IN THE PRECEDING CHAPTER, THE REFORMISTS OF THE FIRST
Biennium (1931–1933) lacked the desire to fully incorporate the new
medium of film into their cultural landscape. Still fiercely wedded to
the word and less touched by the mysticism of moving pictures, the
cultural reformers of the early Second Republic remained committed to
nineteenth-century cultural practices. Therefore, they preached the cult
of the word. Seeing words as the building blocks of culture and civilization, they sought to increase literacy, instill a love of reading, and eventually nurture an appreciation of Castilian literature and language as
embodiments of the Spanish national character. In the process, they
viewed themselves as guardians of the Spanish language and its literature. Reformers believed that if they could increase Spaniards' literacy
and expose them to the canon of Spanish literature, they would be able
to mold a new citizenry ready to take on the responsibilities of living in
and running the modern state. And so reformist Republicans and Socialists lavished the most attention and money on literacy programs and
libraries.

Despite their opposition to the existence of the Republic, anarchists
shared with the cultural reformers many of the same assumptions about
literacy and the power of literature to effect great changes. Although
anarchists distanced themselves from the work of the Republic, they encouraged the growth of literacy among workers and the peasantry, believing that a literate laborer was a revolutionary laborer. They parted
company with the Republican–Socialist coalition, however, when it came

to using literature for nationalistic purposes. In fact, sometimes the anarchists and the Republican–Socialist coalition revered the same books, but drew different lessons from them.

Finally, traditionalist Spaniards opposed the heavy investment of money in literacy programs and libraries developed by the Republican–Socialist coalition because they resented what they saw as a Socialist bias in the book selections and because at the heart of their criticisms lay a fundamental mistrust of literate laborers. Instead of couching their complaints in a language of mistrust, traditionalists resorted to characterizing the peasantry as timelessly stupid, in need of guidance from their social and intellectual superiors.

As with most of the cultural experiments attempted during the Second Republic, the idea of encouraging literacy to chip away at the heavy burden of Spanish degeneracy dates back most clearly to the late nineteenth century. The regenerationist *institucionista*, Joaquín Costa, for example, stood out as the quintessential town crier, admonishing Spaniards to root out all of the rotting structures that threatened to destroy Spain. Education, which required increasing the literacy rate, formed one-half of his two-pronged assault on Spain's infrastructure (see chapter 1). Once again, the Krausists may have been responsible for spawning these ideas and for linking literacy with civilization and literature with the soul of a people.[1] Krausist philosophy inspired the teachers of the Institución Libre de Enseñanza, who sought to cultivate an elite cadre of students willing to tackle Spain's problems: "The Institución hopes that its students will avail themselves quickly and fully of *books* as the greatest font of culture."[2]

But even the *institucionistas* lacked the resources and (at least in the nineteenth century) the will to disseminate their educational philosophy to the less-fortunate members of Spanish society. As Arturo Barea, the working-class boy turned young gentleman turned Republican partisan, chronicled in his autobiography: "I came to feel that the marvelous achievements of Giner de los Ríos had a very serious defect, the basic defect of all Spanish education: the doors were closed to the working people."[3] His assertion was essentially correct. Socialists and anarchists tried to make up for the deficiency of primary schools in Spain by organizing their own educational centers that attempted to equip workers with basic educational and literacy skills. Behind the Socialists' and anarchists' drive to educate the subaltern groups lay a desire to prepare the Spanish have-nots to lead the coming social revolution.

## THE REPUBLIC'S EFFORTS TO COMBAT ILLITERACY

With the advent of the Republic, however, many of the institucionistas and their allies thought it their mission to bring the insights of the Institución Libre to the general population. To supplement the expansion and secularization of the educational system and the construction of new schools, Republican officials sanctioned the expansion of libraries throughout Spain through the channels of the Misiones Pedagógicas and the Junta de Intercambio de Libros para Bibliotecas Públicas (Committee of the Book Exchange for Public Libraries).[4] Once again, the Misiones Pedagógicas provided a model for other state organs to disseminate information.

The plans to expand and reform the library system to combat mass illiteracy were iterated in the decree organizing the Misiones Pedagógicas (May 30, 1931). Government officials impelled organizers of the Misiones Pedagógicas to establish popular libraries, some permanent and others mobile. In another decree of August 8, 1931, the Minister of Public Instruction, Marcelino Domingo, set in motion the act to create libraries in all the national schools and earmarked 100,000 pesetas for the Misiones to collaborate in this project by selecting and acquiring books and giving them to teachers to place in their respective school libraries.[5]

The newly elected officials, many of whom were teachers and professors,[6] placed their faith in books as the saviors of the nation. Some thought that a carefully tended library was an even more beneficial "instrument of culture" than a school was. Marcelino Domingo advanced the cause of building libraries, especially in rural areas, to fulfill the Republic's goal of "bringing the city to the countryside with the object of making the countryside happy, humanized, and civilized."[7] The organizers of the Misiones embraced the "fight against illiteracy" but thought that illiteracy could best be wiped out not necessarily by hiring more teachers but by acquiring more books and libraries. But just teaching the mechanics of reading and writing would not solve Spain's greatest educational and social problems; instead, educators such as the Misioneros needed to awaken in those untouched by schooling "the love of reading, bringing books to the people ... and by reading in a loud voice, as they do in the Misiones, make them enjoy the pleasures enclosed in books."[8] The text prepared by the organization's president, Manuel B. Cossío, and read at the beginning of each session of the Misiones, made explicit the link between the love of reading and social transformation: "Because this is primarily what the Misiones propose: to awaken the desire to read in those who do not feel it, for only when every Spaniard, not only knows how to read—which is not enough—but also has the eagerness to read, to take pleasure and entertain oneself, yes, entertain oneself by reading, will there be a new Spain. For this reason the Republic has begun to distribute books throughout all areas, and for this reason, too, to leave you a small library when we leave."[9]

To realize such a dream, the Misioneros faced formidable obstacles in a country that was estimated to have a 32 percent illiteracy rate.[10] Rhetoric aside, Republicans did not forsake teachers at the expense of books and libraries. Marcelino Domingo, for example, exhorted educators to take up the banner of reform. Citing the university as a conduit for transforming Spanish society, he credited it with the power to "strengthen the national spirit," to "create aristocracies of democracy" that would forge an innovative path for Spain. In essence, he hoped that the new Spain would mirror France's Third Republic by creating a cadre of men ready to deal with all of the "problems and transcendental moments of its history."[11]

But until this transformation could happen, reformers had to sow the seeds of literacy at a more basic and localized level. Hence the focus on developing lending libraries. With the help of government subsidies, the Misiones Pedagógicas developed and ran the Servicio de Bibliotecas, supplying rural areas—some that had scarcely encountered a book— with local libraries. To grasp the importance of the library and literacy projects for the Misiones Pedagógicas, one must realize that despite all the other projects the group sponsored, such as theater, film, folk songs, slideshows, and museums, they spent approximately 60 percent of their entire budget during the course of the first three years on the circulating and fixed libraries.[12]

The most difficult task for the misioneros involved deciding which works best suited the needs of the rural populations. They were aided to some degree by a 1912 study conducted by the Institucionista Rafael Altamira of the circulating libraries created for the Museo Pedagógico Nacional (National Pedagogical Museum) and the advice of experts in the field.[13] Altamira had already published *Lecturas para obreros (Indicaciones bibliográficas y consejos)* [Readings for workers (bibliographical suggestions and advice)] in 1904, in which he suggested a list of authors and books that he deemed necessary for workers to read: anarchist geographer Réclus, Tolstoy, Renan, Kropotkin, Hugo, Darwin, Cervantes' *Don Quixote,* Galdós's *Episodios Nacionales,* and short stories by Poe and Dickens, among others.[14] This short list already displays certain ideological leanings—that is, the books examined and critiqued the social question (Réclus, Tolstoy, Kropotkin, and Hugo), they emphasized a science-centered view of the universe (Darwin), and they celebrated canonical national literary works (Cervantes and Galdós). And, as we will soon see, many of the works listed by Altamira became staples of the libraries distributed by the Misiones Pedagógicas.

But the misioneros could also look to the Socialist Casas del Pueblo as prototypes for their libraries, given that Socialist educators played a large role in organizing and running the Misiones Pedagógicas. Expert librarians also advised the misioneros about works that were most appropriate for the educators' goals. This selection process seems all the more daunting when we realize that each library would initially have only one hundred volumes, a paltry number by today's standards. Administered by inspectors of primary education, the libraries contained an array of subjects, including works of literature from Spain and abroad, art, science, history, geography, and children's books. They attempted to gather works that were "sufficiently simple so that the readers could understand them, and with a content that would help with spiritual elevation."[15] When possible, the Servicio de Bibliotecas established the library in the village school, a step made easier by Marcelino Domingo's decree of August 7, 1931, requiring that all primary schools have a library. Thus the ties between the village and school—and, by extension, the village and the central government—became stronger through this legislation.

The misioneros encouraged this desire to read by placing works in their historical or literary contexts and by reading aloud. In a session of September 18, 1932, in Valle de Arán, for example, the misioneros discussed the concept of the struggle for existence. Now although the written account of this session does not mention him by name, we can infer that the misioneros' discussion of struggle came out of their understanding of Darwin and that their assumptions about the world adhered to a Darwinian rather than a religious framework. After lecturing about the struggle for existence, the misioneros showed a film entitled *The Fight of the Mongoose and the Cobra*, followed by a reading from Kipling's *The Jungle Book*, which recounted the scene rendered on film.[16] In one short session, the misioneros combined lectures, film, and literature to display a worldview that negated the role of religion in the everyday lives of their audiences.

Most of the misioneros' depictions of literary works had to be achieved without the benefit of film, however, and interestingly enough, the works they emphasized tended to be Castilian works or works that glorified Castile and Castilian. They took to heart Cossío's words about present-ing "the most beautiful verses ... of the most glorious Castilian poets."[17] The misioneros tried to contextualize a work as much as possible before actually reading it aloud. Therefore, before they read fragments from the Spanish epic, *El poema de Mío Cid*—an epic that recounts the recon-quest of Spain from the Moors and exalts the centralizing tendencies of Castile—they traced the background of the historical figure of El Cid, as well as the numerous interpretations of the epic in Spanish poetry.[18]

After following the Misiones Pedagógicas on one of their cycles through a region, one journalist, "Raf," writing for the *Diario de Almería*, recorded many of the lessons given by the misioneros to the villagers. His columns provide today's reader with a nice sampling of the misioneros' pedagogi-cal methods. For example, the misioneros spoke about Juan Ramón Jiménez and his children, and they followed the discussion by reading fragments of his work, *Platero y yo*. After a theatrical performance of Calderón's *La vida es sueño*, the misioneros recited verses from the play, thus reinforcing the effect of the words and the sound of the language that the audience had just heard moments before on the stage. They covered the highlights of Castilian poetry, reading works such as the romances of Juan de Encina and stanzas by Quevedo and Antonio Machado (a mem-ber of the Misiones Pedagógicas in his own right). Machado's poetry, a popular subject, was the center of two separate discussions. Because he was best known for his verses glorifying Castile, his poetry embodied the centralizing tendencies of the Misiones Pedagógicas. The misioneros made the most of his poetry by first discussing what they thought were Castile's attributes and then reading some of Machado's verses, thus fusing the poet with the land. Raf marveled at the profound emotions that the misionero Enrique Azcoaga evoked when he read poetry or delivered lectures and was most impressed that the readings were done "without partisanship."[19]

But contrary to Raf's assertion, we know that a system, even if it pro-fesses objectivity and value-neutral education, is based on a series of ideological premises. The people who supplied the list of books that were to be placed in the libraries of the Servicio de Bibliotecas, and those who chose to read certain passages aloud to illiterate peasants, wanted to convey a strong message to their audiences: that is, that literacy would help with Spain's regeneration by nurturing a greater community between the people of the countryside and the city.

By December 1933, the Servicio de Bibliotecas had established 3,151 libraries in rural areas, but the people running the program believed they should do more for those in need. Finding themselves in the midst of a world depression, however, they lacked the financial resources to meet the needs of the entire rural populace. In addition to creating new libraries, they set out to improve the libraries they already had by either increasing the stock of books or replacing the cobweb-gathering works that people had not touched for decades with more current, relevant ones.

The misioneros gathered information about the libraries' readership in the hopes of discovering which books enjoyed the most success. The statistic gatherers classified their subjects into two groups—children and adults—to survey reading practices. They registered the number of readers who checked out books at the respective libraries and wrote down the number of books checked out, as well as the preferred authors and books. Claiming that they could not present a detailed schema of their quantitative and qualitative analyses within the boundaries of their *Memoria,* the misioneros, nevertheless, broadly sketched the results of their surveys (see table 1).

The misioneros stated that children preferred fantasy books and books that looked toward the future (although perhaps this was wishful thinking on the misioneros' part, placing, as it were, the burden of Spanish regeneration in the hands of Spain's future, its youth). Children most often chose the works of Perrault, Grimm, Anderson, Hoffman, Homer and Dante (in versions adapted for children), Poe, Mayne, Reid, Verne, Lagerlöf, and Kipling; the adventure novels of Swift; works of geography; and biographies of famous men such as Alexander the Great, Cervantes, Napoleon, Franklin, Stevenson, and Livingstone. Children apparently had preferences the misioneros found curious, such as their predilection for the biography of the sixteenth-century scientist Miguel Servet. Obviously,

Table 1. Results of Surveys by Misiones Pedagógicas on Reading Habits in Spain, as of December 1933

|  | No. of Readers | No. of Books |
| --- | --- | --- |
| Children | 269,325 | 1,405,845 |
| Adults | 198,450 | 790,650 |
| Total | 467,775 | 2,196,495 |

*Source:* Patronato de Misiones Pedagógicas (1934), 67.

these books did not hew to some nationalistic line but, instead, represented fairy tales and heroic adventure stories in the Western tradition.

Adults, on the other hand, gravitated toward many of the works favored by Altamira when he composed library lists for workers in the early part of the century (see page 146), such as the novel, and, a little less frequently, to poetry and sociological works. They preferred modern novels, with Galdos's *Episodios Nacionales* (a nationalistic, heroic, historical fiction series) taking the lead, closely followed by Valera and Pérez de Ayala. Among the canonized, classic works of Spanish literature, Cervantes and Quevedo led the way. Literate adults did not forsake foreign classics, however; they also read works by Dickens, Tolstoy, Hugo, Remarque, and Wells. Their favorite poets were Bécquer, Machado, and Juan Ramón Jiménez. Sometimes technical books, such as those covering agricultural techniques, were checked out, but these were read on a more localized level, depending on the interests of a particular region.[20] From this list, it looks as if the adults were following the ideological path laid before them by the Republican–Socialist coalition. Although the villagers may not have cut their teeth on Kropotkin or Marx, they were attracted to foreign novels that examined the nineteenth-century social question (which had yet to be resolved in twentieth-century Spain) or that debated the necessity of war (Remarque). And, as the misioneros had hoped, the majority of villagers who could read did target classic Spanish literature. One wonders if these Spaniards' literary tastes would have differed if the libraries had been stocked with an equal number of books that conservatives favored. But that kind of choice is precisely what the misioneros would have wanted to avoid—although they never explicitly said this—because it would have conflicted with the values they wanted the campesinos to absorb.

According to accounts in the *Memoria,* whose interests, of course, lay in showcasing the successes of the Republican cultural reforms, a great number of the new libraries "stimulate[d] the habit of reading in those who did not have it before." To back their assertion, they included some of the enthusiastic reactions from librarians across the country. One anecdote reveals that the local library whipped up such enthusiasm among the villagers that the school (where the library was housed) became the great "meeting point, tightening in this manner the bonds between the school and the family." Another claimed that in the village of De Gualchos (Granada) people harbored "a great love of the book and an increasing interest in reading." Another simply wrote that "the desire to know makes up for the lack of culture." The misioneros also pointed out other signs that gauged the success of their programs: children brought books home for their parents to read; in some places people formed reading societies that would try to acquire new works for the library; in Sabada (Zaragoza), villagers held fundraisers that increased the size of their library to six hundred volumes; and, finally, some libraries had so many readers that there were no more books available to check out.[21]

To supplement the work carried out by the Misiones Pedagógicas, the Republican–Socialist coalition embarked on yet another program that was designed to improve existing libraries, especially those in rural primary schools. This organization, the Junta de Intercambio de Libros para Bibliotecas Públicas, was instituted by decree on November 21, 1931. The project began not as a means to create public libraries but as a way to modernize existing ones and help private institutions create their own libraries. The preamble to the decree cited the abundance of theological texts and books of religious history—a remnant, no doubt, of the religious school system—but lamented that many libraries lacked modern books in science, industry, literature, and history, for example.[22] Once again, in their attempts to clear away old, unread, religious texts to make way for more modern, Enlightenment-influenced texts, the Republican–Socialist coalition appeared ready to sweep away any reminders of Spain's pre-Republican past, a past they associated with religious dogmatism and xenophobia.

The workings of municipal libraries also fell under the auspices of the Junta de Intercambio.[23] On July 13, 1932, the Republic's second Minister of Public Instruction, Fernando de los Ríos, signed a decree authorizing the committee to create a library in municipalities that wanted one. The committee would then supply a new library with a foundation of one hundred fifty to five hundred books, depending on the city's population. Usually libraries in cities with populations of less than three thousand maintained a basic stock of three hundred books. The committee decided that of these allotted books, 60 percent had to be of a recreational nature, that is, books that could be categorized as novels, poetry, theater, travelogues, biography, and folklore. The committee believed that these works lent themselves better than others to create solid reading habits. The remaining 40 percent consisted of classical literature and works that the committee considered to be literary masterpieces. Keeping to its traditional pattern, the committee primarily chose to include in the libraries works that were easy to read and that tended to reflect the more popular authors of the day.

Surprisingly, considering the coalition's effort to engage Spain's youth as the promise of the future, the libraries sorely lacked children's works. One author surmises that the board assumed that the Misiones Pedagógicas were already tackling that problem and therefore felt no need to address children's issues on the municipal level.[24]

The committee hoped to create one hundred municipal libraries a year, a goal it met in 1933, but not in 1934 (only sixty-four were created), and 90 percent of the requests for libraries came from regions dominated by leftist and Socialist political affiliations. Its lack of success after 1933 could perhaps be attributed to the political shift to the right after the November 1933 elections, since factions of the right had little desire to continue funding projects that had been implemented by their opposition.[25]

## REACTIONS TO THESE PROGRAMS

Newspapers such as *El Sol* deemed the Misiones Pedagógicas and the other projects that gave greater numbers access to books to be resounding successes. More conservative groups, in contrast, found these literacy projects inefficient, counterproductive, and sometimes downright offensive. The complaint lodged most often centered around the books selected for the libraries. One writer decried the choice of seemingly leftist partisan works, citing the following as the most egregious choices: Rousseau's *Emile*, Marañón's *Three Essays about Sexual Life*, Ballesteros' *The French and Belgian "Escuelas Únicas,"* G. Deville's *Socialist Principles*, Dewey's *The School and the Child*, Diego Hidalgo's *A Spanish Notary in Russia*, Giner de los Ríos's *Studies on Education*, and Victor Hugo's *Our Lady of Paris*. Calling these works "pedagogically debatable," the author accused the misioneros of engaging in "Socialist labor" and encouraging "the sale of books of [Socialist] friends." While not wishing to rid Spain altogether of the Misiones Pedagógicas, as many of its critics suggested, the author hoped that the organizers would guarantee "impartiality, efficiency and the greatest economy."[26]

Obviously, the works *would be* offensive to traditionalists: they reflected a belief in the Enlightenment roots of education, in frank discussions about sexuality, and in the benefits of revolutionary socialism. For example, Rousseau's *Emile*, primarily, and Dewey's *The School and the Child*, secondarily, focus on child-centered learning, advocating an education that makes learning relevant to children's lives instead of forcing rote memorization on them. Dewey goes even one step further, by promoting the reconstruction, not the reproduction, of the social order, and he sees the classroom as the laboratory for creating a participatory democracy. These ideas, as well as those found in Giner de los Ríos's and Ballesteros's books, went to the heart of the ILE's educational philosophy—transforming the structure of Spanish society through a liberal, and sometimes reformist–socialist education. But, the books listed above represented the bane of the Spanish right—the Enlightenment and the Russian Revolution—and, therefore, they posed a threat to the social order.

The fiercest clashes over the newly established libraries' contents occurred during the Cortes debates of June 26–28, 1935. While acrimoniously debating which cuts to make in the budget for public instruction, conservative delegates suggested slashing, if not eliminating, the budget for the Misiones Pedagógicas. Pedro Sáinz Rodríguez, a member of Acción Española who was to become Minister of Education on the Nationalist side during the Civil War, complained that the members of the Misiones Pedagógicas had far too much autonomy, which allowed them to transport their "political sectarianism" to rural areas. More ridiculous in Sáinz Rodríguez's eyes, however, were the misioneros' efforts to bring such works as those by Oscar Wilde "to the most insignificant villages." These ventures, he believed, only highlighted how far removed the misioneros were from the daily lives of Spanish laborers.[27] Representative Pérez Díaz dismissed such tales carried by Sáinz Rodríguez and his allies as propaganda spewed forth by enemies of the Misiones Pedagógicas. Having visited a library founded by the Misiones himself, Pérez Díaz testified that he saw there "works by Lope, of our classics, primarily, that teach us to think of our Golden Age." More importantly, in his opinion, the library's contents "represent a work of absolute *españolismo*." Despite his praise for the library, others remained convinced that the misioneros' projects reeked of leftist partisanship. Lamamié de Clairac, a Carlist and fellow member of Acción Española, for example, targeted his wrath on writings by Socialists Jean Jaurès, Pablo Iglesias, and Francisco Largo Caballero, considering them works that reflected not only the leftist nature of the literature housed in the libraries but also on the leftist radicals who put them there.[28]

The most vitriolic attack against the Misiones Pedagógicas in general and the Servicio de Bibliotecas, specifically, appeared in the conservative Catholic newspaper *El Debate* shortly after the Cortes debates.[29] The article urged those in charge of the budget to eliminate funding completely for the Misiones Pedagógicas because they lacked "efficaciousness"

and because they hampered Spaniards from funding "other more imperi-
ous necessities of the education of the people." Beginning with an assault
on the economic front, the author of the article criticized the Misiones
as a pork-barrel extravagance. He complained of its nearly 800,000 peseta
budget for the year 1934, of which "apart from many useless expenses,"
75,000 pesetas were spent "in bureaucracy and 10,000! in printing a *Memoria*." The 270,000 pesetas earmarked for libraries infuriated him because
no university library in Spain benefited from this supposed windfall: "the
library of the University of Madrid [received] only 15,000 pesetas!" Of
course his statements illustrate that he missed the entire point behind the
Misiones, namely to bring underprivileged members of society the cultural and educational opportunities that were taken for granted by people
living in cities and attending universities.

But more than the cost of the Misiones, the writer complained that the
peasantry was being exposed to radical ideology under the guise of "spiritual nourishment" and "social formation." He questioned such reading
selections as Devillet's *Socialist Principles,* Kautsky's *The Defense of Workers,* Bebel's *Woman in the Past, Present and Future* (also known as *Woman
and Socialism*), and Engels' *Origin of the Family, Private Property, and the
State.* The author listed the works of universal literature he encountered
in the libraries, only to find the choices shocking and bewildering. He
wrote about, "Poor peasants into whose hands have fallen this collection
of universal literature, of which nine out of the total forty-six works are
Russian." These choices *do* seem a bit far afield from the supposedly apo-
litical works that the misioneros claimed to be distributing to the peasantry. Works such as Bebel's and Engels's—which question the concept of
private property and which tie women's oppression to private property
and the family—are hardly disinterested tracts. But, perhaps we can see
the inclusion of these Socialist works along with classic literary works of
the western European canon as mirroring the difficult need to balance the
political tensions between the reformist Republicans and revolutionary
Socialists in the Republic's coalition government.

Despite the writer's legitimate complaints about the partisan nature
of these library books, he displayed his own ideological biases when he
wrote condescendingly about peasants, "who, scarcely knowing how to
read poorly, have had to decipher *The Iliad* or *The Odyssey,* the tragedies
of Sophocles or the dramas of Shakespeare! Or, finally, they have been
placed in contact with Ibsen's *Ghosts,* Remarque's novel and the works of
Anatole France and Oscar Wilde." Probably as a tongue-in-cheek response

to those who said that the libraries were filled with classic works by Spanish authors, he listed a work by Rodolfo Llopis, the head of the Ministry of Primary Education and a leader in the Socialist Union, the UGT, to illustrate what the misioneros considered to be a contemporary Spanish classic. Completely dismissing the work accomplished by the Servicio de Bibliotecas, the author added that the works harbored in these libraries were "anything but pedagogical."[30]

Just in case anybody reading the article might have thought that the author was cold-hearted in his appraisal of the peasantry's plight, he proposed his own solutions to the "cultural problem" of the peasantry. He wanted to see a version of the Misiones Pedagógicas that suited the peasants' "profession and life." Instead of having a peasant read the works of Sophocles, which, the author claimed, "do not interest him," he should learn more practical skills such as improving cultivation, learning how to work the land, acquiring hygienic habits, strengthening his "moral life," and developing "the feeling of citizenship and patriotism." Not only did it seem illogical to distribute "pedantic and harmful" books in places that lacked agricultural and professional schools, it was, according to our author, positively dangerous: at its best, the library could serve as a "bad seed for tranquil spirits, when it is not a vehicle of unhealthy ideas against morality, the family, society and the state itself." During a period of high unemployment and tightening purse strings, the libraries had to be dismissed as the quixotic dreams of misguided aesthetes.[31]

Regardless of its political motivation, the article in *El Debate* posed some legitimate questions that had to be addressed. Was it reasonable to spend a large percentage of an educational budget on libraries, when a great number of the people for whom the libraries were geared were illiterate? Should a region's spiritual needs—as defined by Krausists and institucionistas—have taken precedence over material or techniçal ones? In other words, was it not more practical to fill the libraries with technical manuals about agriculture than with more novels by Victor Hugo? Historians such as Manuel Tuñón de Lara have certainly criticized the misioneros as misguided because they attempted massive cultural reforms without putting into place the necessary economic reforms first. In his later years, the misionero Antonio Sánchez Barbudo responded to this pointed criticism:

> None of the misioneros that I know of, and I certainly did not, ever confuse "cultural utopia with social justice." We saw the poverty, the backwardness,

the injustices, and all of those things affected us greatly, although we could do little or nothing to help the situation. We were convinced of the need for radical reforms. We knew that the elevation of the cultural level in the villages had to have indispensably at its base the elevation of the economic level. And we knew that the Republic began and planned reforms, although none of them were ever ... as great, quick, or effective as we would have liked. More than anything, we never came to believe that our work was useless.... We did what we could, but we were well aware of the need to do much more, and above all else in the economic sphere.[32]

Despite what Sánchez Barbudo may have thought, the editorial staff of *El Debate* certainly doubted the efficacy of teaching the peasantry the canon of Western thought and proposed, at least superficially, establishing technical schools more suited to the populace's station in life. But if they were sincerely championing the peasantry's rights to a technical education, then why had such institutions not been created in full force prior to the Republic, when the state allied itself more closely with clerical institutions? Posing the question in such a way reveals the duplicitous nature of this article. Moreover, the writers of *El Debate* and their fellow travelers were not adverse to nourishing the spiritual part of Spain in lieu of the material (an accusation they had lodged against the left); they just defined spiritual values differently from their Krausist and institucionista opponents. They believed that Spaniards' spiritual health depended on an undying devotion to the Catholic Church and its precepts, a loyalty to the state (preferably under monarchical rule), and a corporatist social structure, whereby each stratum of society acted harmoniously with the others to ensure a well-functioning organic entity. Unlike the institucionistas who placed their faith in the spiritual values of the Enlightenment literary tradition, Catholics maintained that Spaniards' spiritual sustenance derived purely from the long-established teachings of the church. And to question one's station in life was tantamount to heresy.

Even people who initially supported the Republic but thought that many of its programs needed to be reformed questioned the need for literacy programs. In an article entitled "The Decline of Illiteracy," printed in the Catholic intellectual journal *Cruz y Raya* (founded in 1933), the journal's editor, José Bergamín, presented a convoluted jumble of specious arguments entreating Spaniards to stop encouraging the growth of literacy in Spain.[33] Although the piece was originally read in 1930 in the Residencia de Señoritas, the editorial staff, to which Bergamín belonged, ran it in their journal, presumably because it published articles of the same intellectual caliber as Ortega's *Revista de Occidente,* but with a Catholic bent.

Bergamín began his piece with a discussion of children. Children, he said, do not have the "practical reason" of adults; they have instead a type of reason that is innate, "spiritually immaculate," and "pure"—what he called "illiterate reason." Illiterate reason was not a mark of shame, however, because it reflected a child's blessedness: "It is not that [children] cannot understand the world, but rather that they know it purely: in a manner exclusively spiritual, and not yet literal or lettered or 'literaturized.'" Equating children's reason with play, and play with a state of grace, he called illiteracy "the common poetic denomination of a complete, truly spiritual state."[34]

He lambasted the literate for what he perceived as their persecution of the illiterate and their destruction of world order. The literates' greatest offense, Bergamín claimed, was their suppression of hierarchies: "One rationally loses the sense of hierarchy when one has to order everything alphabetically. Alphabetical order is a false order." He slashed away at the ideas propounded by the French Enlightenment—the real enemy inspiring this article: "Alphabetical order is the greatest spiritual disorder: that of dictionaries or literal vocabularies, more or less encyclopedic, to which literal culture tries to reduce the universe." He argued that while words are things of play, a written letter is a "double-edged sword" that "pierces the illiterate heart of the child," stealing away his spirit. He blamed the Enlightenment for beginning this process of literacy, for encouraging false intellectualism and for making poetry—the embodiment of illiteracy— "sterilized."[35]

In what may be his strangest case for urging a high level of illiteracy, Bergamín uses Jesus as an example of the greatest illiterate ever toppled by the forces of literacy. According to Bergamín, Jesus was illiterate, and because he went to the temple and taught the "doctors of the legal letter" about spiritual matters, he was condemned to death. But because he taught "the spiritual doctrine of innocence," Bergamín implied, these lettered people "literally crucified him, that is, to the letter or letters, placing on his head a poster or sign in which the literate Pilate clearly wrote: I am the King of the Jews."[36] From this curious parable Bergamín hoped to demonstrate that the forces of literacy destroy that which is Divine.

Bergamín continued to rail against the Encyclopediasts—followers of the Enlightenment—for attempting to impose a false order on the universe and for enervating the people's spiritual culture. He ended his article demanding that the people—whom he always compares to children—be granted their rights to illiteracy: "The entire history of Spanish culture, in its purest spiritual values, is formed by way of its constant popular illiteracy." Spaniards must reject what Bergamín called the "cultural alphabetization" that is "the mortal enemy of language as such, in that language is spirit: of the word."[37]

This article begs a serious question. If Bergamín and (presumably) the other Catholic writers who contributed to *Cruz y Raya* felt so opposed to the growth of literacy in Spain, then why were *they* entitled to the privilege or perhaps the "curse" of literacy? Bergamín's article never satisfactorily solves this contradiction. His piece valorizes the spoken word over the written and equates oral culture with blessedness. But it is obvious that he believes that some people, at least, are equipped enough to handle the burden of literacy. Bergamín and other Catholic intellectuals really had no qualms about literacy, per se. But they wanted literacy to be parceled out to small segments of the population that met their spiritual precepts and who would not disturb the social order. And that is why, I believe, they so forcefully rejected the types of books that peasants were reading in the newly formed Republican libraries.

Still, the complaints lodged by the right against such projects as the Servicio de Bibliotecas of the Misiones Pedagógicas deserve some attention. By stocking libraries in economically and educationally destitute areas with works by Tolstoy, Dickens, and Galdós, the misioneros already assumed a high degree of literacy, as well as a penchant for novels that dealt with the social question. One would think that it would seem a bit daunting for a newly literate peasant to have to read 500-plus page tomes instead of more basic primers. One misionero put it best when he was faced with what seemed to be an astounding level of ignorance among the peasantry (and, one might add, among the misioneros): "What they do not know is the total series of suppositions of our culture, the cement that sustains and makes possible our knowledge. For this reason, the first and most anguished impression that one gets from them is the lack of common ground for understanding: that there are not, intellectually, common convictions to depart from."[38] The misioneros began with the premise that the peasantry had only a small base of knowledge from which to fully develop their intellectual potential. The great cultural divide between people in urban and rural areas became even more obvious to the misioneros after their contact with the Spanish peasantry. Literacy could not be taught simply by installing books in rural areas. Teachers had to be the agents of literacy, linking the libraries to villagers. Keeping in mind the misioneros' premise that "only when every Spaniard not only knows how to read ... but has the desire to read ... will there be a new Spain,"[39] we can see that their work could function only to whet the villagers' appetites, to stimulate learning, to showcase works of literature, and to begin to define a canon of Spanish literature. Literacy was merely the beginning of a larger social program.

Like reformists of the Second Republic, the anarchists also stressed the importance of literacy as the backbone of their social programs. As we saw in chapter 1, anarchists set up ateneos and makeshift schools to teach urban and rural laborers to read, and numerous anarchist journals and newspapers sprang up in the late nineteenth century as a way to popularize acratic ideas.[40] Behind the flourishing of workers' ateneos and anarchist print culture lay the hope that a literate labor force would become a revolutionary one.[41] Despite the relative wealth of anarchist journals in circulation, some anarchist writers believed that the literacy revolution had not yet taken place and that more work was needed to bolster the reading skills of the majority of Spain's subaltern population.

One of the greatest complaints lodged by these writers was that even those laborers who knew how to read could not understand what they were reading, or their reading tastes were not very discriminating. For example, one author in *La Revista Blanca* asked if workers were ready to deal with the problems that confronted them: Were they educated enough? He answered "no." In the workers' world, the gap between theory and praxis remained wide. He said that many anarchists had a "horrible aversion" to letters, despite the fact that there were numerous journals and magazines circulating and despite the increasing readership in anarchist ateneos. "It is certain that they read many letters," he said, "but nothing more than letters. And the love of letters does not consist of emitting the corresponding oral signs. The love of letters consists of interpreting the ideas locked inside the letters.... If we do not know the value of words, we will neither be able to understand nor feel the ideas well."[42]

Others were even more contemptuous of workers' literary tastes. Like other European cultural critics of the time, the author Sadi de Gorter decried the "vulgarization of art" led by such culprits as film and radio, and he chided workers who were "poorly informed about artistic and literary expression." In fact, he blamed Socialist publications for "betraying their cultural mission" by not stressing the authors and works that were important for laborers to know, such as Mary Webb, G. K. Chesterton, Heinrich Mann, Stefan Zweig, and John dos Passos.[43]

It may seem odd that these writers were so concerned with developing the workers' literary tastes and urging them to focus on belles lettres instead of dime-store novels. But another writer at *La Revista Blanca* best describes their reasons for encouraging such works:

In the field of art in general, literature occupies an important place.... [Through literature] one can express all of the moral and artistic emotions of the human soul, the aesthetic impulses, as much as ethical anxieties, profoundly more emotionally than the other fine arts.... [Literature] is a sublime, emotional, unique art for reflecting the different mental states of beings, and to shape in beautiful, descriptive pages, nature and all of those things that surround us.

The concept of the beautiful and the good, of the aesthetic and the ethical, of the sublime and the noble, of the romantic and the sentimental, all find their most expressive medium in literature, the art of Letters.[44]

But more interesting than those writers who tried to steer anarchist readers away from literature geared toward a mass readership and toward a more serious form of literature were those who interpreted the canon of Castilian literature for very different purposes from those of the Republican and Socialist misioneros. The most compelling example of revisionist literary criticism that I have encountered is by Ignacio Cornejo, writing, once again, for *La Revista Blanca* about the Spanish classic, *Don Quixote*. Many intellectuals allied with the Republic such as Manuel Azaña, José Ortega y Gasset, and Miguel de Unamuno had already written about *Don Quixote* as the quintessential masterpiece that reflected the Spanish (Castilian) national character, but Cornejo dismissed their interpretations as misguided at best: "Anarchism has to reclaim Don Quixote as one of its own. Don Quixote is not the soul or the prototype of *la raza*, but rather of anarchism. This adventurer has nothing in common with those cruel adventurers and hypocrites who conquered honors for Spain by torturing Indians or ramming the cross down their throats."[45] According to Cornejo, Don Quixote combated the ugliness around him. The windmills he tilted at were not mere illusions, not false giants, but rather, the state. Don Quixote was "an eternal dissident," trying to fight problems that seemed insurmountable. In contrast, Cornejo lambastes Sancho Panza, the one whom critics usually read as Don Quixote's sane companion, by saying that he would have made a good syndicalist, because Sancho would take the small scraps that the government threw at him and would forfeit any chance for real change in the future. In keeping with his supposed anarchist leanings, Don Quixote "does not construct anything because he understands that this is governmental—although he governs Sancho, just as anarchism *governs* the government."[46] One might accuse Cornejo of interpreting Don Quixote anachronistically, but his interpretation provides us with a glimpse of how some anarchist educators hoped to develop critical reading skills in their followers and how canonical literature that had previously been the purview of the ruling classes, could be co-opted for anarchism's revolutionary purposes.

## THE PROBLEM OF REGIONAL LANGUAGES

Obviously, the "literacy question" loomed large in the minds of reformers, radicals, and reactionaries during the Second Republic. But another reason the Republican–Socialist coalition attempted to increase literacy and to build a wide network of libraries has been ignored: the need to safeguard a canon of Spanish (read: Castilian) literature against the splintering effects brought on by the demands of regional nationalists who wanted regional languages taught in the schools. Government officials from across the political spectrum manifested a considerable ambivalence, if not hostility, toward those politicians who favored granting autonomous rights to such regions as Catalonia, Galicia, and the Basque Country. But much of the support for founding the Republic was predicated on the idea that these regions would eventually gain self-rule. A constant tension throughout the Republic's tenure occurred between those who believed that a strong central government was key to the functioning of a powerful modern nation and those who emphasized a plurality of regional identities loosely tied together under the guardianship of Madrid.

Besides insisting on the need for political autonomy, regional nationalists demanded recognition of their respective cultural differences. Language was the primary bone of contention among those who wanted to assert their cultural independence from the centralizing tendencies of Castile. Therefore, officials of the Republic had to grapple with some fundamental questions that threatened to break the tenuous threads holding together the chimera of a centralized state: Should regional languages become official languages? Should they be taught in the schools and universities and used in official correspondence? Should they take precedence over Castilian?

Much debate took place over this issue, for example, during the writing of the Republican constitution at the end of 1931. Although Castilian finally became the official language of Spain, the debate was intense.[47] Miguel de Unamuno, though born in the Basque Country, fiercely defended the need for every Spaniard to know Castilian. He dismissed Basque, for example, as a dead language that was currently being revived artificially, much like Gaelic in Ireland: "Basque, it has to be said, does not exist as a unified language; it is a conglomeration of dialects in which one dialect cannot understand the other."[48] In another instance one year later he said that Basque was a wonderful language for discussing farming techniques, but to grapple with "great thoughts" the language, spoken by a "small" and "local" culture, was appallingly deficient.[49] While he credited Catalonia with having a true, living cultural and linguistic heritage, he still maintained that Castilian should reign, citing Joan Maragall as an example of a Catalan who wrote in the most exquisite Castilian.

For Unamuno, Castilian represented a "work of integration." It welcomed elements of Aragonese and Leonese, and it combined all of these components to make Spanish a living, breathing language. Although he supported an individual's autonomy, he could not abide the cultural nationalists' calls for linguistic autonomy. Using Spain as an analog to language, he contended that Spain was not a nation but a "renation"/rebirth.[50] "Neither an individual, nor a people, nor a language can be reborn," he contended, "without dying; it is the only way to be reborn; fusing oneself with another." Integration, then, was Spain's destiny.[51]

But the most intense discussions over language and national identity came during the debate over Catalonia's Autonomy Statute. The Catalan representatives faced great opposition from many members of the Cortes who feared that the promotion of Catalan language and culture would destroy Castilian hegemony. Even those who supported Catalan political autonomy registered some fear over what they perceived might be overarching demands from the Catalan contingent in the Cortes. For example, shortly before the Cortes's debate on the statute, an interviewer asked the Minister of Public Instruction, Fernando de los Ríos, if he foresaw any problems in the upcoming debate over the question of education in Catalonia. De los Ríos responded: "I think that there will be problems; but I also think that we will solve them. Understanding will prevail. Spanish culture cannot be abandoned. I will defend it.... It is necessary to concede legitimate aspirations; but I will defend the Spanish culture."[52] Because Catalan nationalists had abandoned their claims to an independent Catalan republic in April 1931 in exchange for being allowed to submit an autonomy statute to the Cortes, de los Ríos sought carefully to balance the needs of the precarious Spanish state with the wishes of a Catalan minority that had helped bring about the founding of the Republic.

During the Cortes debates, the Republican Melquíades de Alvarez was even more assertive about the need to keep Spain unified. He did not believe that Catalonia had the same claims to nationhood as Spain: "Spain has all of the characteristics of nationality because of its language, tradition, race, history, the loftiness of its spirit that has left us with great memories, and finally for the wondrousness of this language which, because of its euphony, its ideal nature, is one of the greatest vehicles that serve the supreme interests of civilization."[53]

The *catalanistas* would not easily be dissuaded from their belief that they had to thwart the encroaching Castilianization of Spain. They chose the Catalan language and culture as their weapons. Joan Estelrich, a representative from Girona and a member of the conservative Lliga Catalana, was a major spokesman, both inside and outside the Cortes, for Catalan autonomy and the promotion of Catalan culture. In a work published the same year as the debate over the Catalan Automony Statute, he mirrored the words of Republicans, Socialists, anarchists, and conservatives when he talked about the role of culture in national life: "Culture is the most authentic expression of a people's soul, of a civilization, of a race, manifested in all of the productions of the spirit.... As a creation, we, the Catalans, have only one culture. In the literary sphere ... our language is its sole authentic expression." He moved from this generalized concept of culture as a window into one's soul and civilization to a lament about Castilian hegemony and arrogance: "As Catalans we all need guarantees of the free expression of our spirit. We cannot coexist happily within a compound state while this state does not consider the creations of our autochthonous culture as productions worthy of respect, encouragement, and help as any other culture." He suggested countering this domination by spreading the Catalan language through literature and public education.[54] When the Cortes debated the Autonomy Statute in May and June of 1932, Estelrich fought to protect the cultural rights of his Catalan compatriots. He asked a very compelling question of his fellow representatives: "And I will come concretely to the question of culture. What does a liberal state have to do in the presence of the phenomenon of culture? More concretely: What does the liberal state have to do when within its territory there exist organizations, cultural centers, cultures ... that have a different character, that have a diverse personality?"[55] His question revealed the difficult tensions inherent within the Socialist–Republican coalition. The coalition itself stood on precarious ground, constantly wavering between reformist and revolutionary tendencies. They paid some attention to regional nationalisms, and they claimed they believed that historical minority groups deserved regional autonomy. At the same time, they feared that regional autonomy would destroy that essence which made Spain Spain— the Castilian language and culture. Finding the right balance would be difficult in a liberal framework.

But the right would have none of the equivocating exhibited by the coalition. The right wing insisted even more adamantly on the primacy of Castilian culture and language. Maeztu's *Defensa de la Hispanidad* must be counted among the works that most vociferously defended all aspects of "traditional" Spanish culture in its romanticization of the political unity established by Ferdinand and Isabel. Additionally, columns in *El Debate* lambasted Catalans for discounting the need to learn Castilian. Although they were not trying to denigrate Catalan, writers at *El Debate* thought that Catalans were fooling themselves if they could not see the "practical supremacy of Castilian, that [had] warranted the greatest historical influence, the evident privilege of literature, and above all, of incomparable linguistic expansion. The Catalans themselves must know that learning the Castilian language asserts itself as a cultural imperative."[56]

The Cortes debates fleshed out the right's position without hesitation. Representative Jaén, sounding very much like Melquíades de Alvarez, argued for the unity of Spanish culture and civilization. He accused some members of the Cortes of fighting "against history" and called for "sustaining the imperial nature of the Spanish language." He wanted to make sure that the Catalans maintained Spanish cultural establishments because "Spanish unity is not merely territorial unity, but also the unity of civilization and endeavors."[57] Representative Royo Villanova, besides taking up these same arguments about the sanctity of Spanish and Spain—"It is much more serious to suppress the Patria than to suppress God"[58]—chose to denigrate Catalan culture altogether as an invented culture. He talked about the "poverty" of the Catalan language and how academics at the Institute of Catalan Studies had twisted the language of the people of Catalonia and created a false, academic language. Catalan did not have the "sponteneity which is born of the people." He accused these academics of using a "top-down approach" to artificially impose their idea of a Catalan language on the people and of giving the language an official imprimateur.[59] Of course, he was right about the Catalan nationalists' attempts to forge a national identity by codifying Catalan culture in academic institutions and by creating Catalan myths, but with the exception of the Catalans' standardizing an orthography in the nineteenth century, these approaches were not very different from the traditions that Spanish nationalists invented during the Second Republic.

Given this context of debate over regional languages and culture, then, the Republican–Socialist coalition's subsidy of libraries in the early years of the Republic may have been just what was needed to ensure Castilian cultural hegemony. The links between libraries, literacy, and Castilian centralization became most obvious after the Popular Front (Frente Popular) won the elections in February 1936 and swung the Republic's cultural policies to favor leftist ideas. With the *littérateur,* Prime Minister Manuel Azaña, at the helm once again, Republicans and Socialists sought to make up whatever cultural losses they had incurred from over two years of conservative rule.

In April, Azaña's government embarked on yet another library-related project. By the decree of April 24, 1936, the government wrote into law the formation of a Biblioteca de Escritores Clásicos (Library of Classic Writers). The decree begins with the following statement: "The government of the Republic, keeping vigil over the conservation and diffusion of the monuments of the national language and literature, which are known [to embody] the tastiest fruits of the Spanish spirit and some of the most esteemed titles in the history of civilization, has agreed to create a library of classic writers, directed not solely toward putting good texts at the reach of a mature public of lettered people, but also for the circulation between the school-going youth and the people."[60] This opening sentence crystallized many of the major premises held by leftist reformers. First, wearing the mantle of the nation's educator, the government assumed responsibility for the "conservation" of Spain's language and literature. Second, the Spanish language and literature embodied the nation's spirit. Third, these works that incarnated the nation's spirit had to be accessible to all Spaniards, not just the highly educated ones.

The decree continued along in this same vein. This "work of national character" had to be tackled by the state for two reasons: (1) the destruction wrought by the "corruption of speech" and (2) "the advantage of bringing closer to common knowledge the pure sources of the literary tradition." To facilitate this project, the library would be comprised of three literary series that included volumes containing, whenever possible, an author's complete works; an anthology of authors or genres; and a series of classic "books with exercises for the schools and for popular distribution."[61] Although the decree never defined what it meant by the "corruption of speech," given the politics of regionalism, one could read it to mean that Spanish (Castilian) was being damaged by competing regional languages. Additionally, the decree's wording indicates that the government believed it could create a strong bond among Spaniards if they shared the same set of literary values.

The announcement of this plan brought accolades from Socialist quarters. In explaining the project to its readers, the newspaper *El Socialista* deemed that the pueblo needed to know its geniuses, such as Cervantes, Lope, Quevedo, and Calderón. But most of all, they needed to be aware that these writers were popular, not destined for an elite readership. "Azaña," the column said, "wants to renew the Spanish tradition in one of its broken threads: the word. The beautiful and intimate word that the people speak and the classics bring to their comedies [and] *entremeses*." Like those who believed that Golden Age theater had just as much to offer contemporary popular classes as it had to those of the seventeenth century, the supporters of the Library of Classic Writers contended that the words of Cervantes belonged to all of the people. Once again, Azaña was able to reclaim Cervantes and Lope from the nationalist right, who saw themselves as the inheritors of this literary tradition, and he passed on this literary patrimony to the people. Making the link between language and nation even more explicit than the decree, the writer added: "The idea of the patria cannot be detached from the idea of language. To mystify language is tantamount to dehumanizing us." He called a "community of bad readers" a "failed community," and he took a convoluted swipe at the previous regime headed by the Radical Republican Alejandro Lerroux, blaming his involvement in a corruption scandal over the conferring of gambling licenses on his poor reading habits. Lerroux's soul was lost because his love of popular literature "contaminated politics." According to the author, by proposing this library of classic literature, Azaña "simply wants to repair the damage" wrought by poor readers like Lerroux.[62]

While reformers generally liked the idea of compiling the library, some wished to revise aspects of the proposal. One columnist for *El Sol*, for example, thought that while the Spanish classics had plenty to offer the

public, books that were not considered classics also had much to com-
mend them because they reflected the history and customs of Spain at
particular moments. "Would it not be interesting," he asked, "to know
what [these other authors] have thought about Spain.... What they have
thought about these problems so old and so present: property, the agrarian question ...?"[63]

Even those intimately involved with earlier Republican reforms, such as
Misiones Pedagógicas board member Luis Santullano, had some qualms
about the project. Although he did not object to the materials proposed
for the library—in fact, he was pleased by the government's commitment
to the spiritual values found in literature—he was concerned with how the
materials would be brought to the understanding of the common people.
To make these works accessible to the public as the decree stated, educators had to work hard to close the literacy gap. Santullano suggested many
of the same methods that had already been in effect with the Misiones
Pedagógicas, namely, that these works had to be read repeatedly in public,
at "schools and other centers of learning, in workers' societies, among all
circles of possible readers." Only through this constant exposure to these
works can the "happy objective of bringing the people closer to classic
works" ever be accomplished.[64]

Republicans and Socialists would have done well to heed Santullano's
suggestions, especially in light of his experiences with the Misiones
Pedagógicas. Of course the Spanish Civil War, only three months away,
derailed the Popular Front government's plans to establish the Biblioteca
de Escritores Clásicos. Money had to be channeled to other resources
more pertinent to the war effort. That is not to say that leftist Republicans
supplanted literacy projects with guns; in fact, in many ways, those who
fought on the Republican side believed that the battle to solidify their
vision of cultural unification was more crucial than it had ever been.
Literacy projects, as we will see, continued in full force on the battle-
fields. The fundamental difference, however, lay in the fervor and the tenor
with which those loyal to the Republic attempted to transmit the cultural
values of the left. With a keener eye and more savvy approaches, and in
alliance with leftist intellectuals, the Republicans mastered the art of modern technology and employed propaganda to try to convert the masses to
a radical leftist ideology.

# CHAPTER 6

# Spanish Civil War

## *Culture on the Battlefield*

WITH THE VICTORY OF THE POPULAR FRONT IN FEBRUARY 1936, IT SEEMED as if the cultural programs initiated at the beginning of the Republic were getting a new jump start. The various factions of the left attempted—albeit unsuccessfully—to set aside their doctrinal differences and work together against what they perceived to be an ever-increasing entrenchment of reactionary politics in both Spain and in the rest of Europe. Many on the Spanish left believed that recent events in Germany—where the internecine struggles among Socialist and Communist factions enabled right-wing parties to gain greater political weight and eventually dominate national politics—provided a cautionary tale for Spain. Members of the often fractious Spanish left knew that if any of their programs or ideologies were going to take root on Spanish soil, they had to marshall their forces against the various elements of the Spanish right. Therefore, once the February elections pointed to a Popular Front victory, the prospects for reinvigorating the cultural projects begun by the left during the first part of the Republic looked promising.

But a Popular Front government did not necessarily guarantee political or social stability. On the contrary, social tensions increased and politics became even more polarized on the eve of the Civil War. Street banditry and thuggery by Fascists, Carlists, anarchists, and Socialists alike made the streets of Madrid and Barcelona—as well as other areas in Spain—treacherous and sometimes even deadly places to be. People could no longer choose to remain neutral, as it became increasingly clear to everybody that war would be the only means to settle the vast ideological differences that plagued the people of Spain.

Although plans by right-wing generals to stage a coup d'état, restore the monarchy, and "impose order" on the ever-fracturing Spanish politic had been brewing at least since the February elections, the assassination on July 12 of the intellectual doyen of the right wing, Calvo Sotelo, by Republican Assault Guards, acted as the tinder from which the conflagration of the Spanish Civil War began. On July 17–18, a group of generals led by Emilio Mola and José Sanjurjo, ready to set right the wrongs committed by five years of republicanism, launched their invasion of Spain. Although the generals had counted on a quick victory and subsequent restoration of order, their plans went awry. While managing to capture parts of Castile and Andalusia, the generals failed to quash the main targets of their attacks, Madrid and Barcelona.

The events of July 17–18 triggered a series of responses that, once set in motion, were difficult to control. Almost immediately after the news of Spain's invasion, revolution broke out all over Spain, especially in Catalonia. Workers formed collectives, readying themselves to lead the social revolution and defeat the forces of Spanish "fascism." Moderation no longer lingered in a country beset by such forces tugging at its fray. One was either a "Red" or a "Fascist," and subtle political or ideological differences within the Republican and Nationalist sides, although important within their respective groups, meant nothing to those who wished to cast the other as a monolithic entity of evil.

The destabilizing effects of the war changed the tenor of cultural reform within both the Republican and Nationalist camps. Although this study has focused primarily on the efforts made by multiple groups to achieve a particular vision of unity during the Republic, it cannot end without seeing how these tensions played out in the Civil War. For the war itself, as perceived by its participants, represented more than ever a life-and-death struggle over Spain's future, its "true" identity, and the reconquest of its seemingly forgotten historical traditions. While the Republican–Socialist coalition's vision of Spain during the Republic generally followed the liberal tradition established by the Cortes of Cadiz in 1812, the outbreak of war and the subsequent revolution pushed the leaders of the Popular Front into a more radical stance that was shaped by the ideologies of communism and anarchism. The calls for cultural reform became more shrill, and the programs that the Republicans advocated during the war tended to reflect a more revolutionary than reformist ideology. The Nationalists, in contrast, saw a defeat of the Republic as the chance to annihilate any remnants of the "Red" and "godless" ideology that had been imposed during the five years of Republican rule, and they sought to restore and strengthen what they believed was Spain's real identity: the Catholic, corporatist, and monarchical tradition initiated by the Catholic monarchs, Ferdinand and Isabel.

To detail the numerous cultural programs launched by the various factions fighting the war would be too ambitious and diffuse for the scope of this project.[1] Instead, I will outline broadly the cultural programs endorsed by Republican and Nationalist official channels and then trace the fate of the projects discussed earlier in this book to show how they evolved (or disappeared) with the exigencies of war.

## POLITICS AND CULTURE ON THE REPUBLICAN FRONT

When it became clear that the bombs over Madrid and Barcelona would not cease and that the Nationalist uprising was turning into a full-fledged war, the first wartime Republican government, headed by José Giral, faced the daunting task of trying to organize and run a government amid increasing anarchy. Self-proclaimed "popular tribunals" in the Republican zones took it upon themselves to arrest, try, and kill "enemies of the Republic," while other people, in the midst of revolutionary fervor, burned convents and requisitioned the estates of wealthy Spaniards. Giral's government, a compendium of liberals and institucionistas, was taken aback and paralyzed by the rapidity and turn of events that threatened Spain's social and political order.[2]

While Giral's government attempted to impose a semblance of discipline behind the Popular Front's lines, other groups enlisted their help to achieve the smooth functioning of the government and to defeat the Nationalist forces. On the cultural front, one such group, the Alianza de Intelectuales Antifascistas para la Defensa de la Cultura (Alliance of Antifascist Intellectuals for the Defense of Culture), conveyed shock at the way crowds, in their fervor to burn convents or seize property, mindlessly destroyed Spanish national treasures and monuments. On August 1, 1936, then, the Alianza de Intelectuales Antifascistas, headed by José Bergamín (the Catholic intellectual discussed in the previous chapter) and supported by the Republican Minister of Public Instruction, Francisco Barnés, formed the Junta de Incautación y Protección del Patrimonio Artístico (Committee for Requisition and Protection of Artistic Patrimony) to protect such national treasures as the Prado museum, the Biblioteca Nacional, and other historical monuments.[3]

The committee, headed by the Communist playwright María Teresa León and supported by a plethora of intellectuals whose political sympathies spanned from liberalism to communism to anarchism, worked to protect works of art, rare books, and historic buildings. They assembled trucks to collect whatever valuable works of art or literature they could save from the ravages of Nationalist bombs and Republican revolutionaries, and they stored these works in secure buildings. To aid their effort, the Junta made posters with slogans such as the following:

In a work of religious art, don't look at that which is religious, but rather that which is art.

The national artistic treasure belongs to you as citizens. Help to conserve it!

Any object can have artistic value. Conserve it for the national treasure![4]

The slogans reflected the reverence with which intellectuals allied with the Popular Front treated cultural artifacts.

Although a Spanish outgrowth of the previous year's International Association of Antifascist Writers (which was organized in April 1936 by Communists to gather together intellectuals under the umbrella of the Popular Front), the Alianza de Intelectuales Antifascistas was composed of intellectuals of various leftist stripes who stood in firm opposition to what they termed "fascism." When the war began, approximately sixty intellectuals—the majority of them writers—signed a manifesto denouncing the Nationalist uprising as a "criminal uprising of militarism, clericalism, and pure-bred aristocratism against the democratic Republic and against the people," and they pledged themselves to defend culture and democracy in the name of the Spanish people.[5] They organized branches in Valencia, Barcelona, Madrid, and Alicante and became in many respects the shock troops of the intelligentsia. They contributed their time and energy to the work of the Popular Front by publishing intellectual journals, organizing writing campaigns to rally the outside world to their cause, developing and circulating propaganda, sponsoring films, performing plays, participating in radio programs, and providing morale to the soldiers at the front.[6] At least during the first few months of the war, groups such as the Alianza de Intelectuales Antifascistas, rather than the Republican government, set up the necessary infrastructure to begin disseminating cultural programs aimed at bringing the people to the side of the Popular Front.[7]

The Republican center could not hold for long, however, and by September 4 a new government headed by the UGT leader, Largo Caballero, assembled to impose order on the increasingly anarchic situation behind Republican lines. The people in this cabinet moved farther to the left than any cabinet before it, with a membership of six Socialists, three Republicans, two Communists, one Basque nationalist, and one Catalan nationalist. During his eight-month stint as head of the Republic, Largo Caballero, who had to depend more and more on the aid and advice of the Soviet Union, attempted to unify the forces fighting against the Nationalists. The Communists absorbed the various popular militias and streamlined them into the Ejército Popular (Popular Army) under the direct control of the government. By November, when the Nationalists advanced on Madrid, Largo deemed the crisis serious enough to persuade the Confederación Nacional del Trabajado (CNT; National Confederation of Workers) to join his cabinet. The Republican government then moved its headquarters to Valencia, leaving the people of Madrid on their own to battle Franco's forces.

Although the war and the subsequent move to Valencia had disrupted the functioning of the Republican government, Republican officials still deemed it essential to protect intellectuals loyal to the Republic. With the help of the Quinto Regimiento (Fifth Regiment), the Republicans summoned Madrid's scientists, artists, writers, and other intellectuals loyal to the Republic and escorted them to Valencia where they were housed in the Hotel Palace. The Hotel Palace became the de facto home for the Casa de la Cultura (House of Culture), headed by Antonio Machado and run by these very same intellectuals. The members of the Casa de la Cultura provided studio space for painters, laboratory space for scientists, conferences for writers, and other such amenities. They also published a journal called *Madrid: Cuadernos de la Casa de la Cultura* for intellectuals to publish their articles, poetry, or prose. In general the Casa de la Cultura acted as a safe haven for intellectuals to keep working on independent pursuits, as well as to contribute their intellectual talents to the Republican cause. Due to political shifts in the Republic, however, the Casa de la Cultura was dismantled in July 1937.[8]

The Republican government reached a crisis point again as the rivalry between Socialists and Communists grew more heated. Largo Caballero refused to halt the "people's revolution" that was occurring all over Spain, and thus he incurred the wrath of middle-class Republicans, moderate Socialists, and Communists who felt that the war could be won only by imposing discipline and order in Republican Spain. Largo Caballero was finally forced to resign, and on May 14, 1937, the Communist Juan Negrín replaced him as head of the new cabinet.

Under the streamlining that began with Largo's government came the purging and reshuffling of cultural organizations. The person most responsible for these changes was Jesús Hernández, the twenty-nine-year-old Communist who, educated in Moscow and active in the Spanish Communist Party (PCE; Partido Comunista de España) as its Secretary of Propaganda, became the Minister of Public Instruction. Almost immediately he began to consolidate the diverse educational and cultural programs in hopes of harnessing them for the war effort, believing that the masses were entitled to the cultural works and education that had been denied them over the centuries. On September 15, 1936, Hernández dissolved the various academies and created the Instituto Nacional de Cultura (National Institute of Culture) to act as the umbrella and provide the infrastructure for "all of the cultural, scientific, artistic, educational, and research activities of our country."[9] In addition to reorganizing these institutions, he purged universities and libraries of any professors or functionaries whom he perceived to be at odds with the revolutionary goals of the Republican government. Hernández fought against illiteracy, improved working-class access to higher education, and used all cultural programs and creative acts for propagandistic purposes.[10] To achieve his goals, he and those working for his ministry courted artists and intellectuals and channeled their efforts into organizations such as the Milicias de la Cultura (Cultural Militias) and the Brigadas Volantes (Itinerant Brigades) to bring their brands of culture to the war front and the home front, respectively.[11]

The Milicias de la Cultura—cultural brigades composed of educators, artists, and intellectuals—went to the front to impart lessons on a wide variety of subjects to soldiers with little or no educational background. Although their work mirrored that of the Misiones Pedagógicas in spirit—a group of educated people still brought their idea of culture to those isolated from the culture of the cities—their content was more obviously propagandistic and rife with revolutionary ideology. For example, a circular put out by the Inspector General outlined some of the duties of the Milicias de la Cultura: "The illiterate student ... must always take into account that with arms we will attain the destruction of the old world, but that with Culture a new world will be built; the *Miliciano* should never abandon his rifle, but neither should he abandon his book, which will be tomorrow's rifle."[12] Unlike the misioneros, those working for the Milicias de la Cultura shared in the daily life of the soldiers at the front. Additionally, these groups followed a more militaristic command structure, maintaining a series of divisions for brigades and battalions.

The milicianos labored with soldiers in the trenches, in hospitals, and on military bases, teaching the illiterate ones to read and write and instructing those who had rudimentary skills in subjects such as math, geography, and history. They distributed magazines, newspapers, and leaflets; held conferences; showed films and brought in theatrical troupes such as La Barraca; read poetry; played records; set up libraries and schools; and so on. Their tasks ran the gamut from teaching basic skills to disseminating propaganda.[13] For example, one troupe that performed under the auspices of the Milicias de la Cultura in Barcelona put on a mixture of traditional and revolutionary pieces. An orchestra played "Comintern" and more traditional works by Schubert. They recited "El crímen fue en Granada," a poem about the murder of García Lorca, and performed satirical puppet shows about Franco. And, finally, in a move that revealed the heterogenous makeup of the Republican side, the troupe finished with two pieces: the Communist "International" and the liberal "Hymn of Riego," anthems of revolution and reform, respectively.[14]

On the home front, similar work continued under the auspices of the Brigadas Volantes, which were created on September 20, 1937, by the Ministry of Public Instruction. Their task involved going to "the most isolated corners of [Republican] territory to teach illiterate adults to read and write and to initiate them in the rudiments of culture, completing it with intense methods and of the masses the meritorious work of our teachers."[15] Women and youths of both sexes implemented many of the programs. To qualify as teachers, people had to be at least sixteen years old, loyal to the aims of the Republic, and schooled in basic skills. The Brigadas Volantes, centered prominently in rural areas, waged literacy campaigns and joined their forces with local schools. Often their lessons lasted about an hour and a half—the first half taken up by lessons in reading, writing, and arithmetic; the second half filled with open-air readings of newspapers and magazines and simple talks about subjects such as childcare and domestic labor. They also taught evening classes to workers in the cities.

The propaganda generated by the Ministry of Public Instruction and its subsidiary organizations never ceased to paint the Nationalists as Fascists hell-bent on keeping the working classes and peasantry in docile

Figure 23. Soldiers being educated by the Milicias de la Cultura. Photo by permission of the Biblioteca Nacional, Madrid.

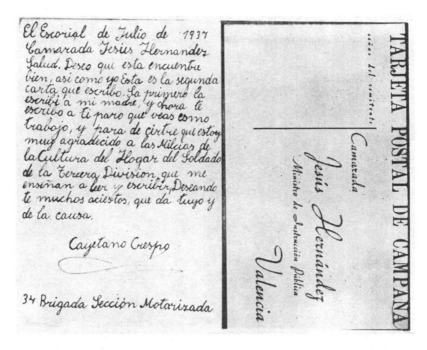

Figure 24. Postcard sent by soldier Cayetano Crespo to the Minister of Public Instruction, Jesús Hernández. Crespo wrote: "This is the second letter that I write. I wrote the first one to my mother, and now I write to you so that you can see how I work and to tell you that I am very grateful to the Milicias de la Cultura of the Soldiers' Third Division, who taught me to read and write." Photo by permission of the Biblioteca Nacional, Madrid.

Figure 25. Soldiers using a library provided by the Milicias de la Cultura. Photo by permission of the Biblioteca Nacional, Madrid.

Figure 26. People being educated by the Milicias de la Cultura. Notice the Zapatista poster on the wall behind the students in the background, which seemingly links the work of the Milicias to that of the Mexican revolution. Photo by permission of the Biblioteca Nacional, Madrid.

ignorance, calling them "the champions of the dark past of ignorance and illiteracy that has been the shame of our patria."[16] In one pamphlet, which seemed to be the basis of at least one *charla popular* (popular talk), Republicans accused the Nationalists of closing down schools, burning libraries, jailing and killing teachers, burning books in public places, and confiscating works of art and sending them to Italy and Germany. The Nationalists engaged in such activities, the Republicans claimed, because "fascism bases its oppression not only in physical terror, but also in the ignorance of the people."[17]

Conversely, the Republicans portrayed themselves as saviors of the people, ready to take up arms to ensure the peoples' rights to culture and democracy. They listed the many accomplishments of the Milicias de la Cultura and the Brigadas Volantes—such as building libraries and schools, teaching literacy, and showing plays and films—to illustrate the Republicans' high esteem for the people: "In this way the workers and peasants that are in the trenches know that they fight not only for liberty and bread, but also for the spiritual goods that had been denied them before." They claimed to have taught 75,000 soldiers to read and write, remarking that 75,000 bayonets "now shine with a new brilliance in front of the enemies of the people."[18]

The Republicans achieved greater success than the Nationalists on the propaganda front. Scholars have attributed this superior strength to the Republicans' location, infrastructure, and alliance with the Soviets. Because the Republicans controlled Spain's major cities (at least until the very end of the war), they had access to great masses of people who were willing to donate their time and experience. The cities also had technology such as printing presses, movie studios, and radio stations, as well as the experienced Soviets' use of agitprop to incite people to a common cause. The bulk of Spain's intellectuals also lived in urban areas. And although certainly not all intellectuals sided with the Republicans, it was easier for the Republicans to draw on the intellectuals residing behind Republican lines than it was for Nationalists to transport *their* intellectuals to the Nationalist front.[19]

## POLITICS AND CULTURE ON THE NATIONALIST FRONT

Although the Nationalists may have had less access to the means necessary to carry out as strong a propaganda campaign as their enemies, their power cannot be discounted. They, too, saw the world of culture as a vital battleground and endeavored to eliminate the "foreign" and "god-less" ideologies that had been foisted on the Spanish people by institucionistas and their perceived successors, the Socialists, Communists, and anarchists.

They concentrated their forces on the educational system, determined to reclaim Spain's youth by erasing any remnants of Institucionismo and reimposing an ideology that fostered the ideals of patriotism based on Hispanidad and fierce Catholicism. Like their Republican counterparts, the Nationalists, in their desire to purge the school system of republicanism and socialism, began to jail and execute teachers and professors who were sympathetic to the aims of the Republic. In a circular of October 7, 1936, the president of the newly formed Commission of Culture and Education under Franco, José María Pemán, justified the purgings as both punitive and preventive measures to protect the Spanish people from those who poisoned "the popular soul," from those who were "most responsible for all the crime and destruction that [had] startled the world and sown the pain of the majority of Spain's honorable households." He couched his attacks on Republicans in the most personal and vitriolic terms: "The individuals who make up these revolutionary hordes ... are simply the spiritual children of professors and teachers who, through institutions such as the so-called 'Libre de Enseñanza' [*sic*], forge unbelieving and anarchic generations. If one wants to make fruitful the blood of our martyrs, it is necessary to combat resolutely the system that has continued for more than a century to honor and elevate the inspirers of evil, while withholding punishment from the mass victims of their deceit."[20] Thus, in order to redeem the Nationalist blood that was being spilled on the battlefield, those elements that the Nationalists held responsible for the fratricide had to be punished severely. The purges, however, resulted in the closing of several elementary schools, as many of these schools had only one teacher.[21]

In the autumn of 1936 Nationalist educators in Zaragoza detailed some of their complaints against Republican schools and presented their plans for revamping the educational system in the *Boletín de Educación de Zaragoza*. They accused Republican educators in Madrid of singing the "International," mistreating people who did not wear the trappings of "Red" clothing, boycotting right-wing teachers, refusing religious books, and destroying works of art (presumably during the church and convent burnings). Republicans, they claimed, wanted to "Sovietize" the school system that is, "to de-Catholicize it, to de-Hispanify it."[22] These educators cast their aspersions in the rhetoric common to both the Falange and the traditionalists, a rhetoric rife with references to Hispanidad, Catholicism, and the Patria.

Godlessness and anarchy could no longer dominate the educational system, they argued, and that was why the uprising against the Republic was absolutely necessary. With Nationalist intervention, Spaniards could now be proud that Spain had "escaped from the dead end in which were sequestered immorality, ignorance and the ungoverning of the perverse enemies, to enter into the open road of Justice, Culture, and Progress." The schools that would work to transform the New Spain (which in National- ists' eyes was the Old Spain) depended on Catholic teachers who would inculcate these values of culture and progress. Teachers had to feel an "inextinguishable love of Spain" in order to prepare citizens who would honor, serve, and defend their Patria against the onslaught of foreign ide- ologies. Upon them was foisted the idea that only they could "recover the ancient splendor" of their nation by executing a "work of spiritual hygiene, a work of purification that wipes away the horrible impressions [of Republicanism] from the childish soul."[23]

To effect the changes they wanted, the Nationalists immediately tackled the two educational issues they found most distressing during the Repub- licans' tenure: coeducation and secularization. Without delay they sup- pressed coeducation, something they had found threatening to children's morality. Additionally, they reinstated religious education, making the precepts of Catholicism and religious history mandatory subjects for all students.[24] The new schools would be run with militaristic precision and discipline, to achieve the "ideal continuation of today's trenches."[25]

By 1938 Franco's government, with a functioning bureaucracy, was firmly entrenched in Burgos. The Ministry of National Education, headed by Pedro Sáinz Rodríguez, reorganized the educational system along Nationalist lines. On May 19, 1938, Sáinz Rodríguez created the Instituto de España as a government body for the stimulation and dissemination of "high" culture and research. By September of that same year, the Nation- alists revoked the educational licenses of all teachers in the Republican zone who had attained their teaching credentials any time between July 18, 1936, and the Nationalist "liberation" of their respective cities.[26]

The battlefront also saw its share of educational proselytizing. Falangist organizations such as the National Delegation of Assistance to the Fronts and Hospitals and the Sección Femenina (the women's subservient coun- terpart to the Falange) carried out much of this work. They visited the trenches and hospitals, disseminated information about hygiene, organized cultural talks, showed films, and performed plays, while at the same time they provided the soldiers with material goods such as clothing, food, and presents to keep up morale. The Ministry of National Education also did its part to educate wounded soldiers. Like the Republicans, the National-ists tried to provide wounded soldiers with the rudiments of literacy and the morale-boosting benefits of theater and film, but, unlike their ene-mies, they emphasized religion and patriotism as the backbone holding Spain together.[27]

Finally, to ensure that Spaniards would have a ready supply of ideo-logical shock troops to carry out the moral and cultural reformation of Spain, the Falange organized paramilitary-type youth groups known as the Frente de Juventudes (Youth Front) and the Sección Femenina (Fem-inine Section)[28] to carry out the Nationalist Crusade. These organizations developed a highly stratified command structure that separated youths into three different age groups. They supplied youths with uniforms and instructed them in military, physical, and moral virtues. These virtues included loyalty to Franco, the Falange, and the Christian faith; the exal-tation of Spain and its imperial traditions and, for girls, the values of domesticity, maternity, and selflessless.[29] Once the war ended with the victory of Franco's forces, these youth organizations became thoroughly institutionalized and served as conduits of cultural unification for Nation-alist ideologies.

As we have seen, both the Nationalists and Republicans sought to attain a unity that had been elusive for approximately the last three centuries by exposing Spaniards to their particular visions of Spanish culture. The ferocity of the Civil War—a war painted strictly in black and white strokes that implied that Spain's fate lay in the hands of its victors—made this quest seem even more urgent than before. The Nationalists fought for an imperial Spain reminiscent of Ferdinand and Isabel, a Spain that was politically and religiously unified under the crown and centered in Castile. Social tensions would be alleviated by a strong authority figure ready to implement a corporatist-type government and a powerful church willing to reinforce its doctrines in the educational sphere. Republicans, at least at the beginning of the war, sought to shape a liberal state based in Castile, free from the shackles of what they considered to be strong religious interference, and they believed they could achieve this goal in great part by exposing uneducated peasants and workers to the varied arts of the Spanish canon. As the war escalated and came more directly under Soviet rule, the cultural projects became geared toward more revolutionary ends, following the agitprop path of the Soviet Union.

## MISIONES PEDAGÓGICAS

The Misiones Pedagógicas had already begun to lose steam during 1935 when the Confederación Española de Derechas Autónomas (CEDA) dominated Cortes, opposed to what they considered to be the extremely leftist character of these projects, drastically cut the Misiones' budget. The misioneros continued to work, albeit sparingly, during 1935 and spring 1936, but they lacked the funds to continue to labor as extensively as they had in their heyday of 1932–1934. They also lost their spiritual guide when Manuel B. Cossío died on September 2, 1935.

Just one week after the war began, Alejandro Casona and Eduardo Torner reassembled the Misiones with fourteen teams composed of three misioneros each to visit various kindergartens in Madrid and entertain the children with gramophones, film, songs, readings, and drawings. Because of wartime conditions, the misioneros could no longer work in the countryside, and thus they limited their scope to Madrid, where they cheered up the wounded brought to the hospitals. Students of both sexes still composed the bulk of the misioneros, but as the men began to go to the front, they were replaced by women.[30]

During the first two months of the war, at least, the misioneros performed works of the Spanish classic theater and sang folk songs. But a few indications that their program had become more radicalized began to surface. For example, by way of introducing the work of the Misiones, Casona explained how the students of Madrid had toured four hundred villages in the last four years to bring these programs to the people; now he overtly injected politics into his speech, adding that the students were working "with the same eagerness to fight against the rebellion" as the rest of Madrid. But even more telling was the group sing-along. Instead of leading the group to sing the "Himno de Riego"—the quintessential song of Republicanism—as they had done countless times before, they sang the "valiant and solemn" "International."[31]

As the Republican government moved further to the left, the work of the Misiones Pedagógicas dissipated to some degree. Many of the functions that earlier were relegated solely to the Misiones were now channeled into other avenues that presented more radical viewpoints. The libraries of the Misiones, for example, fell under the umbrella of the Consejo Central de

Archivos, Bibliotecas y Tesoro Artístico. In October 1936 the Republicans required the Misiones Pedagógicas to have a "Section of Cultural Propaganda" to "organize, direct, and control all of the cultural and artistic activities aimed at strengthening the fighting spirit of the people in the fight against the enemy of the Republic and to popularize with every means the heroic gesture of the Spanish people." The aims of the Misiones Pedagogicas had changed drastically. No longer were the misioneros mere cultural emissaries bringing the fruits of "civilized culture" to ignorant peasants in remote parts of Spain; now they were responsible for strengthening the troops' morale and glorifying the heroic efforts of the Republican fighters. Eventually, the Misiones Pedagógicas (what little remained of the organizational structure) changed their name to the Misiones Culturales and performed in conjunction with the Brigadas Volantes on the home front.[32]

Interestingly enough, the Nationalists created their own form of the Misiones Pedagógicas under the auspices of the Organización Hispana Circumlabor (OHC), an organization created in 1937 to enrich workers' lives by teaching them skills and ideas unrelated to their day-to-day jobs. The OHC and its various components sought to make workers well rounded and to restore to them "the collective expressions that are a product of tradition (festivals, folklore, pilgrimages, etc.)." The group launched a three-pronged program encompassing (1) spiritual education and cultural diffusion, (2) physical education, and (3) social assistance and health. Under the category of "spiritual education and cultural diffusion," the OHC would teach workers art and morals, song and dance, radio, film, theater, patriotic sentiment, "professional perfection" (technical education), and "cultural perfection" (liberal arts education). Under the "art and morals" section, for example, workers would learn about their relationship to popular art and literature by visiting museums of regional art or participating in village festivals or national festivals such as the Día de la Raza (Day of the Race, or Columbus Day) and Dos de Mayo (May 2nd, independence from the French). By extension, it was thought that they would then acquire profound feelings of patriotism because they could see that they were an integral part of Spain's culture and history.[33]

Thus, like the Misiones Pedagógicas, the OHC presumed it could create a collective spirit if the people believed they had a common cultural base. The Nationalists, however, focused on the *völkisch* and Catholic aspects of Spanish culture, whereas the Republicans, although not ignoring these *völkisch* contributions, tended to concentrate on "high," canonized culture as the savior of Spain that would link the cities and the countryside. After the war's end, the Nationalists were able to reorganize the "antinational," "Marxist," and "foreign" Misiones Pedagógicas and change them into a Patronato de Cultura Popular to "bring the spirit of the National Glorious Movement to all the villages of Spain, making them feel the unity, as well as the discipline and loyalty to the Caudillo, Saviour of Spain."[34]

## THEATER

The culture-shapers on both sides of the battlefield still clung to the notion that theater represented the spirit of the people and that, if done properly, it could educate the masses. As one writer sympathetic to the Republicans during the Civil War put it: "Who can deny the great importance of the theater as an instrument of teaching? That which man contemplates with admiration he will tend later to imitate, and our soldiers—simple peasants, workers—feel true admiration for the theater, as they do for all forms of culture."[35] Artists and propagandists on both sides of the ideological divide fancied theater as one of the best avenues to consolidate and shape opinion and, therefore, theatrical troupes flourished during the war. On the Republican side, the theater of the Misiones Pedagógicas and La Barraca, though still functioning at a minimal level, gave way to more radical, propagandistic theater aimed at stirring the sentiments of antifascism in the working classes.[36] The Nationalists also sought to capture the hearts and minds of the working classes, but they chose theatrical pieces that emphasized patriotism and religion or light operas such as the popular zarzuelas.

Although La Barraca continued to function at the beginning of the war, the assassination of its principal founder, García Lorca, in August 1936 dampened the troupe's spirits and movements. The most fertile and active source of Republican theater came not out of La Barraca or the Misiones Pedagógicas, but out of work done by the Alliance of Antifascist Intellectuals. The alliance poured many intellectual resources into creating "theaters of urgency" and "guerrillas" to inspire the soldiers at the front and the citizens at home with revolutionary doctrines. One of the first theatrical troupes borne out of the alliance, headed by Rafael Alberti and María Teresa León, was called Nueva Escena. The set pieces for each performance included one contemporary piece of theater that could "exercise a healthy influence over the people in the present circumstances" and one (generally) classic work that exemplified "the liveliest dramatic literature."[37] The company performed in public squares and villages, and writers such as Alberti, Altolaguirre, Bergamín, Dieste, and Chabás provided much material for Nueva Escena, pledging to write one entremés per week (although this never actually happened).[38]

One example of this type of theater was written by Rafael Dieste. Dieste, who originally ran the puppet shows for the Misiones Pedagógicas, drew from the Spanish literary canon to write a modern day version of Cervantes' entremés, *El retablo de las maravillas,* with a decidedly anti-Nationalist bent. In Cervantes' work, a husband and wife team and a hired helper go from village to village to con the wealthy and powerful residents. They advertise themselves as a troupe that has studied under the great magicians of Europe. They brag that they will show spectators magical sights. They warn, however, that only those who are legitimate and who are free of Jewish blood will be able to see the spectacle; otherwise, the show will appear invisible. The trio also asks to be paid in advance. When the show begins, the members of the audience pretend to see grand spectacles for fear of being thought of as illegitimate or Jewish, and thus losing their standing within the community. When a real military regiment enters the town, the audience believes the trio is continuing to create frightening illusions, and they tell the trio to stop. The trio manages to leave with their money before they are discovered as frauds.

Dieste's modern version, *El nuevo retablo de las maravillas,* is set in an unnamed village in Civil War Spain. The defrauded characters are the general, the gentleman, and the priest. Instead of being skilled at magic like the trio in Cervantes' work, this trio uses science to perpetuate the idea that they can create wondrous illusions. Those who cannot see the wonders before them are those "who have been touched by Marxism, syndicalism, anarchism, and other plagues."[39] The plot remained essentially the same, except that the audience thinks that Nationalist soldiers have conquered Madrid. The poor people in the village know that this is all an illusion, and the play ends with milicianos entering the village. Everybody sings the "International" at the end.

Works such as Dieste's helped Nueva Escena pave the way for other theatrical organizations linked with the Alliance of Antifascist Intellectuals and Jesús Hernández's Ministry of Education. The one that probably received the greatest fame was El Teatro de Arte y Propaganda, headed by María Teresa León. An outgrowth of Nueva Escena, the Teatro de Arte y Propaganda shared a common heritage with García Lorca's La Barraca. Discussing the upcoming creation of María Teresa León's new theater,

Juan Chabás, like many critics before him, waxed eloquently about "the splendid tradition of the Spanish theater" which was "essentially popular." He said that Republican officials were beginning to realize that the Spanish theater was "a national treasure, an essential element of [Spanish] culture," as well as an expression of the passions and heroism they found expressed in their own lives. "Our great classic theater," he said, "is a heroic theater. It is the expression of popular, collective heroism." Therefore, the theater that people needed to see, the theater that most represented the ideals for which Republican soldiers gave their lives, was the classic theater of people (once again) such as Calderón, Lope, and Cervantes, not the "counterrevolutionary" and "fascist" works that spectators often saw in the cities.[40] The Teatro de Arte y Propaganda, therefore, revived the classic works that could best be adapted to the revolutionary spirit of the Republican forces, works such as *Fuenteovejuna* and Cervantes' *Numancia*. They also supplemented their repertoire with works by such non-Spaniards as Twain and Schniztler.[41] Although some of the plays remained relatively untouched, others, such as Alberti's adaptation of *Numancia*, were adapted to fit contemporary circumstances. In Cervantes' play about Spanish resistance to the encroaching Roman Empire, Alberti turned the Romans into "Italians," thus highlighting the Republican struggle against Mussolini's forces.[42]

Another troupe closely linked to the Alliance of Antifascist Intellectuals and the Teatro de Arte y Propaganda was the Guerrillas de Teatro. The Guerrillas, supported by the Ministry of Education, wrote short, polemical pieces that they performed on the war front and in factories. The playwrights wrote pieces meant to educate, to stimulate "anti-Fascist" sentiments and, at the same time, to entertain.[43] Originally each Guerrilla troupe contained fifteen people, with one artistic and political advisor and one administrator. According to an article describing their proposed mission, the Guerrillas would perform short pieces—about twenty minutes each—in the open air and in small gatherings. Not only would they perform political works, but also they would incorporate snippets of classic theater, sticking to short pieces such as entremeses, pasos, and *sainetes* (one-act farces), and to popular songs and dances, without falling into the trap of creating "variety shows." They required that their songs and dances reflect a "popular or revolutionary" spirit.[44]

Finally, the Republican side performed ad hoc theater like *Cuatro batallones de choque* (Four shock battalions) as a way to change the outcome of the war, and they used methods already tried in the Soviet Union to

achieve their goals. The performers, members of the Communist Quinto
Regimiento, hoped to enlist two thousand men in eight days to go to the
front. As the Nationalists were trying to enter Madrid, the troupe performed on the backs of trucks in various neighborhoods and factory
exits in the city. In a pamphlet describing their work, the Quinto Regimiento justified why they performed these plays: "This is the first time
that this type of propaganda and these performances, so extensive and
effective in the Soviet Union, have been tried in Spain.... The Quinto
Regimiento could not ignore such an effective medium as the theater for
its propaganda."[45]

In this play, there are eight characters: a fat, bourgeois man, who
dresses up in working-class clothing; an artist, who needs tranquility to
work; a working-class couple, who believe that they do not need to be
politically involved in the war; a young lady and her "parasitic" gentleman
boyfriend; and a working-class couple, who are enlisted in the Batallones
de Choque and who learn how to use arms during their nonworking
hours. The play takes place literally and figuratively during the defense
of Madrid. The bourgeois man and the artist complain about how the war
is damaging their ability to do work during wartime, but they are not
actively involved in fighting the Fascists. The members of the Batallones
de Choque scold the passive workers for not enlisting or learning to use
arms for the defense of Madrid. "All who do not work at these times for
the war is a Fascist," they are told. They ask the artist what he does, and he
says that he gives free painting classes to children of the milicianos. They
chide him: "The children of the milicianos need you to defend them from
the Fascists," and they tell him that he should be digging trenches instead.
The play ends with the enlisted workers admonishing the people to fight
in the streets and to enlist: "You don't have to abandon your occupations.
We will teach you how to use arms in the hours that are compatible with
your work schedule." According to a caption under a photo taken during
a performance, the public and the artists sang the "International" (again!)
at the end of the performance.[46] This theater eliminated any pretense of
educating through metaphorical tales and, instead, used spare, obvious
drama to present clear messages to its audiences about how they should
act in wartime.

One would expect that the heart of revolutionary Spain—Barcelona—
would be teeming with revolutionary theater. Much to the dismay of
many people, this was not the case. At the beginning of the war, the CNT
nationalized the theater and hoped to create a revolutionary theater along

the lines of those by Piscator and Brecht. But although the theater was collectivized, performers still acted in the same zarzuelas and melodramas that had been playing in Barcelona for years. Piscator actually came to visit the revolutionary city in December 1936 and was appalled that the theater had not been revolutionized: "My fundamental idea is that culture and art cannot remain inactive in a historic moment as important as that in which Catalonia and Spain have entered after the revolution.... Theatrical art, above all, is a weapon."[47] But the CNT was never really successful in organizing a new theater, in part because members struggled with the UGT over control of the theater.

Republican theater in both its traditional and agitprop forms flourished with the aid of committed intellectuals and artists who believed in theater's redemptive qualities. Nationalists, by contrast, lagged considerably behind the Republicans in terms of theatrical output and creativity. Part of the imbalance stemmed, once again, from the Republicans' control of Spain's major cities, the burgeoning of avant-garde theater during the Republic, and the Republicans' ability to garner the sympathy and loyalty of a greater number of intellectuals and artists.

Many of the Nationalists' theatrical activities occurred under the auspices of the Organización Hispana Circumlabor (see above). Like the Republicans, the Nationalists thought that theater was a great vehicle for the education of the masses. They opted to choose or write works that promoted a "national and patriotic sentiment" and that could be adapted to the problems of contemporary society. They focused their attention on comedies and the zarzuela because of their popular appeal and, employing the same tactics as the Republicans, launched their own versions of the farándula in village squares.[48]

Some Nationalist intellectuals such as Dionisio Ridruejo and Gonzalo Torrente Ballestar, who were just as dissatisfied as their Republican counterparts with the state of Spanish contemporary theater, pushed for theatrical renovation and experimentation. Ridruejo, who became the Nationalist head of the Ministry of Press and Propaganda after 1938, said that "the theater should rise up like a belligerant in the field of ideas ... to seize the explosions of patriotism that have been left as an expression of the reconquest of the glorious Spanish people."[49] Torrente Ballester, in words reminiscent of Giménez Caballero's film criticism, viewed theater as a religious spectacle and dreamed that it would function as the "Liturgy of Empire."[50]

The Nationalists had fewer original dramas to work with than the

Republicans because the majority of intellectuals had joined the Republican cause. They therefore relied excessively on the talents of just a few writers, such as José María Pemán, a member of Acción Española and head of the Comisión de Cultura, who wrote works such as *De ellos es el mundo* that glorified the Falange and *La Santa Virreina*, which justified the benevolent colonization of Latin America in contradistinction to the Black Legend of Spain's colonial rapaciousness.[51]

As one would expect, playwrights sympathetic to the Nationalists wrote plays that denigrated the Republican cause and elevated the Nationalists as heroes of a national crusade. Sotero Otero del Pozo's play *España inmortal* (Immortal Spain) was first performed in Palencia on December 12, 1936, while Nationalist troops were very close to entering Madrid. The play is a melodrama about leftists who see the evil of their ways and convert to fascism. Husband and wife, Blas and Rita are syndicalists who want a better Spain for workers. They have a daughter named Conchita, who, much to their chagrin, is seeing a Falangist named Federico. Conchita is also the goddaughter of Doña Concha, a middle-class friend of Blas and Rita. Blas and Rita are hiding syndicalists Eugenio and Juan, who seem to have been involved with the assassination of Calvo Sotelo. On the eve of the war, Eugenio and Juan and some Assault Guards arrest Federico under false pretenses. Blas goes off to war, while Rita is off in hiding. Conchita stays in Madrid with her godmother. Federico escapes from prison and joins the war; Blas is blinded during the war, but by being blinded, he begins to see. He realizes that he was fighting against the true Spain and that Marxism had nothing to offer workers. Rita also reverts back to the Catholic faith she once renounced. The play ends with everybody embracing fascism and with the Nationalist soldiers entering Madrid.[52]

Another play, *En la España que amanece* (In the Spain that dawns), written by Dr. Dalópio, reflected the unification of the Carlists and Falangists that Franco had engineered to strengthen the Nationalist cause. First performed in Avila, the play contained the expected characters: Doña Maria, a widow whose husband was shot in Madrid; Don Pompeyo, an ex-lieutenant colonel; Elisa, María's daughter; Fermín, a Carlist Requeté and María's son; Jacobo, a young merchant who has not been to the front and Elisa's boyfriend; Raquel, Jacobo's sister; Maruso, a Falangist from Galicia; and Juan de Diós, a refugee who had been trapped behind enemy lines in Madrid. In this play everybody is waiting for Fermín to come home from the front. They all praise the efforts of the Nationalists, but Jacobo has not gone to the front, and everybody makes him feel ashamed for not doing so. He and his sister say that he needs to stay home and take care of his business. By the time Fermín comes home, accompanied by his Falangist friend, everybody has convinced Jacobo that he needs to serve his country. Elena is now very happy that she is going to marry somebody who is not a coward. The play is peppered with choruses of "Arriba España" and "Arriba Franco."

The play has its requisite anti-Bolshevism and inclusive nationalism. When Raquel asks Elisa how she has the stomach for visiting wounded soldiers in the hospital, Elisa responds: "You have to see them up close and treat them to be convinced about how good our soldiers are, how good our sons of Spain are. The strength and seriousness of the Castilian, the sweetness of the Galician, the good manners of the Canary Islander, the bravery of the Navarran, the sympathetic nature of the Andalusian or Extremaduran.... Out of curiousity one day, I asked a soldier what he defended in the war since he didn't have anything. Do you know what he said? That he defended his name. That his name was Pérez and that all of the Pérezes had to go to war so that Spain continued to be the Spain of the Pérezes and not of the Lenins and Stalins."[53] In another scene designed to show the unity of Nationalist Spain, Jacobo asks Juan de Diós, "Are you a Falangist or a Requeté?" He answers: "I am Spanish ... and in Madrid nobody distinguishes between classes of Spanish soldiers. There there is nothing more than our soldiers, those who were united before, persecuted later, and ready now and always."[54]

Despite a penchant for melodrama, the Nationalists also resourcefully revived more traditional forms of Spanish theater, concentrating their efforts on resuscitating the auto sacramental. Nationalist intellectuals used the auto as a way to rekindle religious fervor and unity within the community. One Nationalist intellectual, Manuel Machado (brother of Republican Antonio Machado), for example, described the auto as a "mixture of poetic fiction" and religiosity that signified a "marvelous synthesis" of the "Spanish soul returning to its traditional religious fervor and to the Church."[55] Although this portrayal sounds very much like García Lorca's characterization of the Mass as the greatest form of theater (see chapter 3), it leaves out one essential difference: the Nationalists revived the auto because it was a *Catholic* solution for creating unity. Additionally, the auto harked back to a time when politics and religion worked together as one entity. As Ridruejo so well described a rendering of an auto he had recently seen: "The theater and the religious function have been made into one thing, as if we were [living] in the seventeenth century."[56] And although the seventeenth century saw the decline of Spanish power, it did correspond to the apex of the Counter-Reformation. Perhaps the Nationalists viewed the auto sacramental as symbolic of their own desire to impose a form of the Counter-Reformation in Republican Spain.

## FILM

For both Republicans and Nationalists, film played a highly propagandistic role. They used film either to garner foreign support for their respective causes or to shore up the morale of the troops and citizens at home. Scholars writing about this period agree that because they were stationed in the cities that housed the big film studios—Madrid and Barcelona—the Republicans employed film more readily than the Nationalists.[57] Because the political makeup of the wartime Republican government was further to the left than any cabinet during the period of the Second Republic, wartime Republicans chose more radical films to show the public. Nationalists, in contrast, did their best to prevent people from seeing films that might disturb their moral character.

Under the Ministry of Propaganda, later to become the Spanish Cinema of the Subsecretary of Propaganda (headed by film critic and writer Manuel Villegas-López) Republicans began producing and financing newsreels, documentary films, and agitprop trailers both for export and for Republican consumption. Luis Buñuel and Jean Paul Le Chanois made one of the most famous films for the Republican cause, *España 1936* (also known as *Loyal Spain in Arms*). In the hopes of enlisting foreign aid, the directors chronicled in documentary fashion the perceived ideals of the Republic—democracy, peace, et cetera.—and the eventual quashing of Republican freedom by Franco's antidemocratic, Fascist forces. As the war progressed, Republicans, realizing that they would not be receiving any foreign aid outside of the International Brigades, began making and distributing short films that emphasized the valor and bravery of Republican fighters. One film historian argues that as the war continued one can see that the types of films commissioned responded to the needs of the Republican war effort. *España 1936* (1936) represented Republican attempts to show the world the righteousness of the Republican cause. *Madrid* (director and writer Villegas-López, 1937), which portrays the struggle of Madrid's residents as they are bombarded by Nationalist, German, and Italian bombs, showcased the bravery of Madrileños and was intended to give Republicans hope to continue the long fight. Finally, when trying to broker a peace with Franco in May 1938 (Franco had by this time split the Republican zone into two), Negrín outlined a series of accords that Republicans could live with. The Republican government tried to disseminate this information to the general populace in the film *Los trece puntos de la victoria* (The thirteen points of victory; 1938).[58]

In addition to the films produced specifically for the war effort, Republicans also relied on films imported from the Soviet Union. *Battleship Potemkin, October, Chapayev,* and the *Sailors of Kronstadt* made their ways around the cities and trenches. The most popular film in the Republican trenches was *Chapayev* (1934) by the Vasiliev brothers. The story of the brave soldier Chapayev fighting counterrevolutionary forces was supposed to inspire Republican soldiers to resist their Fascist enemies. It is even said that the "invocation of Chapayev in the [battle of] Jarama produced a temporary recovery [of strength] in the Republican troops."[59]

Although Nationalists were just as capable as Republicans of wielding the camera in a propagandistic fashion, their cinematographic output was less prolific. Nationalists had to rely on film studios in Portugal, Germany, and Italy to produce works that reflected Nationalist ideology. Italian filmmakers, for example, documented the first Nationalist victories in such films as *Liberazione di Málaga, Liberazione di Bilbao,* and *Liberazione di Gijón.*[60] They also cleverly used films shot by the enemy to rally like-minded people to the Nationalist cause. For example, they distributed the anarchist film *Report of the Revolutionary Movement,* which, with its convent burnings, looting, and chaos, documented the early days of the revolution in Barcelona. The Nationalists now had a cautionary tale to warn people about what would happen if the "Reds" won the war.

Although the Nationalists did not set up a centralized authority in charge of distributing and producing film until 1938, Falangists and Carlists had already made a series of films meant to chronicle Nationalist victories and to inspire Nationalist sympathizers. Between 1936 and 1938 the Falange Española made seven films: *Heart and Nerve of Spain: Arriba España; The Reconquest of the Patria: Encirclement and Bombing of Madrid; The Conquistadores of the North: Homage to the Navarre Brigades; The Viscayan Front and the 18th of July; The War for Peace; Will;* and *National Council of the Sección Femenina.* The Carlists made two: *With the Navarre Brigades* and *The Taking of Bilbao.*[61]

The Nationalists' strength, however, lay not in filmmaking, but in censorship, where they edited newsreels from abroad that denigrated the Nationalists' efforts, or they refused to show films that might disturb the populace's morals, politics, or patriotism.[62] Even before the Nationalists established their government in Burgos (1938), they had already set up censorship bureaus in Seville and La Coruña. Headed by high-ranking members of the clergy and the Catholic Confederation of the Fathers of the Family (the same people responsible for the journal *Filmor;* see chapter 4), these censorship bureaus eliminated any films that discussed class struggle or sex. After Franco's hold on Spain became stronger, he eliminated the two bureaus and replaced them with one in Salamanca (November 1937); finally, on April 1, 1938, Franco created a National Department of Cinematography which was centered in Burgos under the direction of the Minister of Propaganda; this department took responsibility for distributing, producing, and censoring films.[63] Once the war ended, Franco institutionalized film censorship.[64]

## LIBRARIES AND LITERACY

Republicans had less success creating libraries than they had had during the Republic, due, of course, to the vicissitudes of war that made planning permanent libraries nearly impossible in areas that might readily fall into enemy hands. On February 16, 1937, the Republicans created a Central Council of Archives, Libraries, and Artistic Treasure under whose care the creation and maintenance of libraries would fall. All of the libraries that had been founded by the Misiones Pedagógicas during the Republic now came under the guidance of this central committee. In the space of thirteen months the council established twenty-eight municipal libraries and fifty-two libraries of the Misiones Pedagógicas.[65] The work of increasing the number of libraries fell to an organization known as La Central de Cultura Popular de Madrid, which began its work in April 1936. Until July 1937, its work was prolific. The organization created a total of 780 libraries, each with approximately 120 books. The great majority of the libraries (610) were established on the Republican military front. The rest were divided among hospitals, nursery schools, and workers' libraries.[66]

But the Republican side could not sustain its library-building momentum. When the Nationalists began capturing Republican-held cities and villages, they purged the libraries of any works that contained "immoral" or "Marxist" ideas or anything that showed "disrespect for the dignity of the glorious [Nationalist] Army, assaults to the unity of the Patria, scorn of the Catholic Religion, and anything that opposes the significance and ends of [Franco's] great National Crusade."[67] They also substantially limited the number and types of books that people were allowed to read. Obviously, as the Nationalists gained more ground during the war, the scope of Republican libraries narrowed substantially.

While Republicans could not marshall great forces behind their libraries, they did launch a strong campaign to wipe out illiteracy. With slogans such as "Soldier: teach your comrade to read. In this way you will be better able to win the war," the Republicans, through such organizations as the Milicias de la Cultura, strove to teach soldiers, peasants, and workers across Republican Spain to read.[68]

The reading lessons occurred in the context of political indoctrination. For example, a teacher might write the phrase "Luchamos por nuestra cultura" (We fight for our culture) and then break the sentence down into its requisite letters and syllables. After that, the teacher played with the syllables or letters found in these words to come up with other words such as "Lenin" or "munitions." Each phrase would then be accompanied by a picture that explained the word. All of the "model sentences" they used to teach soldiers, workers, and peasants to read, such as "Obedience to the legitimate government," "Lenin, our great teacher," and "The land for those who work it," dealt with the Republican struggle against the forces of fascism and reflected the Republicans' close alliance with the Soviet Union.[69]

The Nationalists, in contrast, spent little effort in combating illiteracy. They did create a couple of organizations known as the Service of Readings for the Navy and the Service of Readings for the Soldier, but they did not cast their literacy net as widely as the Republicans.[70] Nevertheless, if a source written by Manuel Ballesteros Gaibrois and sponsored by the Sección Femenina is any indication of how the Nationalists taught literacy, then one can see that their methods differed little from those of the Republicans. Their content, however, reflected the ideals of a Nationalist Spain. The letter "I" stood for Empire *(Imperio)* and "Isabel" (the Catholic queen); "F" was for "Falange" and "Franco."[71] And so were imparted the lessons of patriotism and religion.

The Spanish Civil War ended on April 1, 1939, four days after Franco's troops victoriously entered into Madrid. The Republican defeat marked the end of the Republican hopes for creating a unity based on a program of cultural renewal and the beginning of a new Nationalist vision of Spanish regeneration. The Nationalists thought that their victory on the battlefield earned them the right to transform Spain into a nation whose base would be founded on Catholic and traditionalist values. The ideas espoused by the left would have to remain underground until the death of Franco in 1975.

# Conclusion

THE REPUBLICAN SURRENDER TO NATIONALIST FORCES ON APRIL 1, 1939, ended the Republican experiment to refashion Spain into a modern, unified, liberal state through the instruments of education and culture. Instead, numerous Republican intellectuals and artists went into exile in such disparate places as Mexico, Argentina, the Soviet Union, the United States, England, and France; and many spent the last years of their lives urging governments such as the United States to unseat Franco from power. While exiled Republicans wrote memoirs and ruminated over the failure of the Republic, Franco and his sympathizers spent decades eliminating the traces of Republican ideologies from Spanish consciousness, and sought to force his vision for Spain on the defeated population. Nationalist histories of Spain portrayed Franco as El Cid and the Nationalist forces as Christian soldiers who carried out the modern "Reconquest" of Spain from the twin pillars of atheism and communism. Francoists vilified leftist intellectuals—especially those affiliated with the Institución Libre de Enseñanza—and blamed them for tearing apart the social and religious fabric of Spain.[1]

But although Republican reformers were defeated in the war and lost their chance to steer Spain along a course that might have led to a modern centralized state, their methods of reform were not lost on Franco and his cronies. In fact, although Franco despised the ideologies espoused by leftist Republicans, he and his followers studied the left's methods carefully and co-opted them for their own well-orchestrated campaign of cultural unification, a unity they hoped would one day lead to a Spain that was "Una, grande y libre."[2]

Around 1945, for example, the Instituto San José de Calasanz, located where the Residencia de Estudiantes once stood, organized teachers to travel around the countryside for a week and participate in a newly reconstituted Misiones Pedagógicas. Instead of beginning the sessions with the Republican anthem, "El himno de Riego," the Nationalist misioneros began with a Mass. They offered discussions on religion, pedagogy, science, literature, geography, history and patriotic formation, art, folklore, and popular crafts, and quoted the goals of the Republican Misiones almost verbatim: they sought the "elevation of the cultural level of the peoples of Spain" and desired to "establish reciprocal relations between the life of the city and the life of the countryside."[3] Instead of recruiting students and poets to act as cultural emissaries, the organizers sought professionals including priests, professors, teachers, engineers, doctors, and agricultural consultants. The misioneros still donated libraries to rural villages, but the subject matter, which included "history and works of Spanish thought" and "religious culture," differed from that of the previous libraries.[4] Clearly, the Franco regime respected the form, but not the content, of the earlier Misiones Pedagógicas. Similarly, the Social Auxiliary of the Falangist Sección Femenina copied the Republican methods and created their own form of the Misiones Pedagógicas known as Cátedras Ambulantes (Peripatetic Professors).

Because the Franco regime spent the thirty-six years following the Civil War reviling its former enemies and trying to quash any remnants of Republican or Socialist thought in the Spanish populace, it is difficult for the historian to evaluate the Republican era without looking through the historical prism of the Civil War and Francoism. In other words, can we judge the effectiveness of the Republican–Socialist coalition's efforts to create cultural unity when the Republic lasted only five years? On the surface, we would have to say that, given the short tenure of the Republic and the subsequent victory of Franco, the cultural programs launched by the Republican–Socialist coalition were a resounding failure.

But that is too simple an answer. Perhaps if we rephrased the question and embarked on the historian's favorite game of "what if?" we might glean some useful insights: What if the Republicans had won the war and had been able to continue the policies they had begun in 1931 (let us pretend, for a moment, that the radicalization of cultural policies by Republicans during the war had not actually occurred)? Would they have built the foundations of a national revival as they had dreamed?

Given enough time and money, they might have been able to mold

Spaniards into Castilians on the one hand and Europeans on the other, especially if they had concentrated their efforts on the educational system. In France, for example, the Third Republic was quite successful in creating an educational infrastructure that was highly centralized and that closely mirrored the precepts of Republicanism.[5] But there were at least two problems inherent in the Spanish case that make this a flawed comparison: the Republican–Socialist coalition's wish to accommodate regionalist aspirations, and the speed with which they hoped to accomplish their mission.

At first, disparate groups of the left had reason to be optimistic about reforming Spain. When a coalition of Republican, Socialist, and Catalan nationalist leaders signed the Pact of San Sebastian in August 1930, they vowed to establish a Republic. Less then one year later, their plans came to fruition. But once the Republic came into being, the coalition's differences began to overshadow their commonalities, and their ability to create a unified culture by orchestrating consent diminished as problems multiplied during the Republic. For example, the Republicans and Socialists involved in such programs as the Misiones Pedagógicas sought to walk a fine line between presenting a national culture represented by Castile and maintaining a respect for regional cultures. Like today's pundits who debate the question of cultural pluralism in the United States, cultural reformers in Spain faced a quandary when trying to decide how to present Spain's history and its culture to a diverse population with markedly different educational and economic levels. Moreover, there were other actors in the cultural sphere who resisted the attempts of the central government to Castilianize the rest of Spain. If the coalition had been able to continue their programs, they would have had to contend seriously with these regionalist aspirations.

The more pressing problems for Republicans and Socialists, however, was the speed with which they carried out their reforms. When at the beginning of the Republic Manuel Azaña declared that "Spain was no longer Catholic," he underestimated the tenaciousness with which many Spaniards still held their Catholic convictions. The early Republicans' virulent anticlerical policies, especially those that dissolved the religious orders and secularized the educational system, alienated many of the people who were supposed to have been welcomed into the Republican fold. But the reforms of the early Republic did not go far enough or take place fast enough for the anarchists. Given the tricky nature of the coalition, whereby some members believed that Spain needed to undergo revolutionary changes while others preferred a more reformist path, we can see the opposition they would have faced from their opponents on the far right and far left.

Ironically, what may have impeded the progress of Republican-Socialist cultural policies the most was the form of the government itself, namely, liberal democracy. The very nature of liberal democracy presupposes that because they are subject to debate and ratification, policies emerge gradually out of the system through consensus. Therefore, the rapidity with which Republicans and Socialists sought to impose a transformation on Spain could not occur under the auspices of a Republic. Although Spanish intellectuals may have admired the Soviet and Mexican models of political and cultural revolution, they were constrained by the operation of parliamentary politics. That is why, I think, the more radical Republican cultural policies were implemented during the crisis of war.

But the Second Republic did fall at the end of the war, and with it fell the aspirations of at least two generations of intellectuals. Although we cannot really gauge the overall effectiveness of Republican cultural policies on the general population, the period still provides the historian with rich material to study the role that Spanish intellectuals played in fashioning a new vision for the nation. Given the European context into which Spain tried to reinsert itself—the postwar malaise, world depression, and rise of authoritarian and totalitarian governments—the idea that a newly formed Republic with few financial resources was able to survive for any length of time is in itself extraordinary.

And if we look at Franco's legacy, we realize that his attempts to unify the nation under a Castilian and Catholic banner had very little to do with orchestrating consent, and had much more to do with wielding force. The Franco regime became adept at propagating an ideology known as National-Catholicism, but it was always maintained and enforced with the support of violence. Civic institutions, as Gramsci would have defined them—the church and labor unions, for example—could not serve as independent arenas to nurture a counterhegemonic culture, for these institutions no longer existed as entities separate from the state.

After Franco's death in 1975, support for National Catholicism was thin. Just three years later, the Constitution of 1978 established seventeen autonomous communities within the framework of the sovereign state of Spain and it eliminated Catholicism as the official state religion. Although the continued threat of Basque-separatist terrorism demonstrates that the "national problem" has not been completely eliminated from Spain, most people there have reached accommodation with the state, living in a country that promotes both unity and plurality.

Perhaps if leaders of the Second Republic had not had to contend with so many different problems in such a short span of time, they might have been inventive enough to develop programs that celebrated the diversity of regional cultures within the framework of a unified state. Instead, they offended the right by insisting on the primacy of Castilian culture devoid of religion, and they offended regionalists by insisting on the primacy of Castilian culture over regional ones. Unfortunately, it would take over forty years, punctuated by violence and repression, before regional cultures could exist peacefully alongside one another.

Notes

Bibliography

Index

# NOTES

## Introduction

1. There are now works that seek to challenge the monolothic interpretations of fascist and Bolshevik culture. For example, see Marla Stone, *The Patron State: Culture and Politics in Fascist Italy* (Princeton, NJ: Princeton University Press, 1998); Lynn Mally, *Culture of the Future: The Proletkult Movement in Revolutionary Russia* (Berkeley: University of California Press, 1990); and James von Geldern, *Bolshevik Festivals, 1917–1920* (Berkeley: University of California Press, 1993). In contrast with these regimes-in-process, the established French Third Republic faced cultural challenges from marginalized political groups. As Herman Lebovics argues, "From the turn of the twentieth century, when the new leaders of the Third Republic seemed to have succeeded in consolidating a new polity, to at least 1945, the key move of the discontented right was to avoid politics by shifting its ground—and the field of contestation—to culture." Herman Lebovics, *True France: The Wars over Cultural Identity, 1900–1945* (Ithaca, NY: Cornell University Press, 1992), xii–xiii.

2. The first major book to look at cultural studies in Spain is Helen Graham and Jo Labanyi, eds., *Spanish Cultural Studies: An Introduction* (Oxford: Oxford University Press, 1995). A small sampling of cultural histories that influenced my work include Peter Jelavich, *Berlin Cabaret* (Cambridge: Harvard University Press, 1993); Mally, *Culture of the Future;* Michael P. Steinburg, *The Meaning of the Salzburg Festival: Austria as Theater and Ideology, 1890–1938* (Ithaca, NY: Cornell University Press, 1990); Debora Silverman, *Art Nouveau in Fin de Siècle France: Politics, Psychology, and Style* (Berkeley: University of California Press, 1989); and Carl E. Schorske, *Fin de Siècle Vienna* (New York: Vintage Books, 1981).

3. On education during the Second Republic, see, for example, Mercedes Samaniego Boneu, *La política educativa en la Segunda República durante el bienio azañista* (Madrid: Consejo Superior de Investigaciones Científicas, 1977); Mariano Pérez Galán, *La enseñanza en la Segunda República española* (Madrid: Editorial

Cuadernos para el Diálogo, 1975); Manuel de Puelles Benítez, *Educación e ideología en la España contemporánea,* 2d ed. (Barcelona: Editorial Labor, 1986); Fernando Millán, *La revolución laica: De la Institución Libre de Enseñanza a la escuela de la República* (Valencia: Fernando Torres, 1983); Antonio Molero Pintado, *La reforma educativa de la Segunda República: Primer bienio* (Madrid: Santillana, 1977); Carlos Alba Tercedor, "La educación en la Segunda República: Un intento de socialización política," in Manuel Ramírez, ed., *Estudios sobre la Segunda República española* (Madrid: Editorial Tecnos, 1975), 49–85. On the role of intellectuals in the Republic, see Javier Tusell and Genoveva G. Queipo de Llano, *Los intelectuales y la República* (Madrid: Nerea, 1990); Jean Bécarud and Evelyne López Campillo, *Los intelectuales españoles durante la Segunda República* (Madrid: Siglo Veintiuno, 1978).

4. Christopher H. Cobb, *La cultura y el pueblo: España, 1930–1939* (Barcelona: Editorial Laia, 1980); Manuel Tuñón de Lara, *Medio siglo de cultura española (1885–1936)* (Madrid: Editorial Tecnos, 1977) 3d ed. The groundwork in Spanish cultural history is beginning to be laid, however. The most recent attempts to bridge this gap between Spanish cultural history and other European cultural histories are David T. Gies, ed., *The Cambridge Companion to Modern Spanish Culture* (Cambridge: Cambridge University Press, 1999) and Graham and Labanyi, *Spanish Cultural Studies.* Pamela Radcliff also looks at political culture in Gijón in *From Mobilization to Civil War: The Politics of Polarization in the Spanish City of Gijón, 1900–1937* (Cambridge: Cambridge University Press, 1996). Other works in Spanish cultural history include Eduardo Huertas Vázquez, *La política cultural de la Segunda República española* (Madrid: Ministerio de Cultura, 1988); J. L. García Delgado, ed., *Los orígenes culturales de la Segunda República* (Madrid: Siglo Veintiuno, 1993); and *II Comunicación, cultura y política durante la Segunda República y la Guerra Civil: Encuentro de Historia de Prensa.* Bilbao: Departamento de Cultura, Diputación Foral de Bizkaia: Servicio Editorial, Universidad del País Vasco, 1990.

5. See, for example, Carolyn Boyd, *Historia Patria: Politics, History, and National Identity in Spain, 1875–1975* (Princeton, NJ: Princeton University Press, 1997); Clare Mar-Molinero and Angel Smith, eds., *Nationalism and the Nation in the Iberian Peninsula: Competing and Conflicting Ideologies* (Washington, DC: Berg, 1996); Inman Fox, *La invención de España: Nacionalismo liberal e identidad nacional* (Madrid: Cátedra, 1997); Justo G. Beramendi and Ramón Máiz, eds., *Los nacionalismos en la España de la Segunda República* (Madrid: Siglo Veintiuno, 1991); and Andrés de Blas Guerrero, *Tradición republicana y nacionalismo español (1876–1930)* (Madrid: Tecnos, 1991).

6. Helen Graham, "Community, Nation and State in Republican Spain, 1931–1938," in Clare Mar-Molinero and Angel Smith, eds., *Nationalism and the Nation in the Iberian Peninsula: Competing and Conflicting Ideologies* (Washington, DC: Berg, 1996), 136.

7. Benedict Anderson, *Imagined Communities,* rev. ed. (London: Verso, 1991); Ernst Gellner, *Nations and Nationalism* (Oxford: Oxford University Press, 1983); Eric Hobsbawm, *Nations and Nationalism since 1780: Programme, Myth, Reality,* 2d ed. (Cambridge, UK: Canto, 1992); Eric Hobsbawm and Terence Ranger, eds., *The*

*Invention of Tradition* (Cambridge: Cambridge University Press, 1992). For various theoretical approaches to the nationalism question, see Geoff Eley and Ronald Grigor Suny, eds., *Becoming National: A Reader* (New York: Oxford University Press, 1996).

8. Miroslav Hroch, *Social Preconditions of National Revival in Europe* (Cambridge: Cambridge University Press, 1985), and Hroch, "From National Movement to the Fully Formed Nation: The Nation-Building Process in Europe," in Geoff Eley and Ronald Grigor Suny, eds., *Becoming National: A Reader* (New York: Oxford University Press, 1996), 60–77; Anthony Smith, "The Origins of Nations," in Geoff Eley and Ronald Grigor Suny, eds., *Becoming National: A Reader* (New York: Oxford University Press, 1996), 106–130.

9. Hroch, "From National Movement to the Fully Formed Nation," 66.

10. Anthony Smith comments that "nations can be seen as both constructs or visions of nationalist (or other) élites, but equally as real, historical formations that embody a number of analytically separable processes over long time-spans." Smith, "The Origin of Nations," 108.

11. Prasenjit Duara, "Historicizing National Identity, or Who Imagines What and When," in Geoff Eley and Ronald Grigor Suny, eds., *Becoming National: A Reader* (New York: Oxford University Press, 1996), 151–153.

12. Ibid., 153.

13. Although Gramsci uses the terms *hegemony* and *counterhegemony* to discuss how *classes* gain power and attain consent, I prefer to employ the terms more broadly to encompass groups that do not necessarily see their struggle in terms of class. For example, one could find Catalan nationalists in every class of Catalan society.

14. Gramsci refers to the process of building these broad alliances as a *war of position*. Roger Simon, *Gramsci's Political Thought: An Introduction* (London: Lawrence and Wishart, 1991), 25. See also See Quintin Hoare and Geoffrey Nowell Smith , eds. and trans., *Selections from the Prison Notebooks of Antonio Gramsci* (New York: International Publishers, 1971). For a discussion of the application of Gramscian ideas for the study of history, see T. J. Jackson Lears, "The Concept of Cultural Hegemony: Problems and Possibilities," *American Historical Review* 90 (June 1985): 567–593.

15. In Gramsci's terms, civil society includes "the 'so-called private' organizations such as churches, trade unions, political parties and cultural associations which are distinct from the process of production *and* from the public apparatuses of the state." Simon, *Gramsci's Political Thought*, 70.

16. As Pamela Radcliff argues, "This recourse to armed rebellion by both sides signaled the death of the democratic alternative and the triumph of force over consent in the hegemonic struggle." Radcliff, *From Mobilization to Civil War*, 15.

17. Lorenzo Luzuriaga, *Diccionario de pedagogía* (Buenos Aires: Losada, 1960), 99.

18. Many cultural historians in the past twenty years have attempted to define and study culture. Many have forgone the simple dichotomies between elite and popular culture or high and low culture and have lent nuance to the discussion by

expanding the term to include avant-garde, official, and mass culture. Some argue for the elimination of the term *mass culture* altogether, claiming that it reeks of the elitism originally propounded by such intellectuals as Ortega y Gasset. I use *popular culture* to refer to traditional rural culture and *mass culture* to refer to popular urban culture. My explanations of *elite* and *official culture* are found in the text. A small sampling of works dealing with these distinctions includes Peter Burke, *Varieties of Cultural History* (Ithaca, NY: Cornell University Press, 1997); Chandra Mukerji and Michael Schudson, eds., *Rethinking Popular Culture* (Berkeley: University of California Press, 1991); Lynn Hunt, ed., *The New Cultural History* (Berkeley: University of California Press, 1989); Mattei Calinescu, *Five Faces of Modernity: Modernism, Avant-Garde, Decadence, Kitsch, Postmodernism* (Durham: Duke University Press, 1987).

19. José Ortega y Gasset, "Vieja y nueva política," in *Obras Completas,* vol. 1 (Madrid: Revista de Occidente, 1966).

20. See Bécarud and López Campillo, *Los intelectuales españoles,* 33–34.

21. José Alvarez Junco, "Los intelectuales: Anticlericalismo y republicanismo," in J. L. García Delgado, ed., *Los orígenes culturales de la Segund República* (Madrid: Siglo Veintiuno, 1993), 100–126.

22. Ibid., 102.

## Chapter 1. Intellectual and Social Roots of Republican Spain

1. The 1857 Ley Moyano, which was Spain's first comprehensive law of national education, required towns of 500 people or more to provide mandatory primary education. But because the state lacked the resources to build the necessary educational infrastructure, "according to official estimates, in 1895 over 68 percent of children were not in school, in many cases, for lack of school places." Carolyn Boyd, *Historia Patria: Politics, History and National Identity in Spain, 1875–1975* (Princeton, NJ: Princeton University Press, 1997), 5, 9. Adrian Shubert's description of the Spanish railroad system in the nineteenth century exemplifies this problem of Spain's weak and erratic infrastructure. Although much of the railroad network was constructed by 1868, it "was built and controlled by foreign companies." This meant that the network was designed for the interests of foreign economies to the detriment of the Spanish economy. Adrian Shubert, *A Social History of Modern Spain* (London: Routledge, 1992), 17–18.

2. Shubert, *A Social History,* 60.

3. The number of works dealing with the subject of regenerationism is daunting and illustrates how obsessed Spaniards were with the issue of their decline. In his 1925 book, also on the subject of Spain's decline, Pedro Sáinz Rodríguez cited eighty-six works on the theme of Spanish decline and degeneration—which he admitted was not the sum total—in the nineteenth century alone. See Pedro Sáinz Rodríguez, *La evolución de las ideas sobre la decadencia española y otros estudios de crítica literaria* (Madrid: Editorial Atlantida Mendezibal, 1925), 104–112.

4. Mercedes Vilanova Ribas and Xavier Moreno Juliá, *Atlas de la evolución del analfabetismo en España de 1887 a 1981* (Madrid: Centro de Publicaciones del Ministro de Educación y Ciencia, 1992), 232–233.

5. Rodolfo Llopis, "Sanz del Río y el krausismo," *Cuadernos del Congreso por la Libertad de la Cultura* 9 (November–December 1954): 54–55. Sanz del Río appears to have been the first Spanish professor to receive a grant to study abroad since Philip II. See J. B. Trend, *The Origins of Modern Spain* (Cambridge: Cambridge University Press, 1934), 33. Trend also notes that Sanz del Río began a tradition of students going abroad: "The remarkable thing is that they have been nearly all of them either his pupils, or pupils of his pupils" (33).

6. Juan López-Morillas, *The Krausist Movement and Ideological Change in Spain, 1854–1874*, trans. Frances M. López-Morillas (Cambridge: Cambridge University Press, 1981), 8.

7. For an excellent discussion of Krausism's beginnings and for a lucid discussion of Krausist philosophy, especially the concepts of panentheism and harmonic rationalism, see López-Morillas, *Krausist Movement and Ideological Change*, especially chaps. 1 and 2. See also Elías Díaz, *La filosofía social del krausismo español* (Madrid: Cuadernos para el Diálogo, 1973), especially 1–67; Rodolfo Llopis, "Francisco Giner de los Ríos y la reforma del hombre," *Cuadernos del Congreso por la Libertad de la Cultura* 16 (January–February 1956): 60–67; Fernando de los Ríos, *El pensamiento vivo de Giner de los Ríos* (Buenos Aires: Editorial Losada, 1949); Manuel de Puelles Benítez, *Educación e ideología en la España contemporánea*, 2d ed. (Barcelona: Editorial Labor, 1991).

8. María Dolores Gómez Molleda, *Los reformadores de la España contemporánea* (Madrid: Consejo Superior de Investigaciones Científicas, 1966), 34.

9. See Luis Araquistáin, "El krausismo en España," *Cuadernos del Congreso por la Libertad de la Cultura* 44 (September–October 1960): 5: "This philosophy, in effect, is a mystical one, and at its core, it is linked with the Spanish mysticism of the sixteenth century."

10. See Gerald Brenan, *The Spanish Labyrinth*, 2d ed. (Cambridge: Cambridge University Press, 1990), chap. 3.

11. Ibid., 50.

12. Eloy Terrón, *Sociedad e ideolgía en los orígenes de la España contemporánea* (Barcelona: Ediciones Peninsula, 1969), 6–7, as cited in Elías Díaz, *La filosofía social del krausismo español* (Madrid: Cuadernos para el Diálogo, 1973), 28–29.

13. Díaz, *La filosofía social del krausismo español*, esp. part 1.

14. Eloy Terrón, *Estudio preliminar a los "Textos escogidos" de Julián Sanz del Río* (Barcelona: Ediciones de Cultura Popular, 1968), 90–91, as cited in Elías Díaz, *La filosofía social del krausismo español* (Madrid: Cuadernos para el Diálogo, 1973), 60–61.

15. Llopis, "Sanz del Río y el krausismo," 52–53.

16. Llopis, "Francisco Giner de los Ríos y la reforma del hombre," 62.

17. The balance of power during the Second Republic lay with left-liberal intellectuals favorable to programs inspired by the ILE. For example, during the first Cortes of the Second Republic (1931), of the approximately 430 representatives, 64 were teachers. The Cortes also included 45 professors and 47 journalists or writers, 25 of whom were of great notoriety. The list of luminaries included Miguel de Unamuno, José Ortega y Gasset, Fernando de los Ríos (nephew of Giner de los Ríos), Manuel B. Cossío, Luis Bello, and Dr. Gregorio Marañón. See

Jean Bécarud and Evelyne López Campillo, *Los intelectuales españoles durante la Segunda República* (Madrid: Siglo Veintiuno, 1978), 33–34.

18. The ILE became a secondary school with a primary prep school attached. Later still, it developed into solely a primary school. For more biographical information on Giner, see Giner de los Ríos, *El pensamiento vivo de Giner*, and Llopis, "Francisco Giner de los Ríos y la reforma del hombre," 60–67.

19. Llopis, "Francisco Giner de los Ríos y la reforma del hombre," 63.

20. "Estatuos de la Institución Libre de Enseñanza," 1876, as cited in Antonio Jiménez-Landi, *La Institución Libre de Enseñanza y su ambiente*, vol.1 (Madrid: Taurus, 1973), 703.

21. Manuel B. Cossío, *De su jornada (fragmentos)* (Madrid: Impresor de Blass, 1929), 24.

22. Francisco Giner de los Ríos, "Consideraciones sobre el desarollo de la literatura moderna," *Estudios de literatura y arte* (Madrid: Librería de Victoriano Suárez, 1876), 169, as cited in Juan López-Morillas, *The Krausist Movement in Spain, 1854–1874*, trans. Frances M. López-Morillas (Cambridge: Cambridge University Press, 1981), 78.

23. Solomon Lipp, *Francisco Giner de los Ríos: A Spanish Socrates* (Waterloo, Ontario, Canada: Wilfred Laurier University Press, 1985), 47.

24. See Johann Gottlieb Fichte, *Addresses to the German Nation* (Westport, CT: Greenwood Press, 1979), and G. W. F. Hegel, *Reason in History*, trans. Robert S. Hartman (New York: Macmillan, 1953).

25. Francisco Giner de los Ríos, "Consideraciones sobre el desarrollo de la literatura moderna," *Estudios Literarios* (Madrid: R. Labajos, 1866), 92.

26. Ibid., 93.

27. The Radical Republican agenda did change significantly after Barcelona's Tragic Week in 1909. Before this period, radical republicanism, especially as conceived by Alejandro Lerroux, exhorted the working classes to overturn the system through violence. After the convent burnings of Tragic Week, the radicals became more reformist and their approach toward the working classes became more muted, although their anticlericalism remained strong. See José Alvarez Junco, *El emperador del Paralelo: Lerroux y la demagogía populista* (Madrid: Alianza Editorial, 1990); Joaquín Romero Maura, *La rosa de fuego; Republicanos y anarquistas: La política de los obreros barceloneses entre el desastre colonial y la semana trágica, 1899–1909* (Barcelona: Ediciones Grijalbo, 1975); and Joan Connelly Ullman, *The Tragic Week: A Study of Anti-Clericalism in Spain, 1875–1912* (Cambridge: Harvard University Press, 1968).

28. As Prasenjit Duara observes, rival groups can use the same means—in this case, education—to undercut the nationalists' attempts to assimilate people to the nation. Prasenjit Duara, "Historicizing National Identity, or Who Imagines What and When," in Geoff Eley and Ronald Grigor Suny, *Becoming National: A Reader* (New York: Oxford University Press, 1996), 161.

29. For a discussion of the variety of anarchist ideologies competing for dominance in Spain, see George Esenwein, *Anarchist Ideology and the Working-Class Movement in Spain, 1868–1898.* (Berkeley: University of California Press, 1989).

30. Jean Jacques Rousseau, *A Discourse on Inequality* (London: Penguin, 1984), 109.

31. According to Martin Blinkhorn, pre-anarchist rural discontent was channeled into Carlism, the longest lasting counterrevolutionary force in modern European history. Carlists revolted against liberalism and the more egregious problems associated with the Industrial Revolution. Martin Blinkhorn, *Carlism and Crisis in Spain, 1931–1939* (Cambridge: Cambridge University Press, 1975).

32. In strictly Marxist terms, rural laborers cannot be considered a class, but in anarchist terms, both rural and urban laborers comprised the backbone of people exploited by the holy trinity of capitalism, the church, and the state. George Esenwein argues that anarchism "supplied the Spanish working classes with a language of class identity." Esenwein, *Anarchist Ideology*, 6.

33. For a detailed discussion of this debate, see Carolyn Boyd, "The Anarchists and Education in Spain, 1868–1909," *Journal of Modern History* 48 (1976): 125–170.

34. Boyd, "The Anarchists and Education in Spain," 133. See also Pere Solà, *Educació i moviment llibertari a Catalunya (1901–1939)* (Barcelona: Edicions 62, 1980), and Solà, *Els ateneus obrers i la cultura popular a Catalunya (1900–1939)* (Barcelona: Edicions de la Magrana, 1978).

35. According to Boyd, the "unsystematic approach [to anarchist education] was partly the consequence of frequent periods of underground activity and repression; partly the result of the libertarian aversion to bureaucratization of any kind." Boyd, "The Anarchists and Education in Spain," 139.

36. By the end of the first year, enrollment had more than doubled to 70 pupils. By 1904 the total rose to 114, and by 1905 to 126. Paul Avrich, *The Modern School Movement: Anarchism and Education in the United States* (Princeton, NJ: Princeton University Press: 1980), 20.

37. Ferrer's guilt or innocence in this matter is still being contested. Ferrer loyalists contended that he was prosecuted merely because the conservative Spanish government wanted a pretext to stop him from teaching radical ideas. The historian Joaquín Romero Maura argues that Ferrer supplied the bombs and money to facilitate the assassination attempt. Others criticize Maura for accepting uncritically the "truths" revealed in the police files. See Maura, *La rosa de fuego*, and Boyd, "The Anarchists and Education in Spain." For criticism of Maura's view, see Avrich, *Modern School Movement*, 28–29. See also Ullman, *Tragic Week*, and Solà, *Educació i moviment llibertari*.

38. Interview with Valero Chiné, conducted by Martha Ackelsberg, Fraga (Aragón), May 11, 1979. In Martha Ackelsberg, *Free Women of Spain: Anarchism and the Struggle for the Emanicipation of Women* (Bloomington: Indiana University Press, 1991), 60–61.

39. Juan Padreny, *Necesidad del excursionismo y su influencia libertaria en los individuos y los pueblos* (Barcelona: Ateneo Libertario del Clot, "Sol y Vida," Sección excursionismo, 1934), 32, as cited in Martha Ackelsberg, *Free Women of Spain: Anarchism and the Struggle for the Emanicipation of Women* (Bloomington: Indiana University Press, 1991), 61.

40. Journals such as *Ácrata* took their science and revolution seriously, joining the two seamlessly in Teobaldo Nieva's article entitled, "The chemistry of the

social question, that is, the scientific organism of the Revolution. Evidence deduced from natural law of anarcho-collectivist ideas," *Acrata* 9 (Sept. 1886), as cited in Carlos Serrano, "*Acracia*, los anarquistas y la cultura," in Bert Hofmann, Pere Joan i Tous, Manfred Tietz, eds., *El anarquismo español: Sus tradiciones culturales* (Frankfurt am Main: Vervuert; Madrid: Iberoamericana, 1995), 349.

41. The Socialists eventually tried to bring their programs to the peasantry, but those efforts were minimal. See Francisco de Luis Martín, *La cultura socialista en España, 1923–1930* (Salamanca: Consejo Superior de Investigaciones Científicas, 1993), 33–40.

42. For discussions of the so-called failures of Spanish socialism, see Paul Heywood, *Marxism and the Failure of Organized Socialism in Spain, 1879–1936* (Cambridge: Cambridge University Press, 1990), and Paul Preston, *The Coming of the Spanish Civil War: Reform, Reaction, and Revolution in the Second Republic*, 2d ed. (New York: Routledge, 1994). Heywood argues that Spanish Socialists employed revolutionary rhetoric, but their actions tended toward reformist rather than revolutionary policies. This all changed, however, after the October revolution of 1934.

43. Heywood, *Marxism and Failure of Organized Socialism*, 12–20.

44. Ibid., 54.

45. Ibid., 29–58.

46. *El Socialista*, February 30, 1927, as cited in Francisco de Luis Martín, *La cultura socialista en España, 1923–1930* (Salamanca: Consejo Superior de Investigaciones Científicas, 1993), 25. In another work, Luis Martín argues that Spanish Socialists had no original ideas to contribute to pedagogical theory. Luis Martín, *Cincuenta años de cultura obrera en España, 1890–1940* (Madrid: Pablo Iglesias, 1994).

47. For a discussion of the early years of Spanish Socialist culture and education, see Luis Martín, *Cincuenta años de cultura obrera en España;* Manuel Pérez Ledesma, "La cultura socialista en los años veinte," in J. L. García Delgado, ed., *Los orígines culturales de la Segunda República* (Madrid: Siglo Veintiuno, 1993), 149–198; Manuel Tuñón de Lara, "Actitudes socialistas ante la cultura," in Jacques Maurice, Brigitte Magnien, and Danièle Genevois, *Peuple, mouvement ouvrier, culture dans L'Espagne contemporaine* (Saint-Denis: Presses Universitaires de Vincennes, 1990), 141–155; Jean-Louis Guereña, "Les socialistes espagnols et la culture: La 'Casa del Pueblo' de Madrid au début du XXe siècle," in Jacques Maurice, Brigitte Magnien, and Danièle Genevois, *Peuple, mouvement ouvrier, culture dans L'Espagne contemporaine* (Saint-Denis: Presses Universitaires de Vincennes, 1990), 23–37.

48. Of course, this was the cause of Marx's and Bakunin's split during the First International. Bakunin feared that Marx's emphasis on the centralization of power within a proletarian state would lead to an unhealthy concentration of power and an annihilation of individual liberties.

49. For a recent discussion of the debates over educational curriculum in the late nineteenth century and early twentieth century, see Boyd, *Historia Patria*.

50. Pérez Ledesma, "La cultura socialista," 185. Pérez Ledesma characterizes the Casa del Pueblo as representing the "progressive elements of the working class."

51. Luis Martín, *Cincuenta años de cultura obrera*, 125–148

52. Ibid., 142.

53. Recent discussions on the various forms of republicanism can be found in José A. Piqueras and Manuel Chust, eds., *Republicanos y repúblicas en España* (Madrid: Siglo Veintiuno, 1996), and Nigel Townson, ed., *El republicanismo en España (1830–1977)* (Madrid: Alianza, 1994).

54. See, for example, Eugen Weber, *Peasants into Frenchmen: The Modernization of Rural France, 1870–1914* (Stanford, CA: Stanford University Press, 1976).

55. Alvarez Junco says that there was very little correlation between the number of articles and speeches dedicated to the theme of popular education and the number of actual pamphlets and books dealing with scientific dissemination or pedagogy or with the development of popular schools. He also reports that his initial impression, garnered from his research, was that the efforts of the Radical Republicans to educate the working classes were inferior to those of the anarchists and the Socialists, although at the beginning of the century, the influence of Ferrer's schools helped to bring the question of laic school into relief. Alvarez Junco, *El emperador del Paralelo*, 411, 411 n. 119.

56. Solà, *Educació i moviment llibertari*, 23.

57. For the purposes of this study, I am concentrating only on Catalan nationalism, for the Catalans proved to be the most successful in exerting their political clout with the centralizing government, in mobilizing the masses to their cause, and, eventually, in getting a statute for autonomy approved before the Civil War.

58. See Miroslav Hroch, "From National Movement to Fully-Formed Nation: The Nation-Building Process in Europe," in Geoff Eley and Ronald Grigor Suny, eds., *Becoming National: A Reader* (New York: Oxford University Press, 1996), 62–63. Hroch argues that their demands tended to be for (1) development of a national culture based on the local language and its normal use in education, administration, and economic life; (2) achievement of civil rights and political self-administration, initially in the form of autonomy and ultimately of independence; and (3) creation of a social structure out of the ethnic group, including educated elites, an officialdom and an entrepreneurial class, but also—where necessary—free peasants and workers. He also states that it "was only during this final phase that a full social structure could come into being, and that the movement differentiated out into conservative-clerical, liberal and democratic wings, each with their own programmes." The development of Catalan nationalism clearly reflects this pattern. See also Eric Hobsbawm, *Nations and Nationalism since 1780: Programme, Myth, Reality*, 2d ed. (Cambridge, UK: Canto, 1992).

59. There is a large bibliography on Catalan nationalism. For my purposes, the following works proved most helpful: Albert Balcells, *Catalan Nationalism: Past and Present* (New York and Basingstoke: St. Martin's Press and Macmillan, 1996); Daniele Conversi, *The Basques, the Catalans, and Spain: Alternative Routes to Nationalist Mobilization* (Reno: University of Nevada Press, 1997); Juan Díez Medrano, *Divided Nation: Class, Politics and Nationalism in the Basque Country and Catalonia* (Ithaca, NY: Cornell University Press, 1995; Enric Ucelay da Cal, *La Catalunya populista: Imatge, cultura i política en l'etapa republicana (1931–1939)*

(Barcelona: La Magrana, 1982); Ucelay da Cal, "The Nationalisms of the Periphery: Culture and Politics in the Construction of National Identity," in Helen Graham and Jo Labanyi, eds., *Spanish Cultural Studies: An Introduction* (Oxford: Oxford University Press, 1995), 32–39; and Ucelay da Cal, "Catalan Nationalism: Plurality and Political Ambiguity," in Helen Graham and Jo Labanyi, eds., *Spanish Cultural Studies: An Introduction* (Oxford: Oxford University Press, 1995), 144–151.

60. Balcells, *Catalan Nationalism*, 39.

61. Conversi, *The Basques, the Catalans, and Spain*, 15.

62. As Albert Balcells succinctly put it: "This conservative message made it possible to build an ideological bridge linking the Barcelona bourgeoisie to craftsmen and countryfolk in opposition to the urban industrial proletariat. Respect for the church and the sanctification of Catalan civil law were channels uniting the bourgeoisie with the populations of rural and mountainous areas, after the defeat of Carlism at the hands of the centralist liberal state." Balcells, *Catalan Nationalism*, 39.

63. As cited in Balcells, *Catalan Nationalism*, 58. This affiliation with Europe already had a long tradition, given the industrial superiority that Catalonia had over the rest of Spain. As early as 1843 the Catalan philosopher Jaume Balmes said, "It should not be forgotten that Catalonia is the only province that, strictly speaking, forms part of the European industrial movement. On leaving Catalonia for a foreign country, one observes nothing that is not in some way a continuation of what one has seen here: it might be said that the journey is between one province and another of a single nation; but on leaving Catalonia for the Spanish hinterland, one seems really to have left the homeland behind and to have entered foreign lands." Cited in Balcells, *Catalan Nationalism*, 21.

64. Balcells, *Catalan Nationalism*, 27.

65. Conversi, *The Basques, the Catalans, and Spain*, 17–18; Balcells, *Catalan Nationalism*, 35–36.

66. Conversi, *The Basques, the Catalans, and Spain*, 19.

67. Balcells, *Catalan Nationalism*, 36–37.

68. Conversi, *The Basques, the Catalans, and Spain*, 33.

69. Ibid., 31.

70. Ibid., 34–35. This construction of an infrastructure and system of cultural communication illustrate Karl Deutsch's idea—popularized by Miroslav Hroch—that in order to generate patriotism, it is important to have in place social mobility and communications. See Karl Deutsch, *Nationalism and Social Communication: An Inquiry into the Foundations of Nationality* (Cambridge, MA: Technology Press, MIT, 1953), and Miroslav Hroch, *Social Preconditions of National Revival in Europe* (Cambridge: Cambridge University Press, 1985).

71. For a thorough and excellent discussion of Carlism and its role during the Second Republic, see Blinkhorn, *Carlism and Crisis in Spain*.

72. Ibid., 119.

73. Raúl Morodo, *Los orígenes ideológicos del franquismo: Acción Española* (Madrid: Alianza Editorial, 1985), 18.

74. Ramiro de Maeztu, *Defensa de la Hispanidad* (Buenos Aires: Editorial Poblet, 1952), 219.

75. For a discussion of the hybrid nature of fascism, see Zeev Sternhell, *Neither Right nor Left: Fascist Ideology in France* (Berkeley: University of California Press, 1986). See also Stanley Payne, *A History of Fascism, 1914–1945* (Madison: University of Wisconsin Press, 1995. For a discussion of Spanish fascism, see Payne, *Fascism in Spain, 1923–1977* (Madison: University of Wisconsin Press, 1999); Sheelagh Ellwood, *Prietas las Filas: Historia de Falange Española, 1933–1983* (Barcelona: Editorial Crítica, 1984).

76. Raymond Carr, *Spain 1808–1975*, 2d ed. (Oxford: Clarendon Press, 1989), 566, 577–576.

77. Morodo, *Los orígenes ideológicos del franquismo*, 39. Morodo argues that these men under Primo de Rivera represented the ideological links from the Primo de Rivera regime to the Franco regime. Those who served under Primo and were still alive by the end of the Civil War had official positions under Franco.

## Chapter 2. Creating Consent through Culture

1. See, for example, George Esenwein and Adrian Shubert, *Spain at War: The Spanish Civil War in Context, 1931–1939* (New York: Longman, 1995); Paul Preston, *The Coming of the Spanish Civil War: Reform, Reaction, and Revolution in the Second Republic,* 2d ed. ( New York: Routledge, 1994); Edward Malefakis, *Agrarian Reform and Peasant Revolution in Spain* (New Haven, CT: Yale University Press, 1970); Gerald Brenan, *The Spanish Labyrinth: An Account of the Social and Political Background of the Civil War,* 2d ed. (Cambridge: Cambridge University Press, 1990); Gabriel Jackson, *The Spanish Republic and the Civil War, 1931–1939* (Princeton, NJ: Princeton University Press, 1965).

2. Fernando de los Ríos, "The Educational Program of the Spanish Republic." Excerpts from a speech delivered before the students of Sarah Lawrence College, Bronxville, New York, on April 7, 1937. Microfiche 84/3646, The Blodgett Collection of Spanish Civil War Pamphlets, Harvard University.

3. One could see this attempt at integration as an illustration of Antonio Gramsci's idea of attaining a "war of position."

4. Marcelino Domingo, *La experiencia del poder* (Madrid: S. Quemados, 1934), 159. His separation of the ideas of violence and culture is reminiscent of Gramsci's ideas of hegemony, whereby domination can be achieved by measures of violence and consent.

5. Spanish Civil War Archive (Salamanca), PS Madrid 942.

6. Gregorio Marañón, "La obra de todos: La España de hoy y la cultura," *El Sol,* September 18, 1932.

7. Ibid.

8. "Importantísimo acto de cooperacíon intelectual: En un admirable discurso el camarada Fernando de los Ríos resalta el espíritu cultural de la República, que enaltece los valores nacionales," *El Socialista,* March 1, 1932.

9. Ibid.

10. *El Sol,* February 15, 1933.

11. He stated these ideas earlier, too: "The eternal values of culture are those which we have to protect; knowing that only Spain's participation in the cultural

sphere is that which can give us a name in this world." Manuel Azaña, "La República como forma del ser nacional," in vol. 2 of *Obras Completas* (Mexico City: Ediciones Oasis, 1966), 228. Speech originally given at the closure of the Assembly of Acción Republicana, March 28, 1932.

12. Marcelino Domingo, "Discurso leido en la inauguración del curso académico de 1931 a 1932," in *Homenaje a Marcelino Domingo* (Madrid: n.p., 1936), 11.

13. For literacy statistics, see Clara Eugenia Nuñez, *La fuente de la riqueza: Educación y desarrollo económico en la España contemporánea* (Madrid: Alianza Universidad, 1992); Mercedes Vilanova Ribas and Xavier Moreno Juliá, *Atlas de la evolución del analfabetismo en España de 1887 a 1981* (Madrid: Centro de Publicaciones del Ministerio de Educación y Ciencia, 1992), 288–289.

14. Rodolfo Llopis, "La escuela y el pueblo: Lo que hará la República," *El Socialista*, April 19, 1931.

15. See Spanish Civil War Archive (Salamanca), PS Madrid 2116 and 1381, for information about Mexican cultural projects and their application to Spain.

16. Archivo Histórico Nacional (Madrid), Fondo Araquistáin, Legajo 41/Z 18.

17. For a discussion of the Bolsheviks' educational and cultural projects from the Revolution to the 1930s, see Sheila Fitzpatrick, *The Commissariat of Enlightenment: Soviet Organization of Education and the Arts under Lunacharsky, October 1917–1921* (Cambridge: Cambridge University Press, 1970); Fitzpatrick, *The Cultural Front: Power and Culture in Revolutionary Russia* (Ithaca, NY: Cornell University Press, 1992); Lynn Mally, *Culture of the Future: The Proletkult Movement in Revolutionary Russia* (Berkeley: University of California Press, 1990).

18. In fact, after the advent of the Republic, numerous translations of Soviet pedagogy appeared, such as L. Wilson's *Las escuelas nuevas rusas*, translated by Luis Santullano, and A. Pinkevich's *La nueva educación de la Rusia Soviética*, translated by R. Cansinos-Assus, as cited in Mercedes Samaniego Boneu, *La política educativa en la Segunda República durante el bienio azañista* (Madrid: Consejo Superior de Investigaciones Científicas, 1977), 14n. Fernando de los Ríos, the second Minister of Public Instruction, also went to the Soviet Union in 1920 to evaluate the revolution. He was generally more critical of the revolution than his compatriots. See Fernando de los Ríos, *Mi viaje a la Rusia sovietista*, 2d ed. (Madrid: Calpe, 1922).

19. Rodolfo Llopis, *Como se forja un pueblo (La Rusia que yo he visto)* (Madrid: Editorial Espana, 1929), 81–82.

20. Ibid., 72. In Gramscian terms, these are the types of "private" organizations that make up the sphere of "civil society," the sphere where "intellectuals operate specially." Quintin Hoare and Geoffrey Nowell Smith, eds. and trans., *Selections from the Prison Notebooks of Antonio Gramsci* (New York: International Publishers, 1971), 56n.

21. Llopis *Como se forja un pueblo*, 156.

22. For a discussion of the educational and cultural reforms of the Mexican Revolution, see Mary Kay Vaughan, *Cultural Politics in Revolution: Teachers, Peasants, and Schools in Mexico* (Tucson: Arizona University Press, 1997); Marjorie Becker, *Setting the Virgin on Fire: Lázaro Cárdenas, Michoacan Peasants and the Redemption of the Mexican Revolution* (Berkeley: University of California Press,

1995); David Raby, *Educación y revolución social en México, 1921–1940* (Mexico City: Secretaría de Educación Pública, 1974).

23. "Excmo., Sr. Ministro de Instrucción Pública," Spanish Civil War Archive (Salamanca), PS Madrid 2116.

24. Ibid.

25. The great exception here is Catalonia. As we shall see, because Catalan nationalism was firmly entrenched in Spain, and because the Minister of Public instruction was himself a Catalan nationalist, the Republicans proceeded with trepidation in matters concerning education and culture in Catalonia. Republicans walked a fine line between praising the intrinsic and historical value of Catalan culture while simultaneously elevating Castilian culture.

26. See the language used by Cossío in the introduction read by misioneros in the Misiones Pedagógicas in note 32 of this chapter. Almost a year and a half, and one Minister of Public Education later, Spaniards were still studying the Mexican Revolution. The emissary, Julio Alvarez de Vayo, wrote a report to Fernando de los Ríos with more information about the Mexican Revolution, informing de los Ríos that the Spanish government might like to look at what the Mexicans had done in terms of land reform and education, because maybe these lessons could be applied to Spain, "involved in these hours in a similar revolutionary enterprise." "Asunto; La educación rural en México" (January 17, 1933), Spanish Civil War Archive (Salamanca), PS Madrid 1381.

27. Manuel Cossío, "Carácter de la educación primaria" (Madrid: n.p., 1882), as cited in "Cossío y las Misiones Pedagógicas," *Revista de Pedagogía* 165 (1935): 406.

28. *Gaceta de Madrid,* May 30, 1931. The speed with which the Patronato assembled the Misiones Pedagógicas is incredible—less than seven months—especially because the organizers had to find willing participants, such as university students, teachers, set designers, painters, and librarians, as well as having to procure trucks and other supplies for sending the misioneros out to the hinterlands.

29. Ibid.

30. *Patronato de Misiones Pedagógicas* (Sept. 1931–Dec. 1933) (Madrid: n.p., 1934), 14; hereafter *PMP* (1934).

31. Ibid., 34. Compare the preceding sentence to that of Rodolfo Llopis in describing the Bolshevik cultural revolution: "There were always people in the libraries. It is that [the Bolsheviks] have awakened in the Russian people the eagerness to read." Llopis, *Como se forja un pueblo,* 196.

32. See *PMP* (1934) for the following: "abismo en la vida espiritual," "penuria espiritual," and "luces espirituales" (n.p.); "enriquecer las almas" and "aislamiento moral" (x); missionary's office as "duro y de sacrificio" (xix); "obra evangélica" (15); misioneros as "shock troops" (xix); work of "social justice" (n.p.); work of "social solidarity" (5).

33. *PMP* (1934), 11.

34. *El Socialista,* March 1, 1932.

35. *PMP* (1934), 13.

36. *Archivo Histórico Nacional* (Salamanca), Sección Guerra Civil, PS Madrid 2116.

37. *PMP* (1934), 14.

38. Smith speaks of the need for "intellectual-educators" to use both geography and history to "engage the community for their moral and political goals. Both had to be couched in the language and symbolism of the people, in the sense that any novelties must find an echo in popular historical traditions." The landscape, or what he terms "poetic spaces," became one area of manipulation: "A nation, after all, needs before all else a national territory or homeland, and not just anywhere. The geographic terrain must be simultaneously an historic home. How do you create this sense of 'homeland' for people who are either divided into small localities or scattered outside the chosen area? The answer is to endow the chosen home with poetic and historical connotations, or rather with an historical poetry. The aim is to integrate the homeland into a romantic drama of the progress of the nation." Anthony Smith, "The Origin of Nations," in Geoff Eley and Ronald Grigor Suny, eds., *Becoming National: A Reader* (New York: Oxford University Press, 1996), 120.

39. Manuel B. Cossío, "La enseñanza de la historia en la Institución," *De su jornada (fragmentos)* (Madrid: Aguilar, 1966), 29.

40. As Roger Simon so gracefully put it: "It is this strategy of building up a broad bloc of varied social forces, unified by a common conception of the world, that Gramsci called a *war of position.*" Roger Simon, *Gramsci's Political Thought: An Introduction* (London: Lawrence and Wishart, 1991), 25.

41. *Gaceta de Madrid,* May 30, 1931.

42. *PMP* (1934), 14.

43. Ibid., 15.

44. *El Socialista,* March 1, 1932.

45. "Las Misiones Pedagógicas," *El Sol,* July 18, 1931.

46. J. de Izaro, "Arte y fábula por Castilla: Pinturas ambulantes," *El Sol,* October 16, 1932.

47. For discussions of symbolic rituals and visits for political control, see Clifford Geertz, "Centers, Kings and Charisma: Reflections on the Symbolics of Power," in *Local Knowledge: Further Essays in Interpretive Anthropology* (New York: Basic Books, 1983), 121–146. See also David I. Kertzer, *Ritual, Politics, and Power* (New Haven, CT: Yale University Press, 1988).

48. Many studies of national identity formation emphasize that national unification becomes easier after a solid infrastructure has been built. In the case of Spain, where the infrastructure is relatively weak, what I would call "imaginary" or "metaphorical roads" become all that more important for strengthening Spanish national identity.

49. *El Sol,* October 16, 1932.

50. "Por la cultura popular: Interesantes proyectos de Fernando de los Ríos," *El Socialista,* January 14, 1932.

51. Pseudonym of journalist and writer Agustí Calvet Pascual, a center-right Catalanist who directed *La Vanguardia* after 1933.

52. *La Vanguardia,* October 2, 1931; reprinted in *El Sol,* October 3, 1931.

53. Ibid.

54. Francisco de Cossío, "Crisis de lo típico: Información y cultura," *El Sol,* April 20, 1932.

55. "Misiones Pedagógicas en las verbenas," *El Debate,* June 28, 1932.

56. *Diario de sesiones de las Cortes Constituyentes,* March 23, 1932.

57. *Diario de sesiones,* December 21, 1932.

58. *Diario de sesiones,* March 24, 1932.

59. *Diario de sesiones,* March 23, 1932.

60. *Diario de sesiones,* December 21, 1934.

61. Ibid.

## Chapter 3. Return to the Golden Age

1. Benito Pérez Galdós, *Nuestro teatro* (Madrid: Editorial Renacimiento, 1923), 155 and following, as cited in Miguel Bilbatúa, ed., *Teatro de agitación política 1933–1939* (Madrid: Edicusa, 1976), 15.

2. G. G. Brown, *A Literary History of Spain: The Twentieth Century* (London: Ernst Benn, 1972), 110.

3. "Nuestros deseos cumplidos," *El Productor* 7, no. 347, April 20, 1893, as cited in Lily Litvak, *Musa libertaria: Arte, literatura y vida cultural del anarquismo español (1880–1913)* (Barcelona: Antoni Bosch, 1981), 232.

4. Ibid., 213–218

5. Miguel R. Seisdedos, "El teatro socialista: Mi opinión," *El Socialista,* May 1, 1925, 8, as cited in Francisco de Luis Martín, *Cincuenta años de cultura obrera en España, 1890–1940* (Madrid: Pablo Iglesias, 1994), 67–70.

6. Luis Araquistáin, *La batalla teatral* (Madrid: Mundo Latino, 1930), 13–20.

7. Francisco Giner de los Ríos, "Consideraciones sobre el desarollo de la literatura moderna," *Estudios de la literatura y arte* (Madrid, n.p., 1876), 169–170, as quoted and cited in Juan López-Morillas, *The Krausist Movement and Ideological Change in Spain, 1854–1874,* trans. Frances M. López-Morillas (Cambridge: Cambridge University Press, 1981), 78.

8. Rafael Altamira y Crevea, "The Spanish Drama as an Element of Moral Education," in John Drinkwater, ed., *Essays by Divers Hands: Being the Transactions of the Royal Society of Literature of the United Kingdom* (London: Humphrey Milford and Oxford University Press, 1925), 44.

9. Ibid, 46–47.

10. Ibid, 49–51.

11. "Creación del Teatro Nacional": La opinión del gran escritor D. Ramón Pérez de Ayala," *El Liberal,* March 10, 1928, p. 1, as cited in Juan Aguilera Sastre, "El debate sobre el teatro nacional durante la dictadura y la República," in Dru Dougherty and María Francisca Vilches de Frutos, eds., *El teatro de España entre la tradición y la vanguardia (1918–1939)* (Madrid: Tabapress, 1992), 176. For a discussion of the importance of the Soviet model of the theater for Spain, see Rodolfo Llopis, *Como se forja un pueblo (La Rusia que yo he visto)* (Madrid: Editorial España, 1929), chap. 6.

12. Aguilera, "El debate sobre el teatro nacional," 176.

13. Cezar D'Río, "Cuando acabará la 'monarquía literaria'? Sobre un Teatro del Pueblo," *El Socialista,* July 8, 1931.

14. The Casa del Pueblo, a type of Atheneum for the workers organized by

Socialists, performed more politically oriented plays for the workers. For more discussion of revolutionary theater in the Republic and the Civil War, see Bilbatúa, *Teatro de agitación política*. For the *teatro de urgencia*, see Bilbatúa, *Teatro de agitación política*, and Jim McCarthy, *Political Theatre during the Spanish Civil War* (Cardiff: University of Wales Press, 1999).

15. "La Barraca," *El Sol*, January 21, 1934.

16. Enrique Rull Fernández, ed., *Autos sacramentales del Siglo de Oro* (Barcelona: Plaza and Janés, 1986), 17.

17. Ibid., 19.

18. Ibid., 23.

19. Bruce W. Wardropper, *Introducción al teatro religioso del Siglo de Oro* (Madrid: Revista de Occidente, 1953), 87, as cited in Enrique Rull Fernández, ed., *Autos sacramentales del Siglo de Oro* (Barcelona: Plaza and Janés, 1986), 36.

20. Rafael Alberti, *Farsa de los Reyes Magos (Fragmento): "El Espantapájaros,"* in *Octubre* 6, April 6, 1934, 13–15. Reprinted in Enrique Montero, ed., *Octubre*, facsimile (Vaduz: Topos Verlas, 1977), 157–159.

21. Suzanne Wade Byrd, *García Lorca: "La Barraca" and the Spanish National Theater* (New York: Abra Ediciones, 1975), 34.

22. Randall W. Listerman, ed. and trans., *The Interludes (Los Pasos) by Lope de Rueda* (Ottawa: Dovehouse Editions, 1988), 10.

23. Américo Castro and Hugo A. Rennert, *Vida de Lope de Vega* (Madrid: Impr. de los Sucesores de Hernando, 1919); (Salamanca: Anaya, 1968), 263, as cited in Carroll B. Johnson, "The Classical Theater and Its Reflection of Life," in José Rubia Barcia, ed., *Américo Castro and the Meaning of Spanish Civilization* (Berkeley: University of California Press, 1976), 198.

24. It is this type of cultural project that Eric Hobsbawm and other theorists of national identity have emphasized as playing great roles in the growth of national identity in the nineteenth and twentieth centuries. See Eric Hobsbawm, *Nations and Nationalism since 1780: Programme, Myth, Reality*, 2d ed. (Cambridge, UK: Canto, 1992); Eric Hobsbawm and Terence Ranger, eds., *The Invention of Tradition* (Cambridge: Cambridge University Press, 1992); Miroslav Hroch, *Social Preconditions of National Revival in Europe* (Cambridge: Cambridge University Press, 1985).

25. Eugenio Otero Urtaza, *Las Misiones Pedagógicas: Una experiencia de educación popular* (A Coruña: Ediciós do Castro/Ensaio, 1982), 51.

26. *PMP* (1934), 93.

27. Ibid., 94.

28. Ibid., 95.

29. Alejandro Casona, "Nota preliminar," in *Retablo Jovial, Cinco farsas en un acto* (Buenos Aires: El Ateneo, 1949), 10.

30. Enrique Díez-Canedo, "The Spanish Theater," in Thomas H. Dickinson, ed., *The Theater in a Changing Europe* (New York: Holt, 1937), 316.

31. Ibid., 95.

32. For a discussion of the life and work of Eduardo Torner, see María Luisa Mallo del Campo, *Torner más allá del folklore* (Oviedo: Departamento de Arte y Musicología, Servicio de Publicaciones, Universidad de Oviedo, 1980).

33. Ibid., 55.

34. Ibid., 63.

35. *PMP* (1934), 94.

36. Miguel de Unamuno, *En torno al casticismo* (Madrid: Espasa Calpe, 1991).

37. *PMP* (1934), 94.

38. Miguel Cervantes, "The Judge of the Divorce Court," in S. Griswold Morley, trans., *The Interludes of Cervantes* (New York: Greenwood Press, 1969), 19.

39. Casona, "Sancho Panza en la ínsula," 18.

40. Ibid, 25–26

41. Ibid, 27.

42. Casona, "Nota Preliminar," 12.

43. For a comprehensive biography of García Lorca, see Ian Gibson, *Federico García Lorca: A Life* (Boston: Faber and Faber, 1989).

44. Luis Sáenz de la Calzada, *"La Barraca" teatro universitario* (Madrid: Biblioteca de la Revista de Occidente, 1976), 37.

45. Carlos Morla Lynch, *En España con Federico García Lorca* (Madrid: Aguilar, 1958), 127–128.

46. Mildred Adams, "The Theatre in the Spanish Republic," *Theatre Arts Monthly* (March 1932): 238.

47. Ibid.

48. Ibid., 238–239.

49. Ibid., 239.

50. V. S., "Estudiantes de la F.U.E. se echarán a los caminos con 'La Barraca,'" *El Sol,* December 2, 1931.

51. Adams, "Theatre in the Spanish Republic," 239.

52. See Morla Lynch, *En España con García Lorca,* 128.

53. *Obras Completas de Federico García Lorca* (Madrid: Aguilar, 1969), 1747–1748, as cited in Suzanne Wade Byrd, *García Lorca: "La Barraca" and the Spanish National Theater* (New York: Abra Ediciones, 1975), 40.

54. José María Salaverría, "Ideas y notas: El carro de la farándula," *La Vanguardia,* December 1, 1932.

55. Enrique Moreno Báez, " 'La Barraca': Entrevista con su director, Federico García Lorca," *Revista de la Universidad Internacional de Santander* 1 (1933): 69.

56. Taken from private papers, as cited in Luis Sáenz de la Calzada, *"La Barraca" teatro universitario* (Madrid: Biblioteca de la Revista de Occidente, 1976), 124.

57. Francisco Pérez Herrero, "Nuevo carro de Tespis," *La Mañana,* August 1933, as cited in Francisco Calvo Serraller, Ángel González García, and Francisco Javier Rocha, *La Barraca y su entorno teatral* (Madrid: Galeria Multitud, 1975), 36.

58. Salaverría, "Ideas y notas."

59. Sáenz de la Calzada, *"La Barraca,"* 31.

60. For a re-creation of García Lorca's text of *Fuenteovejuna,* see Suzanne Wade Byrd, *La Fuente Ovejuna de Federico García Lorca* (Madrid: Editorial Pliegos, 1984).

61. Joan Tomas, "A proposit de 'La Dama Boba,'" *Mirador,* September 19, 1935.

62. Sáenz de la Calzada, *"La Barraca,"* 74–75.

63. *Heraldo de Madrid,* April 6, 1936.

64. For a discussion of Lorca's collaboration with Falla, see Gibson, *García Lorca,* 108–116.

65. Sáenz de la Calzada, *"La Barraca,"* 71, 95.

66. Ibid., 50.

67. The source of this quotation is difficult to track down. Sáenz de la Calzada paraphrases these words following the quote I previously cited. A short piece that José María Salaverría writes, however, paraphrases the previous quote and attributes them to Lorca, without quoting directly the words I have quoted. See José María Salaverría (1932) in Calvo Serraller et al., *La Barraca y su entorno teatral,* 34.

68. See Friedrich Nietzsche, *The Birth of Tragedy and the Case of Wagner,* ed. and trans. Walter Kaufmann (New York: Vintage Books, 1967).

69. Sáenz de la Calzada, *"La Barraca,"* 95. Here is a complete list of the works that La Barraca performed: Cervantes' entremeses: "La Cueva de Salamanca," "La Guarda Cuidadosa," "Los Habladores," "El Retablo de las Maravillas"; Calderón: *La Vida es Sueño* (auto sacramental), sometimes only the first act; Tirso de Molina: *El burlador de Sevilla;* Lope de Vega: *Fuenteovejuna, Las almenas de toro, El caballero de Olmedo;* Juan del Encina: *Egloga de Plácida y Victoriano;* Lope de Rueda: *Paso de la Tierra de Jauja;* Antonio Machado (the only non–Golden Age writer): "La tierra de Alvargonzález"; "Romance de Conde Alarcos." As listed in Sáenz de la Calzada, *"La Barraca,"* 106.

70. Unión Federal de Estudiantes Hispanos, "Extracto de la Memoria del Teatro Universitario "La Barraca," in Sáenz de la Calzada, *"La Barraca,"* n.p.

71. Ibid., 123, 125.

72. Marino Gómez-Santos, "Alejandro Casona cuenta su vida," *Pueblo,* August 17, 1962.

73. Sáenz de la Calzada, *"La Barraca,"* 45. He states this point more emphatically earlier in a letter to Suzanne Wade Byrd: "Both organizations went to the people of Spain to show the peasants the treasures of our culture, but *La Barraca* revolved integrally on the theater—not always classic—while *Misiones* carried some simple little theatrical piece—some short curtain-raiser—but it presented dances and songs—it was dedicated, also, to gathering together every folkloric aspect of interest (photographs, dances, songs, arts and crafts, etc.), performing a cultural endeavor of the broadest range, but much less deep in the theatrical sense." (Byrd, *García Lorca: "La Barraca,"* 127).

74. Sáenz de la Calzada, *"La Barraca,"* 85.

75. *Patronato de Misiones Pedagógicas: Memoria de la Misión Pedagógico-Social en Sanabria (Zamora). Resumen de trabajos realizados en el año 1934* (Madrid, 1935), 105; hereafter *PMP* (1935).

76. Moreno Báez, "Entrevista con su director," 69.

77. Juan Chabas, "Vacaciones de La Barraca: Federico García Lorca cuenta a *Luz* los triunfos de nuestro teatro universitario," *La Luz,* September 3, 1934, as cited in Francisco Calvo Serraller, Ángel González García, and Francisco Javier Rocha, *La Barraca y su entorno teatral* (Madrid: Galeria Multitud, 1975), 38.

78. "Alejandro Casona frente a su teatro," *Primer Acto* 49 (January 1964): 16.

79. Ibid.

80. E. Díez-Canedo, "La Barraca, teatro universitario," *El Sol*, December 20, 1932.

81. Salaverría, "Ideas y notas."

82. C. Rivas Cherif, "Por el teatro dramático nacional," *El Sol*, July 22, 1932.

83. "La Barraca, teatro de estudiantes," *El Sol*, December 17, 1933.

84. Miguel de Unamuno, "Comentario: Hablemos de teatro," *Ahora*, September 19, 1934.

85. A. Hernández-Cata, "Espejo del mundo: Teatro en Ríofrío," *Ahora*, December 17, 1932.

86. Rivas Cherif, "Por el teatro dramático nacional."

87. See articles in *El Debate* from June 28, 1932; November 31, 1933; and August 7, 1935.

88. A reference is made to this attack in *Luz*, November 6, 1933. Other secondary accounts of this attack place the *El Debate* article at November 6, 1933, but I have not been able to find any such article on this date. See, for example, *Byrd García Lorca: "La Barraca,"* 59, and Sáenz de la Calzada, *"La Barraca,"* 147.

89. "Farsa y farsantes: Embajadores de la farándula," *El Carbayón*, August 16, 1933.

90. *PMP* (1935), 15–16.

91. Mariano Pérez Galán, *La enseñanza de la Segunda República española* (Madrid: Editorial Cuadernos para el Diálogo, 1975), 365–366.

92. Sáenz de la Calzada, *"La Barraca,"* 130; *PMP* (1935), 104.

93. Dionisio Cañas, "La posmodernidad cumple 50 años en España," *El País*, April 28, 1985, as cited in Sultana Wahnón, "Estética y crítica literarias en España (1940–1950)" (Ph.D. diss., Universidad de Granada, 1988), 16–17.

94. For further information about Giménez Caballero's colorful life, see Douglas W. Foard, *The Revolt of the Aesthetes: Ernesto Giménez Caballero and the Origins of Spanish Fascism* (New York: Peter Lang, 1989), and an issue of *Anthropos* entitled "E. Giménez Caballero, Una cultura Hacista: Revolución y tradición en la regeneración de España," *Anthropos* 84 (May 1988).

95. Ernesto Giménez Caballero, *Arte y estado* (Madrid: Gráfica Universal, 1935), 173–175.

96. Ibid., 175.

97. L.B.L., "Mascaras," *Haz* 3, April 9, 1935, p. 2.

98. Ibid.

## Chapter 4. Battle on the Cinematographic Front

This chapter first appeared under the title, "Taming the Seventh Art: The Battle for Cultural Unity on the Cinematographic Front during Spain's Second Republic, 1931–1936," in *The Journal of Modern History* 71 (December 1999): 852–881. It is reprinted here, with slight revisions, by permission of *The Journal of Modern History*.

1. As Eric Hobsbawm says, "The cinema, which would dominate and transform all the twentieth-century arts, was utterly novel, in its technology, its mode of production and its manner of presenting reality." Eric Hobsbawm, *The Age of Empire, 1875–1914* (New York: Pantheon Books, 1987), 238.

2. For a discussion of various European responses to the domination of the U.S. film industry, see Victoria de Grazia, "Mass Culture and Sovereignty: The American Challenge to European Cinemas, 1920–1960," *Journal of Modern History* 61 (March 1989): 53–87.

3. Miguel de Unamuno, "La literatura y el cine," *La Nación* (Buenos Aires: April 29, 1923), as cited in *Obras Completas*, vol. 11 (Madrid: Afrodisio Aguado, 1959), 531–532. "*Película* es lo mismo que *pelleja*, y pelicular una obra literaria es despellejarla," in ibid., 532. Also, 534–535.

4. Ramiro de Maeztu, "El problema del cine," *Nuevo Mundo*, May 15, 1913, as cited in Rafael Utrera, *Modernismo y 98 frente a cinematógrafo* (Sevilla: Universidad de Sevilla, 1981), 88.

5. Some modernist writers—Joyce, Pound, and Eliot, for example—consciously wrote works that were inaccessible to the majority of Europeans. Others expressed cultural anxiety over what they saw as the infiltration of mass values (however defined) in their respective nations. The number of European intellectuals who entered this debate were legion. A small sampling includes Nietzsche, Ortega y Gasset, Shaw, and the Frankfurt School.

6. By 1919 Spain had over 1,000 movie theaters. See Peter Besas, *Behind the Spanish Lens: Spanish Cinema under Fascism and Democracy* (Denver: Arden Press, 1985), 4.

7. For a history of the early years of Spanish film, see Julio Pérez Perucha, "Narración de un aciago destino (1896–1930)," in Román Gubern, ed., *Historia del cine español* (Madrid: Cátedra, 1995), 19–121, and Fernando Méndez-Leite, *Historia del cine español*, vol. 1 (Madrid: Ediciones Rialp, 1965). Valencia gave birth to the first film studio in Spain, Films Cuesta (1904). Barcelona soon followed with Hispano Films (1906), and Madrid lagged far behind, opening its first studio, Patria Films, only in 1915. The Spanish film industry could never compete successfully with France and Italy for domestic or foreign distribution. For the early Barcelona film industry, see Palmira González López, *Els anys daurats del cinema clàssic a Barcelona (1906–1923)*(Barcelona: Institut del Teatre de la Diputació de Barcelona, 1987).

8. For a greater discussion of these problems, see Pérez Perucha, "Narración de un aciago destino," 26–28, 49–56.

9. See, for example, Francisco de Barbéns, *La moral en la calle, en el cinematógrafo y en el teatro* (Barcelona: Librería Católica Internacional, 1914), and Pérez Perucha, "Narración de un aciago destino," 49–53. Government minister Juan de la Cierva y Peñafiel justified the government's censorship of film this way: "So great is the influence of film screenings on the public, especially the youth who are impressionable and predisposed to imitate criminal or immoral acts, that it has been confirmed in many cases that criminal acts perpetrated by children and adolescents were suggested to them by police and horror films." *Gaceta de Madrid*, November 31, 1912, app., 354, as cited in Teodoro González Ballesteros, *Aspectos jurídicos de la censura cinematográfica en España* (Madrid: Editorial de la Universidad de Madrid, 1981), 109.

10. The reasons behind the sudden takeoff in the U.S. film industry are numerous and complex. The most obvious of these has to do with the effects of the war

itself. Many European countries had to abandon filmmaking during the war, and the war damaged or destroyed many of the film studios. Once the war ended, it would take some time for the European economies to recover and to rebuild their film industries. In the meantime, the United States' production could forge ahead. Hollywood understood the postwar global economy and adapted the industry to the workings of monopoly capital. The European film industries, with the exception of Germany's, were tied to an old artisan tradition that prevented them from restructuring their industries to meet the demands of monopoly capital. Additionally, the U.S. government, unlike most European governments (again, Germany was the exception) intervened in the film industry through direct subsidies and protectionist tariffs. With exclusionary distribution networks, Hollywood was able to capitalize on its large home market and the English-speaking colonies, thus dwarfing any markets that France, Germany, or Italy could compete in. Another reason for American dominance may have been the United States' willingness to represent new types of stories. Because the U.S. film industry pulled up stakes from the East Coast to Hollywood, the Hollywood machine may have been able to break more easily from the old theatrical traditions of the East Coast. Conversely, European filmmakers still made films that were wedded to the traditional theater of the big cities. Finally, the U.S. "star system" made actors and actresses into "brand names" that audiences around the world could recognize and consume. For a greater discussion of American hegemony, see de Grazia, "Mass Culture and Sovereignty," 57–66.

11. Spain produced its first sound film in May 1932. That, of course, gave the U.S. a five-year advantage over Spain. But even once Spain produced sound film, the statistics were appalling. Between 1932 and July 18, 1936, Spain produced 109 feature-length sound films. Compare this to 2,001 for the United States, 702 for England, 561 for Germany, 556 for France. Italy trailed Spain with 91 films. Román Gubern, El cine sonoro en la Segunda República, 1929–1936 (Barcelona: Editorial Lumen, 1977), 71.

12. The statistics for Spain show how devastating the American film industry could be. Out of 123 Spanish-language films produced by Hollywood between 1930 and 1936, either in Joinville or in Spanish-language studios in Hollywood, only 16 were directed or codirected by Spaniards. Ibid., 41

13. De Grazia argues that national responses to the American film industry changed from the 1920s to the 1930s. In the 1920s businesses linked to the production and distribution of motion pictures worried about the economic effects of American movie distribution. By the 1930s, governments, intellectuals, and cultural nationalists in Europe began to see a need for national cinemas to shore up their defenses against foreign ideologies. Spanish responses, as we shall see, closely mimicked this pattern. De Grazia, "Mass Culture and Sovereignty," 62–81.

14. In 1925 Spain had 1,497 movie theaters, almost one-tenth of the European total! Pérez Perucha, "Narración de un aciago destino," 88.

15. The following account comes from Gubern, El cine sonoro, 44–52.

16. For a greater discussion of the CHC and its various problems, see Sandie Holguín "The Conquest of Tradition: Culture and Politics in Spain during the Second Republic, 1931–1936" (Ph.D. diss., University of California, Los Angeles,

1994), 193–206. Of course, immorality was only one part of the equation. Access to an audience of over 100 million Spanish speakers had certain financial appeal for Spanish commerce. Gubern, *El cine sónoro*, 50.

17. "Cinema educativo," *El Sol*, May 14, 1933. A small sampling of such articles includes: Luis Angé, "Pedagogía del cinema instructivo," *Popular Film*, February 26, 1931; Luis Angé, "Psicología y pedagogía del cinematógrafo instructivo," *Boletín de la Institución Libre de Enseñanza*, August 31, 1931:233; "¿Que es el cinema educativo?" *El Sol*, November 6, 1932; "El 'cine' como medio instructivo de política internacional," *El Sol*, December 8, 1932.

18. F. Blanco Castilla, *El cinema educativo y Gracián pedagogo* (Madrid: Ed. F. Beltrán, 1933), 13, 15, 17, 18.

19. Ibid., 34, 118.

20. Ibid., 47, 39.

21. Luis Gómez Mesa, *Autenticidad del cinema educativo* (Madrid: Sáez, 1936), 24.

22. Lorenzo Luzuriaga, *La nueva escuela pública* (Madrid: Publicaciones de la Revista de Pedagogía, 1931), 63–68.

23. S. P., "Orientaciones: El cinematógrafo como medio educativo," *El Socialista*, October 4, 1931.

24. *Patronato de Misiones Pedagógicas* (Sept. 1931–Dec. 1933). Madrid: n.p., 1934, 85; hereafter *PMP* (1934).

25. Ibid, 31. Until the end of 1933 the misioneros had at their disposal twenty-six 16-mm and two 35-mm film projectors, and by 1933 they had one sound projector. They showed a total of 174 films. By the end of 1934 they had thirty-six projectors and 411 films, of which 22 were sound films and 15 were documentaries made specifically for the *Servicio del Patronato* (*PMP* [1934], 85–86; *Patronato de Misiones Pedagógicas, Memoria de la Misión Pedagógica-Social en Sanabria (Zamora): Resumen de trabajos realizados en el año 1934* (Madrid: n. p., 1935), 95–96; hereafter *PMP* [1935]). Because Spain did not produce sound films in 1932, the Misiones Pedagógicas imported most of their films from the United States. José Val del Omar, Gonzalo Menéndez Pidal, and Eduardo G. Maroto seem to have been the only documentary filmmakers who produced films for the Misiones. Of the sixteen documentary titles that I have seen specifically mentioned, five came from a series of educational films put out by the Eastman-Kodak Company. These educational films apparently were translated and distributed in foreign countries. See Román Gubern, "El cine sónoro," *Historia del cine español* (Madrid: Cátedra, 1995), 61, and *Historia de las películas pedagógicas Eastman* (Madrid: Eastman-Kodak, n. d.).

26. By the end of 1933, the actual numbers and categories of film shown by the Misiones Pedagógicas were as follows: (1) 16-mm films: agriculture, 19; geography, 34; history, 4; natural science, 20; general lectures, 17; hygiene, 7; industry, 14; cartoons, 12; physics, 8; comedies, 21; and (2) 35-mm films: agriculture, 5; geography, 9; industry, 4. *PMP* (1934), 86. Breakdowns for the films shown in 1934 are not listed in *PMP* (1935).

27. For the relationship between regenerationism and geography, see Josefina Gómez Mendoza and Nicolás Ortega Cantero, "Geografía y regeneracionismo en España (1875–1936)," *Sistema* 77 (1987): 77–89.

28. Raf, "Misiones Pedagógicas," *Diario de Almería*, September 24, 1933.

29. Ibid., September 28, 1933.

30. *PMP* (1934), 31, 48, 34

31. Ibid., 37.

32. "Las parámeras espirituales de España: La maravillosa obra de las Misiones Pedagógicas en nuestras regiones desventuradas," *El Sol*, June 28, 1935.

33. Mateo Santos, "Sugerencias: El cine como instrumento pedagógico," *Popular Film*, February 5, 1931.

34. Isidro R. Mendieta, "Arte social: Propaganda por el cine," *El Socialista*, October 1, 1933.

35. Mateo Santos, "El cinema al servicio del pueblo," *Popular Film*, March 9, 1933.

36. S. P., "Orientaciones: El cinematógrafo como medio educativo," *El Socialista*, October 4, 1931. Although one could argue that some Americans made films that highlighted social injustices, I am not so much concerned with what Americans actually filmed as I am with Spaniards' perceptions of Hollywood.

37. See, for example, Rafael Gil, "Cine documental y educativo," *Popular Film*, September 3, 1931.

38. Mateo Santos, "El cinema al servicio de las ideas," *Popular Film*, July 16, 1931. Republicans sometimes banned certain films for fear of public riots. See my discussion of the *Battleship Potemkin* later in this chapter.

39. Ibid.

40. Rafael Gil belonged to the Grupo de Escritores Cinematográficos Independientes (GECI; Group of Independent Film Writers), a group that Gubern characterizes as decidedly "centrist." Gubern, *El cine sónoro*, 203.

41. He does not actually mention specific names of documentaries produced by Cooper and Schoedsack. Rafael Gil, "Cine documental y educativo," *Popular Film*, September 3, 1931.

42. Ibid.

43. Nazi propaganda minister Goebbels was said to admire *Battleship Potemkin* for its ability to sway the masses, and in a survey of intellectuals and film aficionados taken in 1932 by the film journal, *Nuestro Cinema*, all the respondents replied that *Battleship Potemkin* was destined to be a classic film. On Goebbels, see Angel Rosenblat," ¿Es capaz el fascismo de engendrar una cultura?" *Nuestro Cinema* (April–May 1933), as cited in Carlos Pérez Merinero and David Pérez Merinero, *El cinema como arma de clase: Antología de Nuestro Cinema 1932–1935* (Valencia: Fernando Torres, 1975), 99–103. On responses to the survey, see ibid., 185–209.

44. Luis Buñuel, *Mi último suspiro (memorias),* trans. Ana María de la Fuente (Barcelona: Plaza and Janés, 1982), 88.

45. *Nuestro Cinema* 10 (March 1933), as cited in Gubern, *El cine sonoro*, 225–226. *Battleship Potemkin* was first shown in Spain in May 1931 in the Cineclub Española. Gubern, "El cine sonoro," 162.

46. Stanley Payne says that between February and June of 1933, "the CNT attempted general strikes in at least nine medium or large-sized cities and among peasants in Seville provinces." Stanley Payne, *Spain's First Democracy: The Second Republic, 1931–1936* (Madison: University of Wisconsin Press, 1993), 133.

47. The Spanish Constitution of 1931 called Spain "a government of workers."

48. R.Gil, *Nuestro Cinema* 11 (April–May 1933), 174.

49. Francisco Martínez González, "Cinema Ruso," *Popular Film*, February 16, 1933.

50. S. P., "Orientaciones: El cinematógrafo como medio educativo," *El Socialista*, October 4, 1931.

51. "Estatuos de la Institución Libre de Enseñanza," 1876, as cited in Antonio Jiménez-Landi Martínez, *La Institución Libre de Enseñanza y su ambiente*, vol. 1 (Madrid: Ediciones Taurus, 1973), 703.

52. See, for example, *PMP* (1934), 14.

53. Gubern, *El cine sonoro*, 184–186. As a footnote to this episode, during the Spanish Civil War, Buñuel added a voiceover to indicate that these types of rural problems were not insurmountable. In fact, he claimed, regions similar to Las Hurdes had improved dramatically owing to the actions of the Popular Front. See also Emmanuel Larraz, *Le cinéma espagnol des origines à nous jours* (Paris: Les Editions du Cerf, 1986), 74–76; Larraz, *El cine español* (Paris: Masson et Cie, 1973), 30–34.

54. Gubern, *El cine sonoro*, 69.

55. José María Gil Robles, *No fue posible la paz* (Barcelona: Ediciones Ariel, 1968), 262.

56. Josef von Sternberg, *Fun in a Chinese Laundry* (New York: Macmillan, 1965), 267. The flak surrounding this film might account for another censorship law promulgated in October 1935, which prohibited films that attempted to "denaturalize or diminish the prestige owed to institutions and personalities of our patria." *Historia del cine español,* 453. For other critiques of this film, see "Tu nombre es tentacíon," *Filmor,* July 11, 1935, and "Películas injuriosas para España," *Filmor,* October 31, 1935.

57. "Razón de ser," *Filmor,* June 20, 1935.

58. "Películas injuriosas para España" *Filmor,* October 31, 1935.

59. F. Castello, "Aspectos y remedios de la inmoralidad en el cine," *Filmor,* August 29, 1935.

60. Ibid. Castello's perception belied what was actually happening in the workforce. According to Adrian Shubert: "Overall the number of women in the workforce declined continually between 1877 and 1930, from 1.5 million to 1.1 million, as did the percentage of women who worked, from 17 percent in 1877 to 9 percent in 1930." Adrian Shubert, *A Social History of Modern Spain* (London: Routledge, 1992), 38.

61. Castello, "Aspectos y remedios."

62. Ibid.

63. Ibid.

64. For example, Lluch Garín gave a talk on "Film and Legislation," during the "Week against Immoral Film" (April 23–27, 1935) that was organized by the Juventud Femenina de Acción Católica, a subsidiary of the conservative Catholic organization Acción Católica. For more information on the Week against Immoral Film, see *El Debate,* April 22–27, 1935.

65. Buñuel and Dalí's *An Andalusian Dog,* for example, premiered in Madrid's

Cineclub Español. Members of the Cineclub came from all shades of the political spectrum and included such members as Ramón Gómez de la Serna, Pío Baroja, Federico García Lorca, Rafael Alberti, and Gregorio Marañón. Rafael Utrera, "Cuatro secuencias sobre el cineasta Ernesto Giménez Caballero," *Anthropos* 84 (May 1988): 46–50.

66. See Geoffrey Herf, *Reactionary Modernism* (Cambridge: Cambridge University Press, 1984).

67. See, for example, Ernesto Giménez Caballero, *Genio de España: Exaltaciones a una resurrección nacional. y del mundo* (Madrid: Ediciones de la Gaceta Literaria, 1932); Giménez Caballero, *Manuel Azaña (Profecías españolas)* (Madrid: Ediciones de la Gaceta Literaria, 1932); Giménez Caballero, *La nueva catolicidad: Teoría general sobre el fascismo en Europa: en España* (Madrid: Ediciones de la Gaceta Literaria, 1933); and Giménez Caballero, *Arte y Estado* (Madrid: Gráfica Universal, 1935).

68. Giménez Caballero, *Arte y estado*, 86, 88, 91.

69. Giménez Caballero presents many of the same arguments verbatim in his later work, *El cine y la cultura humana* (Bilbao: Ediciones de Conferencias y Ensayos, 1944).

70. Giménez Caballero, *Art y estado*, 156, 153, 156.

71. Ibid., 160

72. Buñuel, *Mi último suspiro*, 70–71.

73. Giménez Caballero, *El cine y la cultura humana*, 13.

74. Ibid., 45, 48.

## Chapter 5. Literacy and Regeneration

1. See Francisco Giner de los Ríos, "Consideraciones sobre el desarollo de la literatura moderna," *Estudios Literarios* (Madrid: R. Labajos, 1866), 92, and my discussion of his ideas in chapter 1.

2. Manuel B. Cossío, *De su jornada (fragmentos)* (Madrid: Aguilar, 1966), 21.

3. Arturo Barea, *The Forging of a Rebel*, trans. Ilsa Barea (New York: Viking Press, 1943), 354.

4. See, for example, "Informaciones: Lo que hace la República para la difusión del libro español," *Revista de Pedagogía* 161 (May 1935): 227–228.

5. "Decreto organizando el Patronato de Misiones Pedagógicas," *Gaceta de Madrid*, May 30, 1931; "Decreto estableciendo bibliotecas en las escuelas nacionales," *Gaceta de Madrid*, August 8, 1931, as cited in Patronato de Misiones Pedagógicas (Madrid: n.p., 1934); hereafter *PMP* (1934), 153–159.

6. See Jean Bécarud and Evelyne López Campillo, *Los intelectuales españoles durante la Segunda Republica* (Madrid: Siglo Veintiuno, 1978), 33–35.

7. *PMP* (1934), 158.

8. Ibid., xiv.

9. Ibid., 15.

10. Ibid., xxii. More recent studies suggest that the illiteracy rate in 1930 for people ten years or older was 32 percent. In terms of the total population, the illiteracy rate for women was 64 percent and for men it was 36 percent. See Mercedes

Vilanova Ribas and Xavier Moreno Juliá, *Atlas de la evolución del analfabetismo en España de 1887 a 1981* (Madrid: Centro de Publicaciones del Ministerio de Educación y Ciencia, 1992), 289.

11. "Discurso leído en la inauguración del curso académico de 1931 a 1932 por D. Marcelino Domingo, Ministro de Instrucción Pública y Bellas Artes," in *Homenaje a D. Marcelino Domingo* (Madrid: n. p., 1936), 12–13.

12. Hipólito Escolar Sobrino, *La cultura durante la Guerra Civil* (Madrid: Alhambra, 1987), 30.

13. The following information can be found in a section describing the Servicio de Bibliotecas in *PMP* (1934), 61–69.

14. Rafael Altamira y Crevea, *Lecturas para obreros (Indicaciones bibliográficas y consejos)* (Madrid: Biblioteca de "La Revista Socialista," 1904), as cited in José Carlos Mainer, "Notas sobre la lectura obrera en España (1890–1930)," in Albert Balcells, ed. *Teoría y práctica del movimiento obrero en España (1900–1936)* (Valencia: F. Torres, 1977), 211–212.

15. *PMP* (1934), 67.

16. Ibid., 12.

17. Ibid., 14.

18. Ibid., 11.

19. Raf, "Misiones Pedagógicas," *Diario de Almería,* September 28, 1933. A complete listing of the works the misioneros recited can be found in the series of articles written in the *Diario de Almería* by Raf on September 21, 22, 24, 26, and 28 and October 3, 1933.

20. *PMP* (1934), 67–68.

21. Ibid., 68–69.

22. Cited in ibid., 32.

23. Ibid., 36–40.

24. Ibid., 38.

25. Ibid., 39–40

26. "Biblioteca del Patronato de Misiones Pedagógicas," *Atenas,* ca. 1934, 416.

27. *Diario de Sesiones de las Cortes Constituyentes,* June 26, 1935.

28. *Diario de Sesiones,* June 28, 1935.

29. "Una institución ineficaz y superflua," *El Debate,* August 7, 1935.

30. Ibid.

31. Ibid.

32. Interview of Antonio Sánchez Barbudo in John Crispin, "Antonio Sánchez Barbudo, Misionero Pedagógico," in Benito Brancaforte, ed., *Homenaje a Antonio Sánchez Barbudo: Ensayos de literatura española moderna* (Madison: Dept. of Spanish and Portuguese, University of Wisconsin, 1981), 21–22 n. 14. The criticism from Manuel Tuñón de Lara comes from his *Medio siglo de cultura española: 1885–1936,* 3d ed. (Madrid: Tecnos, 1977), 263.

33. José Bergamín, "La decadencia del analfabetismo," *Cruz y Raya* 3 (June 15, 1933): 63–94. Interestingly enough, Bergamín was a staunch supporter of the Republic during the Civil War, when he played a great role in helping to promote cultural activities through his work in the Alliance of Antifascist Intellectuals. For

a discussion of Bergamín's paradoxical role within the Republic, and specifically with *Cruz y Raya*, see Nigel Dennis, *José Bergamín: A Critical Introduction, 1920–1936* (Toronto: University of Toronto Press, 1986), 136–180.

34. Bergamín, "La decadencia," 63–65.

35. Ibid., 67, 69–70. This entire section is a play on the Spanish word for literacy—*alfabetización*—and the alphabet.

36. Ibid., 71.

37. Ibid., 93–94.

38. *PMP* (1934), 37.

39. Ibid., 15.

40. For a thorough discussion of anarchist reading habits, see Lily Litvak, *Musa libertaria: Arte, literatura y vida cultural del anarquismo español (1880–1913)* (Barcelona: Antoni Bosch, 1981).

41. Again, the anarchists adopted the same literacy "technology" as the institucionistas, but for different ends. This illustrates Prasenjit Duara's idea that similar technologies also allow "rivals of the nascent nation-state to construct alternative forms of political and even national identity." Prasenjit Duara, "Historicizing National Identity, or Who Imagines What and When," in Geoff Eley and Ronald Grigor Suny, eds., *Becoming National: A Reader* (New York: Oxford University Press, 1966), 161.

42. Un estudiante de la Normal, "Sobre la cultura de los pueblos," *La Revista Blanca,* May 1, 1931, 563.

43. Sadi de Gorter, "Primacia del factor social en la literatura," *La Revista Blanca,* July 12, 1935, 654.

44. F. Alba, "El orígen de las letras, su proceso de desarollo y las modernas corrientes literarias," *La Revista Blanca,* September 20, 1935, 903.

45. Ignacio Cornejo, "Don Quijote desde el punto de vista anarquista," *La Revista Blanca,* December 27, 1935, 1207.

46. Ibid., 1208.

47. The text of Article 4 of the 1931 constitution reads as follows: "Castilian is the official language of the Republic. Every Spaniard has the obligation to know it and the right to use it, without harming the rights of state laws that recognize provincial or regional laws. Except for that which is set out in special laws, nobody can be required to know or use any regional language." Unamuno had proposed replacing "Castilian" with "Spanish" to make the wording of the Article read, "Spanish is the official language of Spain." See Luis Jiménez de Asúa, *Proceso histórico de la constitución de la República española* (Madrid: Editorial Reus, 1932), 113–114.

48. Reported in "Grand discurso de Don Miguel de Unamuno sobre el castellano como idioma oficial de la República," *El Sol,* September 19, 1931.

49. Reported in "Conferencia de Unamuno: Afirma que del Estatuo le preocupa el problema cultural," *El Socialista,* May 8, 1932.

50. Unamuno's word choice, *renación*, is a pun that does not work in English. It means rebirth, but the root, *nación*, also evokes the idea of a national renewal.

51. "Grand discurso de Don Miguel de Unamuno," *El Sol,* September 19, 1931.

52. "Reforma de la enseñanza española, vista por Don Fernando de los Ríos," *El Sol*, March 27, 1932.

53. *Diario de Sesiones*, June 2, 1932.

54. Juan [Joan] Estelrich, *Temas de nuestro tiempo: Catalanismo y reforma hispánica* (Barcelona: Montaner y Simón, 1932), 97–98.

55. *Diario de Sesiones*, June 30, 1932.

56. "El idioma," *El Debate*, May 29, 1932.

57. *Diario de Sesiones*, May 26, 1932.

58. Ibid., May 27, 1932.

59. Ibid., June 29, 1932.

60. *Gaceta de Madrid*, April 24, 1936. Also duplicated in *El Sol*, April 24, 1936.

61. Ibid.

62. "Un proyecto del Señor Azaña: La vuelta a nuestros clásicos," *El Socialista*, April 24, 1936.

63. Nuñez de Arenas, "Nuestra cultura: Clásicos de todos," *El Sol*, April 24, 1936.

64. Luis Santullano, "La lectura de los clásicos," *El Sol*, May 2, 1936.

## Chapter 6. Culture on the Battlefield

1. Three works that do a thorough job of detailing the myriad projects conceived by the warring factions include: Juan Manuel Fernández Soria, *Educación y cultura en la Guerra Civil (España 1936–1939)* (Valencia: NAU Llibres, 1984); Hipólito Escolar Sobrino, *La cultura durante la Guerra Civil* (Madrid: Alhambra, 1987); Miguel A. Gamonal Torres, *Arte y política en la Guerra Civil española: El caso republicano* (Granada: Diputación Provincial de Granada, 1987).

2. Of Giral's cabinet, four were institucionistas: Giral himself, Francisco Barnés (Minister of Public Instruction), Bernardo Giner de los Ríos (Minister of Communications), and Alvarez Buylla (Minister of Industry and Commerce). José Alvarez Lopera, *La política de bienes culturales del gobierno republicano durante la Guerra Civil española,* vol.1 (Madrid: Ministerio de Cultura, 1982), 24 n.

3. The works done by the Junta de Incautación y Protección del Tesoro Artístico are explained in great detail in Lopera, *La política de bienes culturales.* See also Escolar Sobrino, *La cultura durante la Guerra Civil,* 66–70.

4. Escolar Sobrino, *La cultura durante la Guerra Civil,* 67.

5. Ibid., 107; Fernández Soria, *Educación y cultura,* 123. See also Le Deuxième Congrès International des Écrivains, *Défense de la culture* (Paris: n.p., 1937).

6. Escolar Sobrino, *La cultura durante la Guerra Civil,* 106–114.

7. Alvarez Lopera makes this same point in *La política de bienes culturales,* 26.

8. Fernández Soria, *Educación y cultura,* 120–123.

9. Escolar Sobrino, *La cultura durante la Guerra Civil,* 85.

10. Alvarez Lopera, *La política de bienes culturales,* 28.

11. For general explanations of the Ministry's Cultural Works, see Ministerio de Instrucción Pública y Sanidad, "Charlas populares: Lo que significa la guerra. La República es la cultura para todas" (Barcelona: Ediciones Españolas, c.1938). See also Ministère de l'Instruction Publique de la République Espagnole,

"L'effort culturel du peuple espagnol en armes" (1937). Fundación Pablo Iglesias, FC 1072.

12. Archives of the Federación Anarquista Ibéria-Comité Peninsular, International Institut voor Sociale Geschiedenis, Amsterdam, Netherlands.

13. This discussion of the Milicias de la Cultura and the subsequent discussion of the Brigadas Volantes come from Fernández Soria, *Educación y cultura*, 49–67, and from copies of some of the Milicias de la Cultura papers housed in FAI and CNT archives of the International Institut voor Sociale Geschiedenis, Amsterdam, Netherlands.

14. "Programa del espectáculo que realiza el cuadro artístico," Barcelona, May 1938. Archives of the FAI-Comité Peninsular. Film 175, C3 Cultura, CU4, "Las Milicias de la Cultura." Microfilms in the International Institut voor Sociale Geschiedenis, Amsterdam.

15. Order of 20 September 1937, cited in Fernández Soria, *Educación y cultura*, 60.

16. Ministerio de Instrucción Pública y Sanidad, "Charlas populares," 3.

17. Ibid., 14.

18. Ibid., 8.

19. Escolar Sobrino, *La cultura durante la Guerra Civil*, 101–103.

20. Ibid., 201.

21. Ibid., 190.

22. "El Magisterio de la Provincia de Zaragoza," *Boletín de Educación de Zaragoza* 2 (September–October 1936): 2.

23. Ibid., 3, 5.

24. Escolar Sobrino, *La cultura durante la Guerra Civil*, 189–190.

25. Order of 21 September 1937, as cited in Fernández Soria, *Educación y cultura*, 185.

26. Escular Sobrino, *La cultura durante la Guerra Civil*, 226.

27. Fernández Soria, *Educación y cultura*, 205–206.

28. For a study on the organization and workings of the Sección Femenina, see María Teresa Gallego Méndez, *Mujer, Falange y Franquismo* (Madrid: Taurus, 1983).

29. Fernández Soria, *Educación y cultura*, 205–212.

30. Eduardo de Ontañón, "Las Misiones Pedagógicas, consuelo de heridos de guerra," *Estampa*, September 19, 1936.

31. Ibid.

32. Order of 8 October 1936, as cited in Fernández Soria, *Educación y cultura*, 91–92.

33. Ibid., 221–223.

34. Order of 19 June 1939, as cited in ibid., 226.

35. Antonio Aparicio, "El teatro en nuestro ejército," *Comisario* 4 (December 1938), as cited in Juan Manuel Fernández Soria, "Medios de comunicación y extensión cultural en el ejército republicano," in Carmelo Garitaonaindía Garnacho et al., eds. *Comunicación, cultura y política durante la II República y la Guerra Civil: II Encuentro de la Historia de la Prensa*. (Bilbao: Departamento de Cultura, Diputación Foral de Bizkaia: Servicio Editorial, Universidad del País Vasco, 1990), 396.

36. See, for example, the Quinto Regimiento's "Teatro en la Calle" series: Quinto Regimiento, *Batallones de choque* (Madrid: Ediciones del Quinto Regimiento, n.d.), in the International Institut voor Sociale Geschiedenis, Amsterdam, Netherlands. For a contemporary discussion of revolutionary theater in Catalonia, see Manuel Valldeperes, *La força social i revolucionària del teatre* (Barcelona: Editorial Forja, 1937).

37. *El Mono Azul* 8 (October 15, 1936): 8, as cited in José Monleón, *El Mono Azul: Teatro de urgencia y romancero de la Guerra Civil* (Madrid: Editorial Ayuso, 1979), 190.

38. Monleón, *El Mono Azul*, 190–192. For a detailed discussion of the revolutionary plays of the left during the Civil War, see Jim McCarthy, *Political Theater during the Spanish Civil War* (Cardiff: University of Wales Press, 1999), and Francisco Mundi Pedret, *El teatro de la Guerra Civil* (Barcelona: PPU, 1987).

39. Rafael Dieste, *El nuevo retablo de las maravillas* in Miguel Bilbatua, ed., *Teatro de agitación política 1933–1939* (Madrid: Edicusa, 1976).

40. *El Mono Azul* 31 (September 2, 1937), as cited in Monleón, *El Mono Azul*, 219–221.

41. Monleón, *El Mono Azul*, 241.

42. Fernández Soria, *Educación y cultura*, 153.

43. Rafael Alberti, "Presentación del teatro de urgencia" in Robert Marrast, *Prosas encontradas, 1924–1942*, 193–201, as cited in Monleón, *El Mono Azul*, 202. For examples of the types of plays written for the Guerrillas de Teatro, see Miguel Bilbatúa, ed., *Teatro de agitación política 1933–1939* (Madrid: Edicusa), 1976.

44. Ibid., 203.

45. Quinto Regimento, prologue to *Batallones de choque*.

46. Ibid., 9–14.

47. *Annuari de la Instituciò del Teatre de la Generalitat de Catalunya, curs 1936–1937*, 192–193, as cited in Francesc Burguet i Ardiaca, *La CNT i la política teatral a Catalunya (1936–1938)* (Barcelona: Institut del Teatre de la Diputaciò de Barcelona, 1984), 65.

48. Fernández Soria, *Educación y cultura*, 223.

49. Dionisio Ridruejo, *El Diario Palentino,* collected in Sotero Otero del Pozo's *España inmortal* (Valladolid: n.p., 1937), 151, as cited in Julio Rodríguez-Puertolas, *Literatura fascista española* (Madrid: Akal, 1986), 1:252.

50. Gonzalo Torrente Ballestar, "Razón y ser de la dramática futura," *Jerarquía* 2 (October 1937): 75, as cited in Julio Rodríguez-Puertolas, *Literatura fascista española* (Madrid: Akal, 1986), 254.

51. For a discussion of Pemán's Civil War drama, see Carlos Serrano, "La funcionalidad del teatro en la Guerra Civil y el caso de José María Pemán," in Dru Dougherty and María Francisca Vilches de Frutos, eds., *El teatro en España: Entre la tradición y la vanguardia, 1918–1939* (Madrid: Tabapress, 1992), 393–400.

52. Sotero Otero del Pozo, *España inmortal* (Valladolid, Palencia: Afrodisio Aguado, 1937).

53. Dr. Dalópio, *La España que amanece* (San Sebastian: Bueno Olivan, 1938), 12.

54. Ibid., 15.

55. Manuel Machado, "Intenciones: Teatro español," *ABC*, August 4, 1938, as

cited in Julio Rodríguez-Puertolas, *Literatura fascista española* (Madrid: Akal, 1986), 252.

56. Dionisio Ridruejo, *Casi unas memorias* (Barcelona: Editorial Planeta, 1976), 178, as cited in ibid., 256.

57. Emmanuel Larraz, *Le cinéma espagnol des origins à nos jours* (Paris: Les Editions du Cerf, 1986), 90–94; Escolar Sobrino, *La cultura durante la Guerra Civil,* 101–103;

58. Santos Zunzunegui, "Aparatos de estado y propaganda fílmica: El cine de la República española (1936–1939)," in Carmelo Garitaonaindía Garnacho et al., eds. *Comunicación, cultura y política durante la II República y la Guerra Civil: II Encuentro de la Historia de la Prensa* (Bilbao: Departamento de Cultura, Diputación Foral de Bizkaia: Servicio Editorial, Universidad del País Vasco, 1990), 478–482.

59. José María Caparrós Lera, *Arte y política en el cine de la República (1931–1939)* (Barcelona: Editorial 7 1/2, 1981), 47.

60. Larraz, *Le cinéma espagnol,* 79.

61. Ibid., 90–91.

62. Escolar Sobrino, *La cultura durante la Guerra Civil,* 249; Fernández Soria, *Educación y cultura,* 223.

63. Larraz, *Le cinéma espagnol,* 91–92.

64. See Román Gubern, *La censura: Función política y ordenamiento jurídico bajo el franquismo (1936–1975)* (Barcelona: Peninsula, 1981).

65. Escolar Sobrino, *La cultura durante la Guerra Civil,* 134.

66. See *Realizaciones de la España Leal, La sección de bibliotecas de cultura popular: Un año de trabajo, julio 1936–julio 1937* (Valencia: Ediciones de Cultura Popular, 1938).

67. Escolar Sobrino, *La cultura durante la Guerra Civil,* 212. He does not note the source of his quote.

68. *La Intendencia* 8 (April 1938), as cited in Fernández Soria, "Medios de comunicación y extensión cultural," 387.

69. Fernández Soria, *Educación y cultura,* 53–55.

70. Escolar Sobrino, *La cultura durante la Guerra Civil,* 225.

71. Manuel Ballesteros Gaibrois, *La letra "Y"* (Madrid: Delegación Nacional de la Sección Femenina de F.E.T. de las J.O.N.S., 1939?), Southworth Collection [microform], reel 46, item 1859.

## Conclusion

1. See, for example, Constancio Eguía Ruiz, *Los causantes de la tragedia hispana: Un gran crimen de los intelectuales españoles* (Buenos Aires: Editorial Difusión, 1938); *Una poderosa fuerza secreta: la Institución Libre de Enseñanza* (San Sebastián: Editorial Española, 1940).

2. Some recent studies of Franco's attempts at cultural unification, at least in the sphere of foreign relations, include: Lorenzo Delgado Gómez-Escalonilla, *Imperio de papel: Acción cultural y política exterior durante el primer franquismo* (Madrid: Consejo Superior de Investigaciones Científicas, 1992); María A.

Escudero, "The Image of Latin America Disseminated in Spain by the Franco
Regime: Repercussions in the Configuration of a National Identity" (Ph.D. diss.,
University of California, San Diego, 1993).

    3. *Misiones Pedagógicas* (n.p.: c.1945).

    4. Ibid., 23.

    5. Eugen Weber, *Peasants into Frenchmen: The Modernization of Rural France,
1870–1914* (Stanford, CA: Stanford University Press, 1976).

# BIBLIOGRAPHY

## Archives

Academia de la Historia (Madrid)
Archivo de la Institución Libre de Enseñanza (Madrid)
Archivo Histórico Nacional (Madrid)
Archivo Histórico Nacional (Salamanca)
Arxiu Nacional de Catalunya (Barcelona)
Biblioteca Arus (Barcelona)
Biblioteca Nacional (Madrid)
Centre de Documentació-Històrico-Social-Ateneu Enciclopèdic Popular
  (Barcelona)
Consejo Superior de Investigaciones Científicas (Madrid)
Fundación García Lorca (Madrid)
Fundación Pablo Iglesias (Madrid)
Hemeroteca Municipal (Madrid)
Instituto Municipal de Historia (Barcelona)
International Institut voor Sociale Geschiedenis (Amsterdam)

## Newspapers and Periodicals

*Acción Española*
*Adelantado de Segovia*
*Ahora*
*Anthropos*
*Atenas*
*Boletín de Educación de Zaragoza*
*Boletín de la Institución Libre de Enseñanza*
*El Carbayón*
*Cruz y Raya*

*Cuadernos del Congreso por la Libertad de la Cultura*
*Cuadernos Americanos*
*El Debate* (1931–1936)
*El Defensor de Granada*
*Diario de Almería*
*La Escuela Moderna*
*Estampa*
*Filmor*
*Heraldo de Madrid*
*La Libertad*
*Luz*
*El Mercantil Valenciano*
*Mirador*
*El Noticiero*
*Nuestro Cinema*
*Octubre*
*La Opinión*
*Popular Film*
*Primer Acto*
*Residencia*
*La Revista Blanca*
*Revista de las Españas*
*Revista de Occidente*
*Revista de Pedagogía*
*Revista de la Universidad Internacional de Santander*
*El Socialista* (1931–1936)
*El Sol* (1931–1936)
*Trabajadores de la Enseñanza*
*La Vanguardia*
*La Voz de Galicia*

## Articles and Books

Ackelsberg, Martha. *Free Women of Spain: Anarchism and the Struggle for the Emancipation of Women.* Bloomington: Indiana University Press, 1991.
Adams, Mildred. "The Theatre in the Spanish Republic." *Theatre Arts Monthly* (March 1932): 327–354.
Aguilera Sastre, Juan. "El debate sobre el teatro nacional durante la dictadura y la República." In Dru Dougherty and María Francisca de Frutos Vilches, eds. *El teatro de España entre la tradición y la vanguardia (1918–1939)* (175–187). Madrid: Consejo Superior de Investigaciones Científicas and Fundación Federico García Lorca, 1992.
Alba Tercedor, Carlos. "La educación en la Segunda República: Un intento de socialización política." In Manuel Ramírez, ed. *Estudios sobre la II República española* (49–85). Madrid: Editorial Tecnos, 1975.
Alberti, Rafael. *Farsa de los Reyes Magos (Fragmento): "El Espantapájaros."* In

*Octubre* 6 (April 6, 1934), 13–15. Reprinted in Enrique Montero, ed., *Octubre* (157–159). Facsimile. Vaduz: Topos Verlas, 1977.

"Alejandro Casona frente a su teatro." *Primer Acto* 49 (January 1964): 16–19.

Altamira y Crevea, Rafael. "The Spanish Drama as an Element of Moral Education." In John Drinkwater, ed. *Essays by Divers Hands: Being the Transactions of the Royal Society of Literature of the United Kingdom* (43–61). London: Humphrey Milford and Oxford University Press, 1925.

Alvarez Junco, José. *El emperador del Paralelo: Lerroux y la demagogía populista.* Madrid: Alianza Editorial, 1990.

Alvarez Junco, José. "Los intelectuales: Anticlericalismo y republicanismo." In J. L. García Delgado, ed. *Los orígenes culturales de la II República* (100–126). Madrid: Siglo Veintiuno, 1993.

Alvarez Lopera, José. *La política de bienes culturales del gobierno republicano durante la Guerra Civil española.* Vol. 1. Madrid: Ministerio de Cultura, 1982.

Anderson, Benedict. *Imagined Communities.* Rev. ed. London: Verso, 1991.

Araquistáin, Luis. "El krausismo en España." *Cuadernos del Congreso por la Libertad de la Cultura* 44 (September–October 1960): 3–12.

Araquistáin, Luis. *El pensamiento español contemporáneo.* Buenos Aires: Editorial Losada, 1962.

Araquistáin, Luis. *La batalla teatral.* Madrid: Mundo Latino, 1930.

Arbeloa, Victor Manuel, and Miguel de Santiago, eds. and comps. *Intelectuales ante la Segunda República española.* Santiago: Ediciones Almar, 1981.

Auclair, Marcelle. *Enfances et mort de García Lorca.* Paris: Editions du Seuil, 1968.

Avrich, Paul. *The Modern School Movement: Anarchism and Education in the United States.* Princeton, NJ: Princeton University Press, 1980.

Azaña, Manuel. "La República como forma del ser nacional." In vol.2 of *Obras Completas,* Mexico City: Ediciones Oasis, 1966.

Azcoaga, Enrique. "Las Misiones Pedagógicas." *Revista de Occidente* 7–8 (1981): 222–232.

Azorín. "El teatro nacional." In *La farándula* (102–104). Zaragoza: Librería General, 1945.

Balcells, Albert. *Catalan Nationalism: Past and Present.* New York and Basingstoke: St. Martin's Press and Macmillan, 1996.

Balcells, Albert, and Manuel Tuñón de Lara, eds. *Teoría y práctica del movimiento obrero en España (1900–1936).* Valencia: F. Torres, 1997.

Ballestar Gozalvo, José. *La escuela única.* Valencia: Cuadernos de Cultura, 1930.

Ballesteros Gaibrois, Manuel. *La letra "Y."* Madrid: Delegación Nacional de la Sección Femenina de F.E.T. de las J.O.N.S., 1939? Southworth Collection [microform] reel 46, item 1859.

Barbéns, Francisco de. *La moral en la calle, en el cinematógrafo y en el teatro.* Barcelona: Librería Católica Internacional, 1914.

Barea, Arturo. *The Forging of a Rebel.* Translated by Ilsa Barea. New York: Viking Press, 1943.

Bécarud, Jean. *Cruz y Raya, 1933–1936.* Madrid: Taurus Ediciones, 1969.

Bécarud, Jean, and Evelyne López Campillo. *Los intelectuales españoles durante la II República.* Madrid: Siglo Veintiuno, 1978.

Becker, Marjorie. *Setting the Virgin on Fire: Lázaro Cárdenas, Michoacan Peasants and the Redemption of the Mexican Revolution*. Berkeley: University of California Press, 1995.

Bello, Luis. *Viaje por las escuelas de España*. Madrid: Magisterio Español, 1926.

Ben-Ami, Shlomo. *Fascism from Above: The Dictatorship of Primo de Rivera in Spain, 1923–1930*. Oxford: Clarendon Press, 1983.

Beramendi, Justo G., and Ramón Máiz, eds. *Los nacionalismos en la España de la II República*. Madrid: Siglo Veintiuno, 1991.

Bergamín, José. "La decadencia del analfabetismo." *Cruz y Raya* 3 (June 15, 1933): 63–94.

Besas, Peter. *Behind the Spanish Lens: Spanish Cinema under Fascism and Democracy*. Denver: Arden Press, 1985.

Bilbatúa, Miguel, ed. *Teatro de agitación política 1933–1939*. Madrid: Edicusa, 1976.

Blas Guerrero, Andrés de. *Tradición republicana y nacionalismo español (1876–1930)*. Madrid: Tecnos, 1991.

Blinkhorn, Martin. *Carlism and Crisis in Spain, 1931–1939*. Cambridge: Cambridge University Press, 1975.

Boyd, Carolyn. "The Anarchists and Education in Spain, 1868–1909," *Journal of Modern History* 48 (1976): 125–170.

Boyd, Carolyn. *Historia Patria: Politics, History and National Identity in Spain, 1875–1975*. Princeton, NJ: Princeton University Press, 1997.

Brenan, Gerald. *The Spanish Labyrinth: An Account of the Social and Political Background of the Civil War*. 2d ed. Cambridge: Cambridge University Press, 1990.

Brown, G. G. *A Literary History of Spain: The Twentieth Century*. London: Ernest Benn, 1972.

Buñuel, Luis. *Mi último suspiro (memorias)*. Translated by Ana Maria de la Fuente. Barcelona: Plaza and Janés, 1982.

Burguet i Ardiaca, Francesc. *La CNT i la política teatral a Catalunya (1936–1938)*. Barcelona: Institut del Teatre de la Diputació de Barcelona, 1984.

Burke, Peter. *Varieties of Cultural History*. Ithaca, NY: Cornell University Press, 1997.

Byrd, Suzanne Wade. *La Fuente Ovejuna de Federico García Lorca*. Madrid: Editorial Pliegos, 1984.

Byrd, Suzanne Wade. *García Lorca: "La Barraca" and the Spanish National Theater*. New York: Abra Ediciones, 1975.

Calderón de la Barca, Pedro. *Entremeses, jácaras y mojigangas*. Edited by Evangelina Rodríguez y Antonio Tordera. Madrid: Clásicos Castalia, 1982.

Calinescu, Mattei. *Five Faces of Modernity: Modernism, Avant-Garde, Decadence, Kitsch, Postmodernism*. Durham: Duke University Press, 1987.

Calvo Serraller, Francisco, Angel González García, and Francisco Javier Rocha. *La Barraca y su entorno teatral*. Madrid: Galeria Multitud, 1975.

Capparrós Lera, José María. *Arte y política en el cine de la República (1931–1939)*. Barcelona: Editorial 7½, 1981.

Caparrós Lera, José María. "El Comité de cinema y Laya films, organismos de propaganda de la Generalitat de Catalunya (1932–1939)." In Carmelo Garitaonaindía Garnacho et al, eds. *Comunicación, cultura y política durante la II República y la Guerra Civil: II Encuentro de la Historia de la Prensa* (487–492). Bilbao:

Departamento de Cultura, Diputación Foral de Bizkaia: Servicio Editorial, Universidad del País Vasco, 1990.

Carr, Raymond. *Spain 1808–1975.* 2d ed. Oxford: Clarendon Press, 1982.

Casona, Alejandro. "Nota preliminar," in *Retablo Jovial, cinco farsas en un acto* (9–11). Buenos Aires: El Ateneo, 1949.

Casona, Alejandro. "Sancho Panza en la ínsula." In *Retablo Jovial, cinco farsas en un acto* (16–28). Buenos Aires: El Ateneo, 1949.

Castelló, Antonio. "Proyecto de reforma del teatro español 1920/1939." *Primer Acto* 176 (January 1975): 4–16.

Castilla, F. Blanco. *El cinema educativo y Gracián pedagogo.* Madrid: Ed. F. Beltrán, 1933.

Castro, Américo. "Manuel B. Cossio. Fue él y fue un ambiente." *Revista de Pegogía* 165 (1935): 385–389.

Caudet, Francisco. "Las Misiones Pedagógicas, 1931–1935." *Cuadernos Hispanoamericanos* 453 (1988): 93–108.

Cervantes, Miguel. "The Judge of the Divorce Court." In S. Griswold Morley, trans. *The Interludes of Cervantes* (1–19). New York: Greenwood Press, 1969.

Chartier, Roger, and Lydia G. Cochrane, trans. *Cultural History: Between Practices and Representations.* Cambridge: Polity Press, 1988.

Clifford, James, and George E. Marcus, eds. *Writing Culture: The Poetics and Politics of Ethnography.* Berkeley: University of California Press, 1986.

Cobb, Christopher H. *La cultura y el pueblo: Espana, 1930–1939.* Barcelona: Editorial Laia, 1980.

Conversi, Daniele. *The Basques, the Catalans, and Spain: Alternative Routes to Nationalist Mobilization.* Reno: University of Nevada Press, 1997.

Cossío, Manuel B. *De su jornada (fragmentos).* Madrid: Aguilar, 1966.

Costa, Joaquín. *Joaquín Costa: Oligarquía y caciquismo. Colectivismo agrario y otros escritos.* Edited by Rafael Pérez de la Dehesa. Madrid: El Libro de Bolsillo and Alianza Editorial, 1967.

Crispin, John. "Antonio Sánchez Barbudo, Misionero Pedagógico." In Benito Brancaforte, Edward R. Mulvihill and Roberto G. Sánchez, eds. *Homenaje a Antonio Sánchez Barbudo: Ensayos de literatura española moderna.* Madison: Department of Spanish and Portuguese, University of Wisconsin, 1981.

Dalópio, Dr. *La España que amanece.* San Sebastian: Bueno Olivan, 1938.

Darnton, Robert. "Intellectual and Cultural History." In Michael Kammen, ed. *The Past before Us* (327–354). Ithaca, NY: Cornell University Press, 1980.

Delgado Gómez-Escalonilla, Lorenzo. *Imperio de papel: Acción cultural y política exterior durante el primer franquismo.* Madrid: Consejo Superior de Investigaciones Científicas, 1992.

Dennis, Nigel. *José Bergamín: A Critical Introduction, 1920–1936.* Toronto: Toronto University Press, 1986.

Destree, Jules. "De cinematografía." *Escuela Moderna* 3 (March 1933): 117–119.

Deutsch, Karl. *Nationalism and Social Communication: An Inquiry into the Foundations of Nationality.* Cambridge, MA: Technology Press, MIT, 1953.

Deuxième Congrès International des Écrivains, Le. *Défense de la culture.* Madrid, Valencia, Paris, 1937.

*Diario de Sesiones de las Cortes Constituyentes de la República española, comenzaron el 14 de julio de 1931.* 25 vols. (Madrid, n.p., 1931–1933).

Díaz, Elías. *La filosofía social del krausismo español.* Madrid: Cuadernos para el Diálogo, 1973.

Dieste, Rafael. *El nuevo retablo de las maravillas.* In Miguel Bilbatúa, ed. *Teatro de agitación política 1933–1939.* Madrid: Edicusa, 1976.

Dieste, Rafael. "Testimonio de Rafael Dieste." In *Las Misiones Pedagógicas: Una experiencia de educación popular* (139–154). Sada-A Coruña: Ediciós de Castro/Ensaio, 1982.

Díez-Canedo, Enrique. "The Spanish Theater." In Thomas H. Dickinson, ed. *The Theater in a Changing Europe.* New York: Holt, 1937.

Díez Medrano, Juan. *Divided Nation: Class, Politics and Nationalism in the Basque Country and Catalonia.* Ithaca, NY: Cornell University Press, 1995.

Domingo, Marcelino. *Homenaje a Marcelino Domingo.* Madrid: n.p., 1936.

Domingo, Marcelino. *La escuela en la República (la obra de ocho meses).* Madrid: M. Aguilar, 1932.

Domingo, Marcelino. *La experiencia del poder.* Madrid: S. Quemades, 1934.

Dougherty, Dru, and María Francisca Vilches de Frutos, ed. *El teatro en España: Entre la tradición y la vanguardia, 1918–1939.* Madrid: Tabapress, 1992.

Duara, Prasenjit. "Historicizing National Identity, or Who Imagines What and When." In Geoff Eley and Ronald Grigor Suny, eds. *Becoming National: A Reader.* New York: Oxford University Press, 1996.

Egbert, Donald Drew. *Social Radicalism and the Arts in Western Europe.* New York: Knopf, 1970.

"E. Giménez Caballero, Una cultura Hacista: Revolución y tradición en la regeneración de España." *Anthropos* 84 (May 1988).

Eguía Ruiz, Constancio. *Los causantes de la tragedia hispana: Un gran crímen de los intelectuales españoles.* Buenos Aires: Editorial Difusión, 1938.

Eley, Geoff, and Ronald Grigor Suny, eds. *Becoming National: A Reader.* NewYork: Oxford University Press, 1996.

Ellwood, Sheelagh. *Prietas las Filas: Historia de Falange Española, 1933–1983.* Barcelona: Editorial Crítica, 1984.

Escolano, Agustín. *Leer y escribir en España.* Edited by Agustín Escolano. Madrid: Fundación Germán Sánchez Ruipérez, 1992.

Escolar Sobrino, Hipólito. *Historia del libro y las bibliotecas en el siglo XX.* Madrid: Ediciones Pirámide, 1983.

Escolar Sobrino, Hipólito. *La cultura durante la Guerra Civil.* Madrid: Alhambra, 1987.

Escudero, María A. "The Image of Latin America Disseminated in Spain by the Franco Regime: Repercussions in the Configuration of a National Identity." Ph. D. diss., University of California, San Diego, 1993.

Esenwein, George. *Anarchist Ideology and the Working-Class Movement in Spain, 1868–1898.* Berkeley: University of California Press, 1989.

Esenwein, George, and Adrian Shubert. *Spain at War: The Spanish Civil War in Context, 1931–1939.* New York: Longman, 1995.

Estelrich, Juan [Joan]. *Temas de nuestro tiempo: Catalanismo y reforma hispánica.* Barcelona: Montaner y Simón, 1932.

Fernández Soria, Juan Manuel. *Educación y cultura en la Guerra Civil (España 1936–1939).* Valencia: NAU Llibres, 1984.

Fernández Soria, Juan Manuel. "Medios de comunicación y extensión cultural en el ejército republicano." In Carmelo Garitaonaindía Garnacho et al., eds. *Comunicación, cultura y política durante la II República y la Guerra Civil: II Encuentro de la Historia de la Prensa* (376–401). Bilbao: Departamento de Cultura, Diputación Foral de Bizkaia: Servicio Editorial, Universidad del País Vasco, 1990.

Fichte, Johann Gottlieb. *Addresses to the German Nation.* Westport, CT: Greenwood Press, 1979.

Fitzpatrick, Sheila. *The Commissariat of Enlightenment: Soviet Organization of Education and the Arts under Lunacharsky, October 1917–1921.* Cambridge: Cambridge University Press, 1970.

Fitzpatrick, Sheila. *The Cultural Front: Power and Culture in Revolutionary Russia.* Ithaca, NY: Cornell University Press, 1992.

Foard, Douglas W. *The Revolt of the Aesthetes: Ernesto Giménez Caballero and the Origins of Spanish Fascism.* New York: Peter Lang, 1989.

Fox, Inman. *La invención de España: Nacionalismo liberal e identidad nacional.* Madrid: Cátedra, 1997.

Fuentes, Victor. *La marcha al pueblo en las letras españolas 1917–1936.* Madrid: Ediciones de la Torre, 1980.

*Gaceta de Madrid* (Madrid: n.p., n.d.).

Gallego Méndez, María Teresa. *Mujer, falange y franquismo.* Madrid: Taurus, 1983.

Gamonal Torres, Miguel A. *Arte y política en la Guerra Civil española: El caso republicano.* Granada: Diputación Provincial de Granada, 1987.

García Delgado, J. L., ed. *Los orígenes culturales de la Segunda República.* Madrid: Siglo Veintiuno, 1993.

García Escuderos, José María. *El pensamiento de "El Debate": un diario católico en la crisis de España, 1917–1936."* Madrid: Editorial Católica, 1983.

Garitaonaindía Garnacho, Carmelo, et al., eds. *Comunicación, cultura y política durante la II República y la Guerra Civil: II Encuentro de la Historia de la Prensa.* Bilbao: Departamento de Cultura, Diputación Foral de Bizkaia: Servicio Editorial, Universidad del País Vasco, 1990.

Geertz, Clifford. "Centers, Kings, and Charisma: Reflections on the Symbolics of Power." In *Local Knowledge: Further Essays in Interpretive Anthropology* (121–146). New York: Basic Books, 1983.

Gellner, Ernst. *Nations and Nationalism.* Oxford: Oxford University Press, 1983.

Gibson, Ian. *Federico García Lorca: A Life.* Boston: Faber and Faber, 1989.

Gies, David T., ed. *The Cambridge Companion to Modern Spanish Culture.* Cambridge: Cambridge University Press, 1999.

Gil Cremades, Juan José. *El reformismo español: Krausismo, escuela histórica, neotomismo.* Barcelona: Ediciones Ariel, 1969.

Gil Robles, José María. *No fue posible la paz.* Barcelona: Ediciones Ariel, 1968.

Giménez Caballero, Ernesto. *Arte y estado*. Madrid: Gráfica Universal, 1935.

Giménez Caballero, Ernesto. *El cine y la cultura humana*. Bilbao: Ediciones de Conferencias y Ensayos, 1944.

Giménez Caballero, Ernesto. *Genio de España: Exaltaciones a una resurrección nacional y del mundo*. Madrid: Ediciones de la Gaceta Literaria, 1932.

Giménez Caballero, Ernesto. *La nueva catolicidad: Teoría general sobre el fascismo en Europa—en España*. Madrid: Ediciones de la Gaceta Literaria, 1933.

Giménez Caballero, Ernesto. *Manuel Azaña (Profecías españolas)*. Madrid: Ediciones de la Gaceta Literaria, 1932.

Giner de los Ríos, Francisco. "Consideraciones sobre el desarollo de la literatura moderna." In *Estudios literarios*. Madrid: R. Labajos, 1866.

Giner de los Ríos, Francisco. *Estudios de literatura y arte*. 2d ed. Madrid: Librería de Victoriano Suárez, 1876.

Gómez Mendoza, Josefina, and Nicolás Ortega Cantero. "Geografía y regeneracionismo en España (1875–1936)." *Sistema 77* (1987): 77–89.

Gómez Mesa, Luis. *Autenticidad del cinema educativo*. Madrid: Sáez, 1936.

Gómez Mesa, Luis. "España en el mundo sin fronteras del cinema educativo." *Revista de las Españas* 98–100 (1935): 431–434.

Gómez Molleda, María Dolores. *Los reformadores de la España contemporánea*. Madrid: Consejo Superior de Investigaciones Científicas, 1966.

Gómez-Santos, Marino. "Alejandro Casona cuenta su vida." *Pueblo*. August 17, 1962.

González Ballesteros, Teodoro. *Aspectos jurídicos de la censura cinematográfica en España*. Madrid: Editorial de la Universidad de Madrid, 1981.

González Lopez, Palmira. *Els ans duarats del cinema clàssic a Barcelona (1906–1923)*. Barcelona: Institut del Teatre de la Diputació de Barcelona, 1987.

Graham, Helen. "Community, Nation and State in Republican Spain, 1931–1938." In Claire Mar-Molinero and Angel Smith, eds. *Nationalism and the Nation in the Iberian Peninsula*. Washington, DC: Berg, 1996.

Graham, Helen, and Jo Labanyi, eds. *Spanish Cultural Studies: An Introduction*. Oxford: Oxford University Press, 1995.

Grazia, Victoria de. "Mass Culture and Sovereignty: The American Challenge to European Cinemas, 1920–1960." *Journal of Modern History* 61 (March 1989): 53–87.

Gubern, Román. "El cine sonoro." In Román Gubern, ed. *Historia del cine español* (123–179). Madrid: Cátedra, 1995.

Gubern, Román. *El cine sonoro en la Segunda República, 1929–1936*. Barcelona: Editorial Lumen, 1977.

Gubern, Román. *La censura: Función política y ordenamiento jurídico bajo el franquismo (1936–1975)*. Barcelona: Peninsula, 1981.

Guereña, Jean-Louis. "Les socialistes espagnols et la culture: La 'Casa del Pueblo' de Madrid au début du Xxe siècle. In Jacques Maurice, Brigitte Magnien, and Danièle Genevois, eds. *Peuple, mouvement ouvrier, culture dans l'Espagne contemporaine* (23–37). Saint-Denis: Presses Universitaires de Vincennes, 1990.

Guixé, Juan. *Le vrai visage de la Republique espagnole*. Paris: Imprimerie Cooperative Etoile, 1938.

Hegel, G. W. F. *Reason in History.* Translated by Robert S. Hartman. New York: Macmillan, 1953.

Herf, Geoffrey. *Reactionary Modernism.* Cambridge: Cambridge University Press, 1984.

Herr, Richard. *An Historical Essay on Modern Spain.* Berkeley: University of California Press, 1971.

Heywood, Paul. *Marxism and the Failure of Organized Socialism in Spain, 1879–1936.* Cambridge: Cambridge University Press. 1990.

*Historia de las películas pedagógicas Eastman.* Madrid: Eastman-Kodak, n.d.

Hoare, Quintin, and Geoffrey Nowell Smith, eds. and trans. *Selections from the Prison Notebooks of Antonio Gramsci.* New York: International Publishers, 1971.

Hobsbawm, Eric. *The Age of Empire, 1875–1914.* New York: Pantheon, 1987.

Hobsbawm, Eric. *Nations and Nationalism since 1780: Programme, Myth, Reality.* 2d ed. Cambridge, UK: Canto, 1992.

Hobsbawm, Eric, and Terence Ranger, eds. *The Invention of Tradition.* Cambridge: Cambridge University Press, 1992.

Holguín, Sandie. "The Conquest of Tradition: Culture and Politics in Spain during the Second Republic, 1931–1936." Ph.D. diss., University of California, Los Angeles, 1994.

Honig, Edwin. *García Lorca.* Norfolk, CT: New Directions, 1944.

Hroch, Miroslav. "From National Movement to the Fully Formed Nation: The Nation-Building Process in Europe." In Geoff Eley and Ronald Grigor Suny, eds. *Becoming National: A Reader.* New York: Oxford University Press, 1996.

Hroch, Miroslav. *Social Preconditions of National Revival in Europe.* Cambridge: Cambridge University Press, 1985.

Huerta, Luis. "Nota profesional: Misiones Pedagógicas." *Trabajadores de la Enseñanza* 4 (1934).

Huertas Vásquez, Eduardo. *La política cultural de la Segunda República española.* Madrid: Ministerio de Cultura, 1988.

Hunt, Lynn, ed. *The New Cultural History.* Berkeley: University of California Press, 1989.

Iglesias Rodríguez, Gema. "Las Misiones Pedagógicas: Un intento de democratización cultural." In Carmelo Garitaonaindía Garnacho et al., eds. *Comunicación, cultura y política durante la II República y la Guerra Civil: II Encuentro de la Historia de la Prensa* (337–365). Bilbao: Departamento de Cultura, Diputación Foral de Bizkaia: Servicio Editorial, Universidad del País Vasco, 1990.

Jackson, Gabriel. *The Spanish Republic and the Civil War, 1931–1939.* Princeton: Princeton University Press, 1965.

Jelavich, Peter. *Berlin Cabaret.* Cambridge: Harvard University Press, 1993.

Jiménez de Asúa, Luis. *Proceso histórico de la constitución de la República española.* Madrid: Editorial Reus, 1932.

Jiménez Fraud, Alberto. "The 'Residencia de Estudiantes.'" *Texas Quarterly,* special issue "Image of Spain" 4 (1961): 48–54.

Jiménez García, Antonio. *El krausismo y la Institución Libre de Enseñanza.* Madrid: Editorial Cincel, 1986.

Jiménez-Landi, Antonio. *La Institucion Libre de Ensenanza y su ambiente.* Vol. 1. Madrid: Ediciones Taurus, 1973.

Jobit, Pierre. *Les éducateurs de l'Espagne contemporaine.* Paris: E. de Boccard, 1936.

Johnson, Carroll B. "The Classical Theater and Its Reflection of Life." In José Rubia Barcia, ed. *Américo Castro and the Meaning of Spanish Civilization.* Berkeley: University of California Press, 1976.

Kertzer, David I. *Ritual, Politics, and Power.* New Haven, CT: Yale University Press, 1988.

Lannon, Frances, and Paul Preston, eds. *Elites and Power in Twentieth-Century Spain: Essays in Honour of Sir Raymond Carr.* Oxford: Clarendon Press, 1990.

Larraz, Emmanuel. *El cine español.* Paris: Masson et Cie, 1973.

Larraz, Emmanuel. *Le cinéma espagnol des origines à nos jours.* Paris: Les Editions du Cerf, 1986.

L.B.L. "Máscaras." *Haz* 3 (April 9, 1935): 2.

Lears, T. J. Jackson. "The Concept of Cultural Hegemony: Problems and Possibilities." *American Historical Review* 90 (June 1985): 567–593.

Lebovics, Herman. *True France: The Wars over Cultural Identity.* Ithaca, NY: Cornell University Press, 1992.

Lipp, Solomon. *Francisco Giner de los Ríos: A Spanish Socrates.* Waterloo, Ontario, Canada: Wilfred Laurier University Press, 1985.

Listerman, Randall W., ed. and trans. *The Interludes (Los Pasos) by Lope de Rueda.* Ottawa: Dovehouse Editions, 1988.

Litvak, Lily. *Musa libertaria: Arte, literatura y vida cultural del anarquismo español (1880–1913).* Barcelona: Antoni Bosch, 1981.

Llarena Lluna, Juan. "Misiones Pedagógicas." *La Escuela Moderna* 1 (1933): 35–39.

Llopis, Rodolfo. *Como se forja un pueblo (La Rusia que yo he visto).* Madrid: Editorial España, 1929.

Llopis, Rodolfo. "Francisco Giner de los Ríos y la reforma del hombre." *Cuadernos del Congreso por la Libertad de la Cultura* 16 (1956): 60–67.

Llopis, Rodolfo. *Hacia una escuela más humana.* Madrid: Editorial España, 1934.

Llopis, Rodolfo. *La revolución en la enseñanza.* Madrid: Bolanos Aguilar, 1933.

Llopis, Rodolfo. "Sanz del Río y el krausismo." *Cuadernos del Congreso por la Libertad de la Cultura* 9 (1954): 50–56.

Lope de Vega. *Fuenteovejuna.* Edited by Jesús Cañas Murillo. Barcelona: Plaza and Janés, 1984.

López-Morillas, Juan. *The Krausist Movement and Ideological Change in Spain, 1854–1874.* Translated by Frances M. López-Morillas. Cambridge: Cambridge University Press, 1981.

Lozano Seijas, Claudio. "La prensa pedagógica durante la II República." *Perspectivas Pedagógicas* 11 (1978): 193–203.

Luis Martín, Francisco de. *Cincuenta años de cultura obrera en España, 1890–1940.* Madrid: Pablo Iglesias, 1994.

Luis Martín, Francisco de. *La cultura socialista en España, 1923–1930.* Salamanca: Consejo Superior de Investigaciones Científicas, 1993.

Luzuriaga, Lorenzo. *Diccionario de pedagogía.* Buenos Aires: Losada, 1960.

Luzuriaga, Lorenzo. "Ideas pedagógicas de Cossío." *Revista de Pedagogía* 165 (1935): 410–419.

Luzuriaga, Lorenzo. *La Institución Libre de Enseñanza y la educación en España.* Buenos Aires: Universidad de Buenos Aires, 1957.

Luzuriaga, Lorenzo. *La nueva escuela pública.* Madrid: Publicaciones de la Revista de Pedagogía, 1931.

Machado, Antonio. "Sobre la defensa y la difusión de la cultura. Discurso pronunciado en Valencia en la sesión de clausura del Congreso Internacional de Escritores." *Hora de España* 8 (August 1937): 11–19.

Madariaga, Benito, and Celia Valbuena. *La Universidad Internacional de Verano en Santander, (1933–36).* Madrid: Ministerio de Universidades e Investigación, 1981.

Maeztu, Ramiro de. "El arte y la moral: Discurso leido ante la Academia de Ciencias Morales y Políticas en el acto de su recepción el día 20 de marzo de 1932." *Acción Española* 2 (1932): 193–210.

Maeztu, Ramiro de. *Defensa de la Hispanidad.* Buenos Aires: Editorial Poblet, 1952.

Mainer, José Carlos. *La edad de plata (1902–1939): Ensayo de interpretación de un proceso cultural.* Madrid: Cátedra, 1983.

Mainer, José Carlos. "Notas sobre la lectura obrera en España (1890–1930)." In Albert Balcells and Manuel Tuñón de Lara, eds. *Teoría y práctica del movimiento obrero en España (1900–1936)* (175–239). Valencia: F. Torres, 1977.

Malefakis, Edward. *Agrarian Reform and Peasant Revolution in Spain.* New Haven, CT: Yale University Press, 1970.

Mallo del Campo, María Luisa. *Torner más allá del folklore.* Oviedo: Departamento de Arte y Musicología, Servicio de Publicaciones, Universidad de Oviedo, 1980.

Mally, Lynn. *Culture of the Future: The Proletkult Movement in Revolutionary Russia.* Berkeley: University of California Press, 1990.

Marichal, Juan. "La europeización de España (1898–1936)." *Sistema* 86–87 (November 1988): 53–60.

Marichal, Juan. *El intelectual y la política.* Madrid: Publicaciones de la Residencia de Estudiantes, Consejo Superior de Investigaciones Científicas, 1990.

Mar-Molinero, Claire, and Angel Smith, eds. *Nationalism and the Nation in the Iberian Peninsula: Competing and Conflicting Ideologies.* Washington, DC: Berg, 1996.

Marrast, Robert. *El teatre durant la Guerra Civil espanyola: Assaig d'història i documents.* Barcelona: L'Institut del Teatre, 1978.

Martínez Cuadrado, Miguel. *La burguesía conservadora (1874–1931).* Madrid: Alianza, 1986.

Martínez-Bretón, Juan Antonio. *Iglesia católica en la cinematografía (1951–1962).* Madrid: Harofarma, 1987.

Maurice, Jacques, ed. *Peuple, mouvement ouvrier, culture dans L'Espagne contemporaine.* Saint-Denis: Presses Universitaires de Vincennes, 1990.

McCarthy, Jim. *Political Theatre during the Spanish Civil War.* Cardiff: University of Wales Press, 1999.

Méndez-Leite, Fernando. *Historia del cine español.* Vol. 1. Madrid: Ediciones Rialp, 1965.

Menéndez Pidal, Ramón. *Poesía juglaresca y juglares.* 4th ed. Madrid: Espasa-Calpe, 1956.

Millán, Fernando. *La revolución laica: De la Institución Libre de Enseñanza a la escuela de la República*. Valencia: Fernando Torres, 1983.

Ministère de l'Instruction Publique de la République Espagnole. *L'effort culturel du peuple espagnol en armes*. N.p.: Ministère de l'instruction publique de la République espagnole, 1937.

Ministerio de Instrucción Pública y Sanidad. *Charlas populares: Lo que significa la guerra. La cultura es la cultura para todos*. Barcelona: Ediciones Españoles, c.1938.

*Misiones Pedagógicas*. Madrid: n.p., c.1945.

Molero Pintado, Antonio. *Lorenzo Luzuriaga y la política educativa de su tiempo*. Primeras Jornadas de Educación. Ciudad Real: Biblioteca de Autores y Temas Manchegos, 1986.

Molero Pintado, Antonio. *La reforma educativa de la Segunda República: primer bienio*. Madrid: Santillana, 1977.

Monleón, José. *El Mono Azul: Teatro de urgencia y romancero de la Guerra Civil*. Madrid: Editorial Ayuso, 1979.

Moreno Baez, Enrique. "'La Barraca': Entrevista con su director, Federico García Lorca." *Revista de la Universidad Internacional de Santander* 1 (1933): 68–69.

Morla Lynch, Carlos. *En España con Federico García Lorca*. Madrid: Aguilar, 1958.

Morodo, Raúl. *Los orígenes ideológicos del franquismo: Acción Española*. Madrid: Alianza Editorial, 1985.

Morris, C. B. *This Loving Darkness: The Cinema and Spanish Writers 1920–1936*. Oxford: Oxford University Press, 1980.

Mukerji, Chandra, and Michael Schudson, eds. *Rethinking Popular Culture*. Berkeley: University of California Press, 1991.

Mundi Pedret, Francisco. *El teatro de la Guerra Civil*. Barcelona: PPU, 1987.

"Nacionalismo integral." *Acción Española* 1 (1932): 225–232.

Navarro Tomás, T. *Spanish in the Talking Films*. Translated by Aurelio M. Espinosa. Madrid: Tipografía de Archivos, 1930.

Nietzsche, Friedrich. *The Birth of Tragedy and The Case of Wagner*. Edited and translated by Walter Kaufmann. New York: Vintage Books, 1967.

Nuñez, Clara Eugenia. *La fuente de la riqueza: Educación y desarollo económico en la España contemporánea*. Madrid: Alianza, 1992.

Ortega y Gasset, José. *España invertebrada: bosquejo de algunos pensamientos históricos*. 8th ed. Madrid: Espasa-Calpe, 1921.

Ortega y Gasset, José. "La pedagogía social como programa político." In *Obras Completas*, vol.1, 494–513. Madrid: Revista de Occidente, 1910.

Ortega y Gasset, José. "Vieja y nueva política." In *Obras Completas*, vol.1, 267–308. Madrid: Revista de Occidente, 1966. Originally published in 1914.

Otero del Pozo, Sotero. *España inmortal*. Valladolid, Palencia: Afrodisio Aguado, 1937.

Otero Urtaza, Eugenio. *Las Misiones Pedagógicas: Una experiencia de educación popular*. A Coruña: Ediciós do Castro/Ensaio, 1982.

Otero Urtaza, Eugenio. "El Patronato de Misiones Pedagógicas y los nuevos medios de comunicación social." *Bordón* 36 (1984): 193–203.

Paredes, Javier, ed. *España Siglo XIX*. Madrid: Actas, 1991.

Patronato de Misiones Pedagógicas. *Memoria de la Misión Pedagógica-Social en Sanabria (Zamora): Resumen de trabajos realizados en el año 1934*. Madrid: n.p., 1935.

Patronato de Misiones Pedagogicas. *Patronato de Misiones Pedagogicas (septiembre de 1931–diciembre de 1933*. Madrid: n.p., 1934.

Paucker, Eleanor Krane. "Cinco años de misiones." *Revista de Occidente* (Extraordinario 1) 7–8. (November 1981): 233–268.

Payne, Stanley. *Fascism in Spain, 1923–1977*. Madison: University of Wisconsin Press, 1999.

Payne, Stanley. *A History of Fascism, 1914–1945*. Madison: University of Wisconsin Press, 1995.

Payne, Stanley. *Spain's First Democracy: The Second Republic, 1931–1936*. Madison: University of Wisconsin Press, 1993.

Pérez de la Dehesa, Rafael. *El pensamiento de Costa y su influencia en el 98*. Madrid: Sociedad de Estudios y Publicaciones, 1966.

Pérez Galán, Mariano. *La enseñanza en la II República española*. Madrid: Editorial Cuadernos para el Diálogo, 1975.

Pérez Ledesma, Manuel. "La cultura socialista en los años veinte." In J. L. García Delgado, ed. *Los orígenes culturales de la II República*. Madrid: Siglo Veintiuno, 1993.

Pérez Merinero, Carlos, and David Pérez Merinero. *El cinema como arma de clase: Antología de Nuestro Cinema 1932–1935*. Valencia: Fernando Torres, 1975.

Pérez Perucha, Julio. "Narración de un aciago destino (1896–1930)." In Román Gubern, ed. *Historia del cine español* (19–121). Madrid: Cátedra, 1995.

Piqueras, José A., and Manuel Chust, eds. *Republicanos y repúblicas en España*. Madrid: Siglo Veintiuno, 1996.

Preston, Paul. *The Coming of the Spanish Civil War: Reform, Reaction, and Revolution in the Second Republic*. 2d ed. New York: Routledge, 1994.

Preston, Paul. "The 'Moderate' Right and the Undermining of the Second Republic in Spain 1931–1933." *European Studies Review* 3 (1973): 369–394.

*Primer Congreso Hispanoamericano de Cinematografía: Madrid, 2–12 octubre. Conclusiones*. Madrid: n. p., 1931.

Puelles Benítez, Manuel de. *Educación e ideología en la España contemporánea*. 2d ed. Barcelona: Editorial Labor, 1991.

Quinto Regimiento. *Batallones de choque*. Madrid: Ediciones del Quinto Regimiento, n.d.

Raby, David. *Educación y revolución social en México, 1921–1940*. Mexico City: Secretaría de Educación Pública, 1974.

Radcliff, Pamela. *From Mobilization to Civil War: The Politics of Polarization in the Spanish City of Gijón, 1900–1937*. Cambridge: Cambridge University Press, 1996.

Ramírez, Manuel, ed. *Estudios sobre la II República española*. Madrid: Tecnos, 1975.

Ramsden, H. *The 1898 Movement in Spain*. Manchester: Manchester University Press, 1974.

*Realizaciones de la España Leal, La sección de bibliotecas de cultura popular: Un año de trabajo, julio 1936–julio 1937*. Valencia: Ediciones de Cultura Popular, 1938.

Rennert, Hugo Albert. *The Spanish Stage in the Time of Lope de Vega*. New York: Dover Publications, 1963.

Río, Angel del. "Fernando de los Ríos." *Cuadernos del Congreso por la Libertad de la Cultura* 18 (May–June 1956): 69–79.

Ríos, Fernando de los. *El pensamiento vivo de Giner de los Ríos*. Buenos Aires: Editorial Losada, 1949.

Ríos, Fernando de los. *Mi viaje a la Rusia sovietista*. 2d ed. Madrid: Calpe, 1922.

Robinson, R. A. H. *The Origins of Franco's Spain*. London: Newton Abbot, David and Charles, 1970.

Robinson, Richard. "The Parties of the Right and the Republic." In Raymond Carr, ed. *The Republic and the Civil War in Spain* (46–78). London: Macmillan, 1971.

Rodríguez-Puertolas, Julio. *Literatura fascista española*. 2 vols. Madrid: Akal, 1986.

Romero Maura, Joaquín. *La rosa de fuego; republicanos y anarquistas: La política de los obreros barceloneses entre el desastre colonial y la semana trágica, 1899–1909*. Barcelona: Ediciones Grijalbo, 1975.

Rousseau, Jean Jacques. *A Discourse on Inequality*. London: Penguin, 1984.

Rubía Barcia, José, ed. *Américo Castro and the Meaning of Spanish Civilization*. Berkeley: University of California Press, 1976.

Rull Fernández, Enrique, ed. *Autos sacramentales del Siglo de Oro*. Barcelona: Plaza and Janés, 1986.

Sáenz de la Calzada, Luis. *"La Barraca" teatro universitario*. Madrid: Biblioteca de la Revista de Occidente, 1976.

Sáinz Rodríguez, Pedro. *La evolución de las ideas sobre la decadencia española y otros estudios de crítica literaria*. Madrid: Editorial Atlantida Mendezibal, 1925.

Sáinz Rodríguez, Pedro. *La tradición nacional y el estado futuro*. Madrid: Cultura Española, 1935.

Sáinz Rodríguez, Pedro. *Testimonio y recuerdos*. Barcelona: Editorial Planeta, 1978.

Samaniego Boneu, Mercedes. *La política educativa en la Segunda República durante el bienio azañista*. Madrid: Consejo Superior de Investigaciones Científicas, 1977.

Santullano, Luis A. "Cossío y Las Misiones Pedagógicas." *Revista de Pedagogía* 165 (1935): 405–410.

Santullano, Luis A. "Patronato de Misiones Pedagógicas." *Residencia* 4 (1933): 1–21.

Santullano, Luis. *Pensamiento vivo de Cossío*. Buenos Aires: Editorial Losada, 1946.

Schorske, Carl E. *Fin de Siècle Vienna*. New York: Vintage Books, 1981.

Sender, Ramón J. *Teatro de masas*. Valencia: Ediciones Orto, 1932.

Serrano, Carlos. "*Acracia*, los anarquistas y la cultura." In Bert Hofmann, Pere Joan i Tous, and Manfred Teitz, eds. *El anarquismo español: sus tradiciones culturales*. Frankfurt am Main: Vervuert; Madrid: Iberoamericana, 1995.

Serrano, Carlos. "La funcionalidad del teatro en la Guerra Civil y el caso de José María Pemán." In Dru Dougherty and María Francisca Vilches de Frutos, eds. *El teatro en España: Entre la tradición y la vanguardia, 1918–1939* (393–400). Madrid: Tabapress, 1992.

Shubert, Adrian. *A Social History of Modern Spain*. 2d ed. London: Routledge, 1992.

Silverman, Debora. *Art Nouveau in Fin de Siècle France: Politics, Psychology, and Style*. Berkeley: University of California Press, 1989.

Simon, Roger. *Gramsci's Political Thought: An Introduction.* London: Lawrence and Wishart, 1991.

Smith, Anthony. "The Origins of Nations." In Geoff Eley and Ronald Grigor, eds. *Becoming National: A Reader.* New York: Oxford University Press, 1996.

Solà, Pere. *Educació i moviment llibertari a Catalunya (1901–1939).* Barcelona: Edicions 62, 1980.

Solà, Pere. *Els ateneus obrers i la cultura popular a Catalunya (1900–1939).* Barcelona: Edicions de la Magrana, 1978.

Somolinos d'Ardois, Germán. "Las Misiones Pedagógicas de España (1931–1936)." *Cuadernos Americanos* 71 (September–October 1953): 206–224.

Steinburg, Michael P. *The Meaning of the Salzburg Festival: Austria as Theater and Ideology, 1890–1933.* Ithaca, NY: Cornell University Press, 1990.

Sternhell, Zeev. *Neither Right nor Left: Fascist Ideology in France.* Berkeley: University of California Press, 1986.

Stone, Marla. *The Patron State: Culture and Politics in Fascist Italy.* Princeton, NJ: Princeton University Press, 1998.

Townson, Nigel, ed. *El republicanismo en España (1830–1977).* Madrid: Alianza, 1994.

Trend, J. B. *The Origins of Modern Spain.* Cambridge: Cambridge University Press, 1934.

Trepanier, Estelle. "Federico García Lorca et La Barraca." *Revue d'Histoire du Théatre* 8 (1966): 163–181.

Tuñón de Lara, Manuel. "Actitudes socialistas ante la cultura." In Jacques Maurice, Brigitte Magnien, and Danièle Genevois, eds. *Peuple, mouvement ouvrier, culture dans l'Espagne contemporaine* (141–155). Saint-Denis: Presses Universitaires de Vincennes, 1990.

Tuñón de Lara, Manuel. *Medio siglo de cultura española (1885–1936).* 3d ed. Madrid: Editorial Tecnos, 1977.

Tusell, Javier, and Genoveva G. Queipo de Llano. *Los intelectuales y la República.* Madrid: Nerea, 1990.

Ucelay da Cal, Enric. "Catalan Nationalism: Cultural Plurality and Political Ambiguity." In *Spanish Cultural Studies: An Introduction* (144–151). Edited by Helen Graham and Jo Labanyi. Oxford: Oxford University Press, 1995.

Ucelay da Cal, Enric. *La Catalunya populista: Imatge, cultura i política en l'etapa republicana (1931–1939).* Barcelona: La Magrana, 1982.

Ucelay da Cal, Enric. "The Nationalisms of the Periphery: Culture and Politics in the Construction of National Identity." In Helen Graham and Jo Labanyi, eds. *Spanish Cultural Studies: An Introduction* (32–39). Oxford: Oxford University Press, 1995.

Ullman, Joan Connelly. *The Tragic Week: A Study of Anti-Clericalism in Spain, 1875–1912* Cambridge: Harvard University Press, 1968.

Unamuno, Miguel de. *En torno al casticismo.* Madrid: Espasa Calpe, 1991.

Unamuno, Miguel de. "La literatura y el cine." In *Obras Completas* (vol. 11, 531–535). Madrid: Afrodisio Aguado, 1959.

*Una poderosa fuerza secreta: La Institución Libre de Enseñanza.* San Sebastian: Editorial Española, 1940.

Utrera, Rafael. "Cuatro secuencias sobre el cineasta Ernesto Giménez Caballero." *Anthropos* 84 (1988): 46–50.

Utrera, Rafael. *Modernismo y 98 frente a cinematógrafo.* Seville: Universidad de Sevilla, 1981.

Valldeperes, Manuel. *La força social i revolucionària del teatre.* Barcelona: Editorial Forja, 1937.

Vaughan, Mary Kay. *Cultural Politics in Revolution: Teachers, Peasants, and Schools in Mexico.* Tucson: Arizona University Press, 1997.

Vicens, Juan. *L'Espagne vivante: Le peuple à la conquête de la culture.* Paris: Editions sociales internationales, 1938.

Vilanova Ribas, Mercedes, and Xavier Moreno Juliá. *Atlas de la evolución del analfabetismo en España de 1887 a 1981.* Madrid: Centro de Publicaciones del Ministro de Educación y Ciencia, 1992.

von Geldern, James. *Bolshevik Festivals, 1917–1920.* Berkeley: University of California Press, 1993.

von Sternberg, Josef. *Fun in a Chinese Laundry.* New York: Macmillan, 1965.

Weber, Eugen. *Peasants into Frenchmen: The Modernization of Rural France, 1870–1914.* Stanford, CA: Stanford University Press, 1976.

Whanón, Sultana. "Estética y crítica literarias en España (1940–1950)." Ph.D. diss., University of Granada, 1988.

Xirau, Joaquín. *Manuel B. Cossío y la educación en España.* Barcelona: Ariel, 1969.

Zapatero, Virgilio. *Fernando de los Ríos: Los problemas del socialismo democrático.* Madrid: Editorial Cuadernos Para el Diálogo, 1974.

Zuloaga, Eusebio. "Unos motivos de acción política: Interpretación moderna de la tradición española." *Acción Espanola* 2 (1932): 571–583.

Zulueta, Luis de. "Cossío, artista de la educación." *Revista de Pedagogía* 165 (1935): 399–402.

Zunzuneguí, Santos "Aparatos de estado y propaganda fílmica: El cine de la República española (1936–1939)." In Carmelo Garitaonaindía Garnacho et al., eds. *Comunicación, cultura y política durante la II República y la Guerra Civil: II Encuentro de la Historia de la Prensa* (478–482). Bilbao: Departamento de Cultura, Diputación Foral de Bizkaia: Servicio Editorial, Universidad del País Vasco, 1990

# INDEX